Lecture Notes of the Institute for Computer Sciences, Social Informatics and Telecommunications Engineering

157

Edito

Ozgu
  Mi
Paolo
  Un
Jiann
  Ho
Falko
  Un
Dome
  Un
Mario
  UC
Hisas
  Pr
Sergi
  Ur
Sarta
  Ur
Xuen
  Ur
Mirc
  Ur
Jia X
  Ci
Albe
  Ui
Geof
  Li

More information about this series at http://www.springer.com/series/8197

Joshua I. James · Frank Breitinger (Eds.)

Digital Forensics and Cyber Crime

7th International Conference, ICDF2C 2015
Seoul, South Korea, October 6–8, 2015
Revised Selected Papers

 Springer

Editors
Joshua I. James
Digital Forensic Research Laboratory
Hallym University
Kangwon
Korea (Republic of)

Frank Breitinger
University of New Heaven
West Haven, CT
USA

ISSN 1867-8211   ISSN 1867-822X   (electronic)
Lecture Notes of the Institute for Computer Sciences, Social Informatics
and Telecommunications Engineering
ISBN 978-3-319-25511-8   ISBN 978-3-319-25512-5   (eBook)
DOI 10.1007/978-3-319-25512-5

Library of Congress Control Number: 2015951394

Springer Cham Heidelberg New York Dordrecht London

Springer International Publishing AG Switzerland is part of Springer Science+Business Media
(www.springer.com)

Preface

With approximately 40 % of the world's population now connected to the Internet, many people have unprecedented access to education, commerce, and cultural exchange. As new technologies allow more people to connect, these opportunities will continue to grow well into the future. However, the same opportunities that allow legitimate businesses to reach new customers online also allow opportunities for cyber criminals to perpetrate large-scale fraud, intrusions, and data theft.

Beyond what could be considered traditional cybercrime, the actors, and their motivations, are changing. Perpetrators of cybercrime are increasingly organized and global. Governments are investing heavily in military-grade cyber-offensive and defensive capabilities. Unfortunately, average businesses and Internet users are still largely unaware of the potential dangers of cyber crime and how to protect themselves. Governments are still largely uncooperative and ineffectual during the majority of international cyber crime investigation requests, and some countries still lack legislation on cyber crime.

While progress is being made in national investigation capacities, cyber criminals are taking advantage of the weak cooperation between countries. Unsecured infrastructure and poor policies allow civilian and government infrastructure to become part of criminal organizations' or foreign military assets.

Indeed, improved information security and cyber crime investigation education is needed, as well as a better understanding of such crimes, refined investigation techniques, and an increase in global cooperation from all stakeholders.

In an attempt to raise awareness and improve cultural understanding and international cooperation in cyber crime investigations, the 7th International ICST Conference on Digital Forensics and Cyber Crime (ICDF2C 2015) was held in Seoul, Republic of Korea; the first time ICDF2C was hosted in Asia.

This volume contains papers presented at ICDF2C 2015, held October 6–8, 2015 in Seoul, Republic of Korea. Unlike other conferences in the field of digital forensics, ICDF2C focuses on the applications of digital forensic research, providing a forum where practitioners can learn how the latest research results can be used in everyday investigations of cyber crimes and corporate misconduct.

The 14 papers and three abstracts contained in this volume cover a variety of topics ranging from tactics of cyber crime investigations to digital forensic education, network forensics, and international cooperation in digital investigations. Each paper was reviewed in a double-bind peer review process. We sincerely thank the Technical Program Committee for their hard work in reviewing the submissions. We thank the Organizing Committee, Sang-Jin Lee, Pavel Gladyshev, Frank Breitinger, Yunsik "Jake" Jang, Taeshik Shon, Kisik Chang, YooJin Kwon, Young-jin Son, Songmin Lee, Jae Hyeok Bang, and Boyoung Lim, as well as ASCO, the Korean National Police, the Korean Digital Forensics Society, and the Seoul Tech Society for their tireless efforts in managing all of the arrangements required for a successful conference. We would also like to thank JETCO and DUZON for sponsoring the event. Finally, we offer special thanks to all the staff at EAI who made this conference possible.

August 2015

Joshua I. James
Frank Breitinger

Organization

ICDF2C 2015 was organized by the Digital Forensic Investigation Research Laboratory in the College of International Studies at Hallym University, Chuncheon, Republic of Korea, in cooperation with the Korean Digital Forensic Society (KDFS).

Steering Committee

Sanjay Goel	University at Albany, State University of New York, USA
Imrich Chlamtac	CREATE-NET, Italy
Pavel Gladyshev	University College Dublin, Ireland
Marcus Rogers	Purdue University, USA
Ibrahim Baggili	University of New Haven, USA
Joshua I. James	DFIRE Labs, Hallym University, Republic of Korea

Organizing Committee

Conference Chair

Joshua I. James	DFIRE Labs, Hallym University, Republic of Korea

Advisory Board

Sang-Jin Lee	Korea University, Republic of Korea
Pavel Gladyshev	University College Dublin, Ireland

Technical Program Chair

Frank Breitinger	University of New Haven, USA

Workshop Chair

Yunsik "Jake" Jang	Hallym University, Republic of Korea

Publicity Chairs

Taeshik Shon	Ajou University, Republic of Korea
Kisik Chang	Korean National Police Agency, Republic of Korea
YooJin Kwon	Korea Power Electric Research Institute & Korea University, Republic of Korea

Web Chair

Young-Jin Song	Korean National Police University, Republic of Korea

Translators

Young-Jin Song, Korean
Songmin Lee, Chinese
Jae Hyeok Bang, Japanese
Boyoung Lim

Reviewers

Ahmed F. Shosha	Irfan Ahmed	Nicole Beebe
Andrew Marrington	Jill Slay	Pavel Gladyshev
Bruce Nikkel	Kam Pui Chow	Petr Matousek
Christian Winter	Kathryn Seigfried-Spellar	Shahzad Saleem
David Dampier	Mark Scanlon	Simson Garfinkel
Ernest Foo	Martin Mulazzani	Thomas Kemmerich
Farkhund Iqbal	Martin Olivier	Timothy Vidas
Frank Adelstein	Michael Losavio	Vassil Roussev
Hossain Shahriar	Michal Rzepka	Zeno Geradts
Ibrahim Baggili	Neil Rowe	

Sponsoring Institutions

DUZON IT Group
JETCO Technology, Inc.
CREATE-NET

Contents

X   Contents

Digital Forensics Education

Digital Forensics Education: A Multidisciplinary Curriculum Model

Imani Palmer[1], Elaine Wood[2], Stefan Nagy[1], Gabriela Garcia[3], Masooda Bashir[4(✉)],
and Roy Campbell[1]

[1] Department of Computer Science, University of Illinois at Urbana-Champaign,
Urbana-Champaign, IL 61801, USA
{ipalmer2,snagy2,rhc}@illinois.edu
[2] Department of English, University of Illinois at Urbana-Champaign,
Urbana-Champaign, IL 61801, USA
wood10@illinois.edu
[3] Illinois Science, Technology, Engineering, and Mathematics Education Initiative,
University of Illinois at Urbana-Champaign, Urbana-Champaign, IL 61801, USA
gjuare3@illinois.edu
[4] Graduate School of Library and Information Science,
University of Illinois at Urbana-Champaign, Urbana-Champaign, IL 61801, USA
mnb@illinois.edu

Abstract. This paper reports experiences and lessons learned in the process of developing and implementing an undergraduate curriculum for digital forensics over the last three years at the University of Illinois at Urbana-Champaign. The project addresses the challenges of developing a higher-education standardized curriculum for digital forensics that meets the needs of the digital forensics community. The curriculum provides degree options and considers the growing employability of digital forensics students in an increasing range of jobs. The approach builds on the multidisciplinary nature of the field. The findings include a curriculum model, detailed course content, exams, and an evaluation package for measuring how students respond to the courses. This paper summarizes the model, results, challenges, and opportunities.

Keywords: Digital forensics · Standardization · Higher education · Portable curriculum · Multidisciplinary approach

1 Introduction

Digital forensics involves the investigation of data/evidence from computers, networks, and other electronic devices. It is multidisciplinary in the sense of depending not only on technical aspects of investigation, but on a combination of skills and knowledge of application areas including mathematics, statistics, law and courtroom procedure, government policies, psychology, library science, and finance. Efforts to establish a cohesive body of knowledge and standard curriculum practices remain largely under-developed because digital forensics, and forensics itself, is a new science, quickly

© Institute for Computer Sciences, Social Informatics and Telecommunications Engineering 2015
J.I. James and F. Breitinger (Eds.): ICDF2C 2015, LNICST 157, pp. 3–15, 2015.
DOI: 10.1007/978-3-319-25512-5_1

developing, with applications for all sorts of uses in society. This project argues that computer forensics education is not the same as computer security although it shares many common techniques. The difference lies in the nature and process of digital evidence when it is used by society for social processes, whereas, security concerns information assurance and availability.

Members of the digital forensics community are concerned by the relative absence of digital forensics practitioners training [1–4]. There is a broad need for higher-education standards and curricula. To address the need for a standardized high-quality digital forensics education program, this project, in conjunction with the National Science Foundation (NSF), is developing and piloting a curriculum package in digital forensics suitable for adoption by other institutions. Research by Woods et al. [9, 26], Ismand and Hamilton [27], Al Amro et al. [28], describe a technical foundation for the development of digital forensics education programs. Their scholarly findings provide a basis for this program's development, detailed below.

A Digital Forensics program could be organized in a number of ways. The proposed and adopted approach encourages widespread distribution. Specifically, the Digital Forensics curriculum is offered as a specialization to an existing degree within a department of a university. The project has designed a three-course series of study to prepare students for an increasing number of digital forensics related job openings. The design includes multidisciplinary themes within the curriculum model. The curriculum can be taught as a specialization within just one department or shared between any or all of the multidisciplinary degrees. The project's progress in establishing and implementing a standardized curriculum over the past three years is elaborated in the remainder of this paper. The following sections discuss findings and issues concerning this curriculum.

2   Related Work

Research investigators discuss different approaches to introduce digital forensics in higher education. Chi et al. [6] reported on the challenges of teaching computer forensics at Florida A&M University to students without a strong technical background. To supplement the students' need for technical knowledge, Chi et al. created preparatory courses for students to bolster their prerequisite knowledge of computer forensics before introducing the more technical components of the field. In contrast, Srinivasan [7] described a course on computer forensics at the University of Louisville available only to computer information systems students concentrating in information security. Bashir et al. [5] published research findings on a more multidisciplinary approach.

Other research investigations focus on building a curriculum around industry needs and fortifying the employability of their students in fields related to digital forensics. Liu's baccalaureate program in digital forensics at Metropolitan State University adopted a "practitioner's model," aimed to prepare students for their target industries [20]. This approach failed to recruit the necessary qualified faculty for implementing the model. Wassenaar et al. [8] discusses an approach by Cypress College that prepares students for professional certification. The program required instructors that are digital forensics practitioners. The program's credibility relied on instructors' abilities to communicate their industry experience.

This project's design and development was influenced by challenges to digital forensics education already identified, discussed, and published by Bashir [5], Lang et al. [10], Woods [9], Walls et al. [11], Beebe [12], Kwan et al. [13], Bishop [14], Craiger et al. [15], Nance et al. [16], and Burnett [17]. Further, this project identified challenges faced by institutions involved with implementing digital forensics programs. These include: balancing training and education [18, 19], lack of an adequate textbook on digital forensics [20], finding qualified faculty [19, 20], lab setup [19, 20], selecting appropriate prerequisites [6, 20], and absence of widely accepted curriculum standards [21–24].

3   Background

To help address the need for qualified digital forensics professionals, this project develops an adoptable curriculum. The goal is to distribute it as a self-contained curriculum package. This includes an instructor handbook, a lab instructor handbook, lecture slides, and question sets. This will be a significant contribution to the digital forensics education community [2]. When complete, the program will consist of an introductory, an advanced course in digital forensics with accompanying hands-on laboratory sessions, and a special topics course. The introductory course is accessible to a wide range of students from many disciplines and valuable as a stand-alone offering. The second course is more technically intensive, but it is intended to be accessible and valuable to students from non-technical disciplines. The third course is a purely technical course, and it focuses on new relevant topics of digital forensics [2].

This DF program is not necessarily a job-track training program intended to prepare students to directly enter the job market as digital forensic examiners and analysts. Instead, it provides a broadly applicable education in the field of digital forensics that will be valuable for students going into many disciplines related to digital forensics, such as law, in addition to forensic analysts. It is expected that these students will receive additional education training specific to their career paths and some on-the-job training specific to their eventual professional roles. At the time of writing, this project developed curriculum for the introductory and advanced course. The pilot courses of both were taught and in the process of curriculum revision for distribution to other institutions [2]. The content includes modules developed collaboratively by faculty experts in multiple fields of computer science, law, psychology, social sciences, and accountancy.

4   Methodology

The vision and strategy for this standardized Digital Forensics education curriculum proposes that digital forensics would be best suited as a *specialization* within a technical domain. The curriculum design envisioned a three-course sequence. The hallmarks of the program include a multidisciplinary approach to digital forensics education. Also, domain experts from multiple fields related to digital forensics develop and teach the curriculum. The course work is modular and portable. Also, live evaluation feedback of the curriculum and teaching was part of the entire design for this project from the beginning.

The modules are combined to form a coherent narrative and introduce students to the complex and multiple dynamics of digital forensics. The laboratory assignments from the project's introductory course solely use open source content (detailed below). Further, the modular course content is designed with the intention of being easily adaptable and integrated at various educational institutions.

Digital Forensics is essentially multidisciplinary – encompassing evidence collection, evidence preservation, evidence presentation, forensic preparation [2] – the research team for this project is also multidisciplinary and includes computer science, electrical and computer engineering, criminal justice, law, psychology, and educational assessment experts. The proposed curriculum introduces students to various application areas of digital forensics, including topics such as fraud investigation and digital archives, with the aim of demonstrating the breadth of application for diverse knowledge in the field. The sections below will detail the specifics for Digital Forensics 1, Digital Forensics 2, and Digital Forensics 3.

To satisfy the multidisciplinary aims of this three-course curriculum sequence, professors and experts in digital forensics and related fields deliver subject-specific course material during lectures. The fields of study mentioned above, including technical and non-technical topics, were carefully chosen as the result of an extensive review of literature that outlined relevant intersecting topics in the expansive field of digital forensics. Experts, who attended the Digital Forensics Research Workshop (DFRWS 2011 – 2013), confirmed the accuracy of structuring the course to include these specific fields.

4.1 Digital Forensics 1

Digital Forensics 1 is an introductory course designed to offer an initial overview of the field to students from a broad range of disciplines. Designing a digital forensics curriculum that is appropriate for a large target audience creates particular problems and challenges. It is difficult for a single class to offer a comprehensive introduction to a field as complex as digital forensics; however, the pilot course covered the major forensics-related fields – computer, network, and mobile device – precisely because its pedagogical strategy focuses on education rather than training.

The introductory course was taught in 2013 and 2014. The classes consisted of two 75-min lecture sessions and an hour-long laboratory session each week for a 16-week term. To create a multidisciplinary and modular-based curriculum to correspond with the multidisciplinary nature of the field, the project assembled a development team to include domain experts in computer security, computer networks, law, civil and criminal justice, fraud investigation, and psychology. This approach allows the content developers to receive feedback from student interactions and more efficiently revise their materials. Various modules were combined to form a coherent narrative and introduce students to various perspectives of the field.

The learning objectives that guided the curriculum development were that students should understand: (a) Common terminology, techniques, and investigative procedures of digital forensics, including the related disciplines of computer forensics, network forensics, and mobile device forensics; (b) Applications of the scientific method to digital forensics investigation and its importance; (c) Various types of digital forensics evidence acquired and the limitations of current techniques; (d) Basic operations of the

U.S. justice system and court proceedings; (e) Areas related to digital forensics, such as data recovery, psychology, cyber crime, and fraud examination.

4.2 Digital Forensics 2

Digital Forensics 2 (DF2) is an advanced lecture and lab course designed to offer students an in-depth look at particular multidisciplinary topics related to digital forensics. The class consists of two 50-min lecture sessions and two hour-long laboratory sessions each week for a 16-week term. The learning objectives that guided the curriculum development were that students: (a) Should be familiar with the known barriers and challenges in digital forensics research; (b) Should be able to use their investigative skills in real-world scenarios; and (c) Should be able to contribute research to the digital forensics community. DF2 includes greater focus on technical topics and more rigorous laboratory assignments than the introductory course. It also requires students to complete a research project. Notably, despite recent consumer trends, research continues to neglect the forensics of non-Windows operating systems, file systems, and user applications. The course aims to encourage students to research Linux, Mac, and iOS operating systems as they become increasingly prominent in our daily lives. Students' understanding of multiple operating systems contributes to their ability to adapt the digital forensics investigative process for use in different systems.

Another design decision that is important to the curriculum and this advanced course is the inclusion and option for students to learn in a virtual laboratory environment. The program established a virtualized laboratory called ISLET. ISLET allows professors to demonstrate various digital forensics tools and students to complete their laboratory exercises remotely. ISLET is a container-based virtualization system for teaching Linux-based software with minimal participation and configuration effort. The participation barrier is set very low, and students need only a Secure Shell (SSH) client in order to participate [25].

Inspired by the extensive range of open research questions in the field of digital forensics, this curriculum requires students to contribute to solutions rather than only learn about the issues. To achieve this end students chose a topic for a semester-long research project. Students were guided to design manageable and relevant research topics and were provided with a list of research project ideas. Students formed groups and submitted a project proposal. Each proposal was scrutinized to establish feasibility and likelihood of contributing to digital forensics research and/or education community. The midterm progress report indicates whether students are on-track for the semester. Significantly, the report reveals any particular challenges experienced by the students at that point in the semester. This offers an opportunity for instructors to help students develop strategies for addressing challenges as they continue working on their projects. Near the end of the semester, students present their research projects in the form of oral presentations to their peers and instructors. Ultimately, they submit final project reports.

4.3 Digital Forensics 3

Digital Forensics 3 (DF3) is an advanced topics course specifically designed to include a substantial research component, challenging students to investigate, develop, and design a research project that focuses on a particular aspect related to the multidisciplinary field of digital forensics. This course aims to enroll advanced undergraduate and graduate students to develop topic-specific research that is related to their fields of study. Students will read and examine the latest research in the area of digital forensics. They will be asked to analyze and critique an array of papers, and from this analysis, they will choose a research topic. The strategies for DF3 curriculum design are in development and will focus primarily on enhancing digital forensics research.

4.4 Evaluation Methodologies

The construction, modifications, and updates to the curriculum are based on workshops, surveys, student evaluations and performance. The construction of the initial curriculum vision is based on summaries of a series of workshops (the proceedings are now in press) that included experts in the field of digital forensics. Findings and guidance gathered from these workshops significantly added to the curriculum development process. An external evaluation team was hired to conduct a formal evaluation of the initiative by providing: (a) Ongoing feedback to inform the implementation and delivery of the curriculum, and (b) Comprehensive assessment of program effectiveness and outcome attainment. Being responsive to the multiple groups of individuals involved with the initiative helps to legitimize a diversity of perspectives and experiences and contribute to a comprehensive understanding of the curriculum being developed. To that end, the evaluation design includes both quantitative and qualitative methods developed in collaboration with the initiative's leadership team.

Three student surveys were developed, which were distributed throughout the academic semester. The initial paper-based survey is administered to registered students during the first week of the course. Its purpose is to gather initial information about enrolled students, including major, technical background, ethnicity, and gender. The second survey is administered mid-course and online after the midterm exam. This survey records how students are experiencing the course. The third survey is an end-course survey administered online during the last week of class. Its aim is to gather information about students' perspectives, experiences, and suggestions. All surveys include multiple-choice questions whereby students indicate their level of agreement with a statement on a scale from 1 to 5. Surveys also included open-ended items, inviting students to include additional comments about specific aspects of the course.

The evaluation team observed most of the lecture and lab sessions. The purpose of these observations was to assess the delivery of the curriculum content, and students' engagement and experience with the course. Information related to the following categories was noted during the observations: (a) Social or interpersonal setting: how groups and individuals were situated; (b) Activities: a systematic description of activities and time-frames; (c) Content: a description of resources and materials used and discussed; and (d) Interactions: a description of student-professor verbal and nonverbal interactions.

Group or individual interviews were conducted in the middle and at the end of the course to explore students' experiences, reactions to, and opinions on the course in detail. Each group or individual interview involved a dialogue between students and one of the evaluators, who prompted conversations about course-related topics. In an effort to maintain student confidentiality and privacy, there were no members of the course's staff or instructors present during the interviews.

5   Results, Opportunities, Challenges

This project found Digital Forensics to be a complex curriculum to teach in a higher-education institution. This curriculum model and course outlines contribute to a stronger basis for a standardized curriculum. The results are based on teaching the first course twice and the second course once and the results are supplemented with evaluations, surveys and exam results. Below is a summary of the project's findings so far, commenting on opportunities to improve the curriculum, and outlining some challenges that remain.

5.1   Findings About Students

The program attracted students from various majors, including law, psychology, math, computer engineering, and computer science. Perhaps unsurprisingly, a major problem with designing a curriculum for multiple majors is that there was a wide difference in students' expectations. Students with a technical background desired to learn more about technical topics, and typically they failed to understand the importance of non-technical topics. Students with a non-technical background and interest tended to appreciate the course overall; however, they struggled with the technical concepts and assignments of the course. The large number of possible careers includes digital forensics analyst, examiner, practitioner, security specialist, expert witness, security researcher, digital archivist, and fraud investigator added to student expectations.

5.2   Team Development of a Course

Lacking any individual with the full range of Digital Forensics expertise, the course sequence is team-taught. The project struggled to present a cohesive course and maintain course integrity related to the differing approaches of the team. Multiple professors did achieve the aim to provide students with a broader understanding of the topics presented. However, many students failed to grasp all of the connections. The intention for the final product is that one instructor will be able to teach all the materials. Part of this project involves providing background material as a teaching aid.

5.3   Digital Forensics Theory and Practice

Approaching Digital Forensics education using a scientific approach requires evaluation of methods and experimental results. However, scientifically evaluating Digital Forensics methods and reasoning about that evidence using logic is immature in theory and in practice. The project introduced a module in Digital Forensics 2 on "Reasoning about Evidence" with the intention of promoting a more scientific approach to digital forensics research than was offered in the introductory course. The following challenges resulted from this approach. First, the time limitations of a 16-week course limited covering several topics in depth. Second, digital forensics practitioners, educators, and researchers identified that a robust scientific basis for the evaluative methods involved with digital forensics investigations was ongoing research. The Scientific Working Group on Digital Evidence (SWGDE), for instance, have released several documents since 1999 concerning digital forensics standards, best practices, testing, and validation processes, and these were considered in the development of our curriculum. Additionally, in 2001, the U.S. National Institute of Standards and Technology (NIST) began the Computer Forensic Tool Testing (CFTT) Project. It subsequently established and implemented validation test protocols for several digital forensics tools. Moreover, DF2 includes a module entitled tool validation but remains challenging because tool evaluation technologies are unavailable.

The first Digital Forensics Research Workshop (DFRWS 2011) initiated a gathering of over 50 researchers, investigators, and analysts. It aimed to establish a research community that would apply the scientific method in finding focused near-term solutions that were based on practitioner requirements. The community addressed future aims for developing the field of digital forensics. The related curriculum emphasizes the need to bring rigorous scientific methodological approaches to evidence evaluation. One example is "fuzzy logic," a particular form of reasoning about digital evidence. Fuzzy logic allows elements to be identified as true or false *to some degree*. A "fuzzy engine" provides a solution to human errors (such as word misspellings) that might skew the results of analysis by selecting an acceptable degree of "fuzziness." A fuzzy expert system regards a misspelled or mistaken word as input and then finds relationships for it with other similar words.

5.4 Project Opportunities

The Digital Forensics 2 advanced course implements a semester-long research project. This provided the students with opportunities to explore different concerns of Digital Forensics. For example, several students decided to develop a case study as their research project that will be available to other institutions to be used in future work and may also be incorporated into the next iteration of the introductory course, Digital Forensics 1. A group interested in social media investigated the amount of shared information by considering application programming interfaces that could potentially be used to extract data about individuals. The project involves the creation of a correlation engine that would be able to demonstrate a connection between application programming interfaces and the ability to extract information about an individual from an online environment. Another group of students introduced digital forensics to high school students. Modeled on their own abbreviated curriculum they also created challenge exercises for the high school students. The goal of the students is to produce outcomes of their project that will contribute to outreach programs that engage students of all ages in digital forensics education. Yet another research group designed a lab for students to examine Mac operating system malware and relevant legal aspects of an investigation.

5.5 The Laboratory Environment: Results and Challenges

The collaborative virtual lab environment also led to some challenges. It requires students to be knowledgeable about the Linux command-line, which is a challenge for many non-technical students. This will hopefully be overcome in the future by designing a laboratory assignment based on an introduction to the Linux command-line.

5.6 Evaluation Methodology Challenges

The evaluation progressed with some challenges. As the aim of the evaluation is to provide ongoing feedback to the initiative's leadership team, a mid-course survey is administered to students during each course. Much of the feedback provided by students is related to the structural organization of the course, which is not feasible to change in the middle of the semester. Another challenge is the variability in student participation. Encouraging students to participate in surveys and interviews was difficult as students' participation declines closer to the end of the semester. Different strategies are being explored to maintain and encourage student participation. Another challenge is that the data gathered are representative of the perspectives and experiences of students enrolled at a particular university. As an alpha version of the curriculum is in the process of being distributed, the goal is to also gather data from institutions adopting the curriculum. Gathering a broad range of data will potentially provide support for the initiative's goal of the curriculum's acceptance as a national standard.

The course enrolls students from various majors, including law, psychology, math, computer engineering, and computer science. Conducting course and lab session observations yielded a significant amount of insight about the curriculum being implemented. First, these observations offered an immediate impression of how the courses are progressing, which informs and further enlightens data gathered from surveys and interviews. For instance, during the evaluation of the introductory course in the fall of 2014, it was observed that students struggled with answering and finishing lab assignments. Students were asked in an open-ended question format about the pace and structure of the lab, especially if they were dissatisfied with the lab section. Second, conducting observations allowed for the evaluation team to further understand the curriculum because it was situated within a classroom environment. Observing the curriculum's implementation and development progress revealed how it was being structured, delivered and received by students. Third, classroom presence, for the purposes of observation, helped to build rapport between the evaluation team and enrolled students. Conducting observations is time consuming, but it is an important method as it helps to situate the program overall.

6 Conclusion

This proposed project offers a standardized multidisciplinary curriculum model for digital forensics education. It is being made available to institutions for adoption. This project transformed the multidisciplinary undergraduate education at a Midwest university in the United States by institutionalizing this program and the collaborations upon which it is built. In accordance with the multidisciplinary nature of the field of digital forensics, the curriculum development team included domain experts in computer security, computer networks, law, civil and criminal justice, fraud investigation, and psychology. The modular approach to curriculum development is organized by a three-course digital forensics education sequence, and the modules are combined to form a coherent narrative, thus exposing students to multiple perspectives on digital forensics. The curriculum package provides a strong theoretical foundation for the techniques learned by the students as well as an array of studies in fields related to digital forensics. Hopefully this paper will initiate a conversation with the international community, note that standards need to continue to be developed for digital forensics curriculum, and recognize the multidisciplinary need for this field of study. This project, curriculum, and course outline are available on the website http://publish.illinois.edu/digital-forensics/ and a content package containing all of these materials will be posted there in the near future.

Appendix A. Digital Forensics Curriculum Topics

See Tables 1 and 2.

Table 1. Topics for digital forensics 1

Introductory course topic list by module

Introduction and Concepts of Forensics
Define digital forensics
Process of forensics investigation
Review of case studies

Sociological Aspects of Digital Forensics

Legal Aspects of Digital Forensics
Fourth Amendment
Evidence
Privacy laws
Cyber crimes

Computer Forensics
Introduction to computer forensics
Introduction to file system forensics
NTFS analysis
File carving
Windows analysis and application

Psychological Aspects of Digital Forensics
Forensics psychology and cyber crime
Psychological profiling of cyber criminals

Network Forensics
Network fundamentals
Evidence acquisition
Packet analysis

Fraud Investigations
Introduction to fraud examination
Nature and extent of fraud; Benford's Law

Mobile Forensics and Malware
Mobile device forensics
Mobile network forensics
Malware

Table 2. Topics for digital forensics 2

Advanced course topic list by module
Sociological Perspectives on DF-related Cases
Computer Fraud and Abuse Act
Privacy
Incident Response
Reasoning about Digital Evidence
File System Forensics
Timeline analysis
Tool Validation and Anti-Forensics
Linux/Mac operating system analysis
Mobile (Android/iOS) OS analysis
Network Forensics
Network log analysis
Traffic pattern analysis
Network protocol analysis
Unknown network protocol analysis
Wireless traffic analysis
Psychology of Cyber Crime
Understanding hackers
Human heuristics and biases
Digital Archives
Basics of archival perspective
Digital forensics hardware and software in archives
Reverse-Engineering Malware
Overview of malware analysis
Case Study

References

1. Meyers, M., Rogers, M.: CF: the need for standardization and certification. Int. J. Digital Evid. **3**(2), 1–11 (2004)
2. Yasinsac, A., Erbacher, R.F., Marks, D.G., Pollitt, M.M., Sommer, P.M.: Computer forensics education. IEEE Secur. Priv. **1**(4), 15–23 (2003)
3. Bem, D., Huebner, E.: Computer forensics workshop for undergraduate students. In: Proceedings of the Tenth Conference on Australian Computing Education, vol. 78, pp. 29–33. Australian Computer Society, Inc., January 2008
4. Kessler, G.C., Schirling, M.E.: The design of an undergraduate degree program in computer and digital forensics. J. Digital Forensics Secur. Law **1**(3), 37–50 (2006)

5. Bashir, M., Applequist, J., Campbell, R., DeStefano, L., Garcia, G., Lang, A.: Development and dissemination of a new multidisciplinary undergraduate curriculum in digital forensics. In: ADFSL, Richmond, Virginia, 28–29 May 2014

6. Chi, H., Dix-Richardson, F., Evans, D.: Designing a computer forensics concentration for cross-disciplinary undergraduate students. In: Information Security Curriculum Development Conference, pp. 52–57. ACM (2010)

7. Srinivasan, S.: Computer forensics curriculum in security education. In: Information Security Curriculum Development Conference, pp. 32–36. ACM (2009)

8. Wassenaar, D., Woo, D., Wu, P.: A certificate program in computer forensics. J. Comput. Sci. Coll. **24**(4), 158–167 (2009)

9. Woods, K., Lee, C.A., Garfinkel, S., Dittrich, D., Russel, A., Kearton, K.: Creating realistic corpora for forensic and security education. In: Proceedings of the ADFSL Conference on Digital Forensics Security and Law, pp. 123–134 (2011)

10. Lang, A., Bashir, M., Campbell, R., DeStefano, L.: Developing a new digital forensics curriculum. In: DFWRS, Denver, CO, 3–6 August 2014

11. Walls, R.J., Levine, B.N., Liberatore, M., Shields, C.: Effective digital forensic research is investigator-centric. In: HotSec (2011)

12. Beebe, N.: Digital forensic research: the good, the bad and the unaddressed. In: Peterson, G., Shenoi, S. (eds.) IFIP WG. IFIP AICT, vol. 306, pp. 17–36. Springer, Heidelberg (2009)

13. Kwan, M., Chow, K.-P., Law, F., Lai, P.: Reasoning about evidence using bayesian networks. In: Ray, I., Shenoi, S. (eds.) Advances in Digital Forensics IV. IFIP, vol. 285, pp. 275–289. Springer, Heidelberg (2008)

14. Bishop, M.: Education in information security. IEEE Concurrency **8**(4), 4–8 (2000)

15. Craiger, P., Ponte, L., Whitcomb, C., Pollitt, M., Eaglin, R.: Master's degree in digital forensics. In: System Sciences, HICSS 2007, 40th AHIC, pp. 264b. IEEE (2007)

16. Nance, K., Armstrong, H., Armstrong, C.: Digital forensics: defining an education agenda. In: System Sciences, HICSS 2010, 43rd AHIC, pp. 1–10. IEEE (2010)

17. Burnett, S.F.: Computer security training and education: a needs analysis. In: 2012 IEEE Symposium on Security and Privacy, p. 0026. IEEE Computer Society (1996)

18. Cooper, P., Finley, G.T., Kaskenpalo, P.: Towards standards in digital forensics education. In: Proceedings of the 2010 ITiCSE Working Group Reports, New York, pp. 87–95. ACM (2010)

19. Gottschalk, L., Liu, J., Dathan, B., Fitzgerald, S., Stein, M.: Computer forensics programs in higher education: a preliminary study. In: SIGCSE Bulletin, vol. 37, pp. 147–151 (2005)

20. Liu, J.: Implementing a baccalaureate program in computer forensics. J. Comput. Sci. Coll. **25**(3), 101–109 (2010)

21. FEPAC Accreditation standards Technical report. AAFS (2012)

22. Curricula, C.: Report of ACM/IEEE-CS Joint Curriculum Task Force (1991)

23. WVUFSI: Technical working group for education and training in digital forensics technical report. U.S. Department of Justice, August 2007

24. Scientific Working Group on Digital Forensics. SWGDE/SWGIT guidelines and recommendations for training in digital and multimedia evidence technology (2010). https://www.swgde.org/documents/CurrentDocuments

25. Schipp, J., Dopheide, J., Slagell, A.: ISLET: an isolated, scalable and lightweight environment for training. In: The Proceedings of XSEDE 2015, St. Louis, MO, July 2015

26. Woods, K., Lee, C., Garfinkel, S., Dittrich, D., Russel, A., Kearton, K.: Creating realistic corpora for forensic and security education. In: ADFSL Conference on Digital Forensics, Security and Law (2011)

27. Ismand, E.S., Hamilton, J.A. Jr.: A digital forensics program to retrain America's veterans. In: 5th ASIA, pp. 62–66 (2010)
28. Al Amro, S., Chiclana, F., Elizondo, D.A.: Application of fuzzy logic in computer security and forensics. In: Elizondo, D.A., Solanas, A., Martinez, A. (eds.) Computational Intelligence for Privacy and Security. SCI, vol. 394, pp. 35–49. Springer, Heidelberg (2012)

Development and Initial User Evaluation of a Virtual Crime Scene Simulator Including Digital Evidence

Alleyn Conway[1], Joshua I. James[2], and Pavel Gladyshev[3(✉)]

[1] IT Planning, an Garda Síochána, Phoenix Park, Dublin 8, Ireland
alleyn.conway@ucdconnect.ie
[2] DigitalFIRE, Hallym University, Chuncheon, South Korea
joshua@cybercrimetech.com
[3] DigitalFIRE, University College Dublin, Dublin 4, Ireland
pavel.gladyshev@ucd.ie

Abstract. Imagine the following scenario: an inexperienced law enforcement officer enters a crime scene and – on finding a USB key on a potential suspect – inserts it into a nearby Windows desktop computer hoping to find some information which may help an ongoing investigation. The desktop crashes and all data on the USB key and on the Windows desktop has now been potentially compromised. However, the law enforcement officer in question is using a Virtual Crime Scene Simulator and has just learned a valuable lesson. This paper discusses the development and initial user evaluation of a Virtual Crime Scene Simulator that includes the ability to interact with and perform live triage of commonly-found digital devices. Based on our experience of teaching digital evidence handling, we aimed to create a realistic virtual environment that integrates many different aspects of the digital and physical crime scene processing, such as physical search activities, triage of digital devices, note taking and form filling, interaction with suspects at the scene, as well as search team training.

Keywords: Virtual crime scene simulator · Digital forensic training · Unity3D · Digital evidence

1 Introduction

As with any discipline, the opportunity to practice, learn and apply such learning to a real-life scenario instills confidence within oneself. It allows mistakes to be made, actions to be evaluated and tasks to be set. In the sometimes high-pressure environment of a crime scene search involving complex physical and digital evidence, one incorrect action can be detrimental to any future judicial proceedings.

There have been a number of projects that attempt to virtualise crime scenes either for entertainment, educational or, more recently, for law enforcement training purposes. The examples of entertainment involving crime scene simulations include the popular Facebook game 'Criminal Case' [1] and the Interview Simulator game [2]. The Interview Simulator is a relatively simple, static interaction that attempts to simulate interviews in the

© Institute for Computer Sciences, Social Informatics and Telecommunications Engineering 2015
J.I. James and F. Breitinger (Eds.): ICDF2C 2015, LNICST 157, pp. 16–26, 2015.
DOI: 10.1007/978-3-319-25512-5_2

context of police investigation. While such entertainment represents some educational value for law enforcement, it does not accurately represent real crime scenes.

The F.B.I. realised the need to accurately represent real crime scenes, and began working with Epic Games' Unreal Engine 3 [3] in an effort to create realistic, complex 3D simulations of crime scene activities in a first-person point of view. Such an effort is similar to the 3D game released by the U.S. Army, called 'America's Army' [4]. Other simulator games specifically for law enforcement include firearms and other tactical training [5].

Although existing specialised simulators are valuable as educational tools, there are problems hindering their practical usage for digital forensics training. First and foremost, existing crime scene simulators do not normally represent digital evidence in the crime scene but rather cover crime scene reconstruction and investigation, e.g., Crime Scene Virtual Tour [6]. Also, these systems do not easily allow for the modification of scenarios that can match the training course. Overcoming these challenges, while preserving the realism and complexity of the simulated experience has been the focus of the work described in this paper.

1.1 Contribution

This work contributes to the field of digital forensic investigation by providing considerations for crime scene investigation training that includes digital evidence; providing a 3D virtual environment in which law enforcement can practice learned crime scene search and seizure procedure; and evaluating such systems with law enforcement officers during classroom training.

2 3D Technology and Crime Scene Simulation

With the advent of software such as Unity 3D, a powerful cross-platform 3D engine and Virtual Reality (VR) headsets such as Oculus Rift a developer now has access to technology that only a few years ago would have been the preserve of a Hollywood film studio.

There are multiple examples of 3D technology been employed by law enforcement, military and educational institutes. Whilst all have varying end users the methods the applications employ allow for effective knowledge transfer.

Crime Scene Virtual Tour (CSVT) [6] allows the user to reconstruct a 3D crime scene using photos, provides a 3D measurement feature and thereafter walks through the scene. By uploading photos of the crime scene the user is able to zoom, pan, tilt and rotate the scene and relive the crime scene. Unlike the Virtual Crime Scene Simulator developed as part of this project, however, it does not offer the ability to interact with devices found at the scene. Another solution is offered by AI2-3D [7], a Canadian company, specialising in the reconstruction of crime scenes using 3D forensic visualisation for court presentations.

Beginning in 1960 "the armed forces took the lead in financing, sponsoring, and inventing the specific technology used in video games" [8]. Spacewar!, which some historians would consider the first video game, was developed by graduate students at MIT who were funded by the Pentagon. Forward 50 years and we now see sophisticated First Person Shooter games such as American's Army or Full Spectrum Warrior being played by gamers but also being used by military forces for training [9].

3   Development of the Virtual Crime Scene Simulator

There are a number of reasons as to why a new Virtual Crime Scene Simulator is needed for digital forensic investigation training. First, crime scene processing is a vital part of investigator training that can only be learned through practice. The initial aim of the project described in this paper was to create a virtual environment that would allow distance-learning students to familiarize with and practice the key elements of the crime scene search before a trip to a dedicated training facility for hands-on training.

In comparison with physical crime scene simulations, virtual environments have a number of distinct advantages:

- virtual crime scenes are less expensive and faster to setup;
- virtual crime scenes could be big, complex, and/or highly unusual;
- virtual crime scenes can be used to perform joint training sessions where team members are geographically far apart;
- virtual crime scene could allow straightforward simulation of live triage and crime scene processing using virtual machines.

These reasons provide the motivation for development of the Virtual Crime Scene Simulator, and minimum final functionality for the system.

Unity3D was chosen as the base platform for the Virtual Crime Scene Simulator because it comes with a free feature-complete development environment. Another advantage is support for multiple platform development. Applications can be created for iOS, MACs, PCs, Steam, Xbox and others.

The Virtual Crime Scene Simulator provides a realistic crime scene with configurable search options. In addition to physical crime scene simulation it encapsulates virtual machines, imitating digital devices in a crime scene along with an Artificial Intelligence Markup Language (AIML) based chatbot [10] providing interactivity with an avatar.

Before commencing development, a 3D representation of a house was created containing three rooms, a hallway, a hidden room and outside scenery. The creation of such scenery is a straightforward application of Unity3D and can be created without any development experience whatsoever. Following the creation of the scenery the next step was the creation of game objects. These set the scene for the user and included items such as:

- Furniture
- Props
- Hardware devices, e.g., mobile phone, desktop, hidden laptops
- An avatar for interrogating

The intelligence and internal logic of the game objects was written mostly in Javascript (Unityscript), which is built into Unity 3D engine. The following gaming actions were developed and applied to the game objects:

- Issuing of a warrant before a search could commence
- Physical searching of game objects
- Labeling, exhibiting of possible evidential item
- Dismantling, examining and seizure of game objects
- Note taking during crime scene searching
- Interactive avatar who can be treated as a suspect and/or witness and questioned appropriately
- Live examination of digital devices such as mobile phones, desktops, laptops, Smart TVs using multiple options
- Live feedback with reference to ACPO principles [11] depending on device interaction

The Virtual Crime Scene Simulator is an open source project. The source code and the binary installers can be downloaded from the project website [12].

If a trainer needs to amend the scene then he or she will need to be familiar with the scene functionality in Unity3D along with knowledge of how the scripts in the application interact with each other. Should the trainer need to add logic over and above what the application does then the existing Javascript can be amended or new code added. Once this is achieved the trainer has the ability to create additional devices or delete existing ones, add new rooms, create new tasks, etc.

Figure 1 shows the initial screen of the current version of Virtual Crime Scene Simulator. Upon installation the user can select various setup options via an administration menu. These options allow the user to

- turn on/off background noise
- turn on/off virtual integration with external devices
- detail what OS should be used on simulated digital devices – there is a separate configuration option per each simulated device.
- choose type of pre-programme search scenario – urgent or routine.

3.1 Sample Walk-Through

Upon entering the crime scene the user is presented with a number of tasks she or he is required to perform. Currently, these include

- Exhibit at least 3 items
- Discover a hidden object
- Begin an interrogation
- Get suspect's date of birth
- Save log files

Once the simulator commences, the user has the ability to walk around all rooms within the scene but can only start interacting with the game objects once a warrant has been presented to the avatar. Once done, a suite of options are now available.

Fig. 1. Opening presented to the trainee when starting the virtual crime scene simulation in single-user mode.

Fig. 2. Virtual environment shown to the trainee when choosing to analyze the suspect computer in the virtual crime scene simulator.

If the user wishes to interact with a digital device an option "Interact with <device>" is available in the list of actions for each digital device. Currently device interaction is fully realized only on the Microsoft Windows version of the Virtual Crime Scene Simulator. It is implemented using Virtual Machines running under VirtualBox. During the device interaction phase, the user is shown the console of the virtual machine in a full-screen mode (see Fig. 2). The user may now interact with the VM and upon finishing return to the crime scene. Through the Admin menu the trainer can elect which operating system (either Microsoft Windows or Ubuntu Linux) particular devices will be running when called, e.g., the laptop could be running Ubuntu whilst the desktop could be running Windows.

Fig. 3. A list of action options that is available when interacting with the suspect desktop on-scene.

Virtualbox VMs are called from the simulator using Windows shell scripts (.BAT files), which can be adapted to use a different virtualisation manager. Nircmd utility [13] was also utilised to ensure that the virtual client is always displayed on top of the Unity backdrop and is centered appropriately.

When the user interaction with the virtual device is finished the virtual client is rolled back to its original snapshot and the user is returned to the crime scene. The snapshot rollback ensures that the trainer does not need to restore all the virtual clients back to their original state for the next training session

In addition to interacting with digital devices there is also the ability to search for, manipulate and examine game objects, e.g., moving a bookcase reveals a hidden room or examining a bed reveals a laptop under the covers (see Fig. 3 as an example).

As well as interacting with inanimate and digital objects, the user has the option to interrogate an avatar. The avatar's intelligence is simulated using a back-end chatbot application. The chatbot responds to questions which are pre-programmed using Artificial Intelligence Markup Language (AIML). The user can choose whether to question the avatar as either a suspect or a witness. All questions and responses are logged in a time-stamped log file.

Upon completion of the user's session the application saves the following log files:

- Action log detailing all options selected by the user and feedback from the application
- Notes log detailing any notes taken by the user
- Interrogation log detailing all questions and responses from the avatar
- Communications log detailing all chat which took place with other search team members

These log files can then be analysed by a trainer and used to give detailed feedback to the individual students and the team as a whole.

4   Evaluation of the Virtual Crime Scene Simulator

In August 2014 the opportunity arose to have the application tested by members of Law Enforcement from a developing country. These law enforcement officers were in the process of receiving a 5 month in-house training course on digital forensic and cyber-crime investigations. Such training included a crime scene investigation component.

In the current version of the Virtual Crime Scene Simulator, virtual machine integration executes on a Windows OS only, so the ability to launch a VM was excluded from the training exercise. However, all other device interaction functionality, such as switching devices on and off and connecting USB sticks to it, was available.

Overall, 6 participants used the Virtual Crime Scene Simulator. Each had various levels of experience with computers in general and with computer games.

Before training, the trainees had at least 3 years experience as criminal investigators. Three out of the group had some experience with digital devices, but considered themselves 'beginner' level. The remaining trainees had no experience with digital investigations.

After lectures on related topics, the trainees were instructed to install the Virtual Crime Scene Simulator (VCSS) on their laboratory workstations. Each trainee was able to download, install and run the VCSS with no issues.

As mentioned, each of the trainees were experienced law enforcement officers with very different computing backgrounds. This was immediately apparent once the VCSS was started. Those with little computing experience, especially those that claimed to have never played video games before, found it difficult to interact with the VCSS. The trainees with computer gaming experience were able to use the system with no issues. Trainees with little-to-no experience took approximately 30 min to get familiar with the controls.

The exercise goal was to complete the previously mentioned pre-defined tasks. The system provided an automatic checklist of tasks, and indicated whether they have been completed or not. The trainees were instructed to let the teacher know when they have finished.

Like a normal crime scene, there are a number of objects in the virtual crime scene that may be related, but are not explicitly listed as objectives. The trainees could choose whether to seize, analyse, deconstruct or leave any other objects they found.

After each trainee finished, we collected Virtual Crime Scene Simulator log files detailing each trainee's search and seizure activity, and had each student fill out a survey relating to their experience.

4.1   Virtual Crime Scene Simulator Questions

This section covers the virtual crime scene simulator survey results from the trainees immediately after using the VCSS followed by a brief analysis of the results.

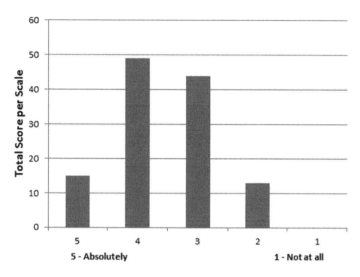

Fig. 4. Allocation of scores combined from 20 questions from all respondents.

Twenty questions were posed to the trainees, which covered the following areas:

- User Interaction
- Educational Value
- Technical aspect of the application

The trainees were asked to assess each question based on a scale of 5 (Absolutely) to 1 (Not at all).

In addition to these questions the trainees were also asked to (1) detail what modifications they would like to see added to the application, (2) what functionality did they particularly like and (3) to document issues which they had with the application (Fig. 4).

As can be seen from the above graph the application achieves a high score in the 4 to 5 scale. The fact that some of the participants were never used to play FPS (First Person Shooter) games needs to be taken into account when viewing the 2–3 scale totals (Figs. 5, 6 and 7).

4.2 Survey Analysis

The use of Linux version for the evaluation highlighted a number of bugs which did not exist on the Windows OS version of the VCSS and is an area which needs further improvement for future releases.

One student, who had computer experience and had used a FPS game before, scored the application high. It is possible that the average scoring attributed by the non-computer experienced users related more to their lack of experience with computers and FPS games. Possibly, with more experience such trainees would focus on the scene search rather than concentrating on manipulating the game for the first time.

The results in Sect. 4.1, on average, score highly amongst the participants in relation to the educational purpose of the application and indicate that there are enough tasks to

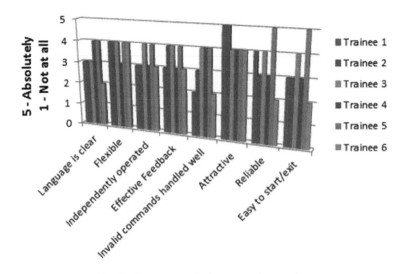

Fig. 5. Responses relating to user interaction.

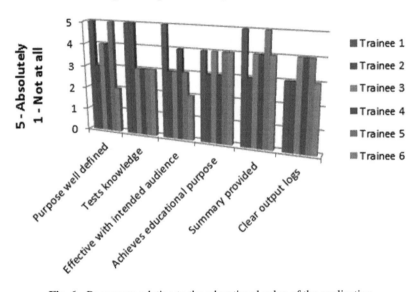

Fig. 6. Responses relating to the educational value of the application

motivate the users to continue using the program. This is very encouraging given the usability bugs within the Linux version of the application.

It is worth noting that one participant marked the application with a mark of 2 in 9 questions but yet scored it 4 when it comes to stating that the program achieves its purpose from an educational viewpoint.

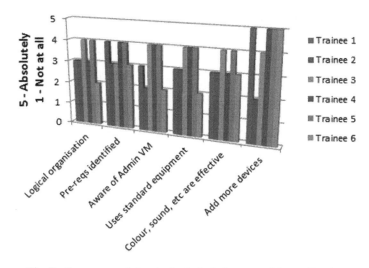

Fig. 7. Responses relating to the technical aspect of the application.

5   Trainer Comments

From a training perspective, the VCSS was very useful for reinforcing the theoretical concepts presented to students prior to the exercise. No students had experience with digital evidence seizure in a crime scene, and their reactions to the VCSS were very much like what we have seen with inexperienced investigators in the field. Specifically, rushing straight to digital devices, non-structured searching, not adhering to ACPO or similar guidelines, etc.

From a trainer's perspective, the logs that are produced by the VCSS provide a clear indication of what the trainee was trying to achieve, as well as the crime scene search process (or lack thereof). This information proved to be extremely valuable for identifying areas of confusion, and was used both to discuss such concepts again, and to better illustrate how such concepts would be conducted in a real crime scene.

6   Conclusions and Future Work

The application, even when used by participants with little prior computer experience, offered a valuable insight into real crime scene processing with digital devices, and the options faced by an investigator upon entering a possible crime scene. Notwithstanding the Linux-specific issues which arose and the lack of computer experience amongst the participants it was encouraging to note that users still got benefit from the application.

As with any application there is always room both for improvement and expansion. It is now planned to incorporate functionality to make the application more versatile which will include, though not limited to, the following:

- Creation of independent game objects so they can be placed into any Unity Scene for re-use

- Customize setup using configuration files, e.g., localisation of narrative, task creation, scenario types, etc.
- Extending interaction with virtual environments for Linux and OSX operating systems
- Incorporating Oculus Rift plug-in
- Record and playback for further training purpose.

Further enhancements and plug-ins are planned for further releases to ensure that this application over time will become a best-in-practice learning application for crime scene investigators.

References

1. Criminal Case Game. https://www.facebook.com/CriminalCaseGame (2014)
2. Interview Simulation. http://www.horton.com/portfoliointerview.htm (2013)
3. Makuch, E.: FBI using Unreal Engine 3 crime scene sim. http://www.gamespot.com/articles/fbi-using-unreal-engine-3-crime-scene-sim/1100-6368256/ (2012)
4. Osborne, S.: Americas Army. http://www.gamespot.com/reviews/americas-army-operations-review/1900-2895424/ (2002)
5. Lee, C.: Police simulator training more than just a video game. http://www.dailyillini.com/news/campus/crime/article_1cdc97e1-3d6a-5df4-9fdc-1f394c2a8d44.html?mode=story (2013)
6. Crime Scene Virtual Tour. http://www.crime-scene-vr.com/ (2011)
7. AI2-3D. Forenisc Mapping, Analysis & Visualization. http://ai2-3d.com/ (2014)
8. Mead, C.: War Play: Video Games and the Future of Armed Conflict. Eamon Dolan/Houghton Mifflin Harcourt, Boston (2013)
9. Perez, M.: Military Advertising and Simulation Training: U.S. Army's Use of Video Games. http://www.academia.edu/6823477/Military_Advertising_and_Simulation_Training_U.S._Armys_Use_of_Video_Games (2012)
10. Shawar, B.A.: A Corpus Based Approach to Generalising a Chatbot System: Applying Simple Natural Language Processing Techniques to Build Knowledge Base of ALICE Chatbot System LAP Lambert Academic Publishing. dl.acm.org/citation.cfm?id=2132757 (2011)
11. Association of Chief Police Officers. ACPO Good Practice Guide for Digital Evidence. http://www.acpo.police.uk/documents/crime/2011/201110-cba-digital-evidence-v5.pdf (2012)
12. Open Source Digital Forensics Reference Site. www2.opensourceforensics.org (2014)
13. NirSoft. NirCmd v2.75. http://www.nirsoft.net/utils/nircmd.html (2013)

Computational Forensics

Detection of Frame Duplication Type of Forgery in Digital Video Using Sub-block Based Features

Vivek Kumar Singh[✉], Pallav Pant, and Ramesh Chandra Tripathi

Department of Information Technology, Indian Institute of Information Technology,
Allahabad India
vivekkr.singh@hotmail.com, pallav.pant@gmail.com,
rctripathi@iiita.ac.in

Abstract. With the easy availability and operability of video editing tools, any video could be edited in short span of time. Sometimes, these modifications change the actual meaning of targeted video. Hence, before making any judgment and opinion about such multimedia contents, it is necessary to verify their genuineness. A video can be tampered by various different attempts. Each different attempt derives a new type of forgery in videos. Among various types of attack on video, frame duplication is a common type of attack. Frames are duplicated and pasted into same video in order to either hide or add false information. We propose Sub Blocked based features to detect frame duplication. The experimental results show higher accuracy that not only detects but also localize duplicated frames as well.

Keywords: Frame duplication · Image forensic · Sub-blocking method · Video forgery · Correlation

1 Introduction

In the recent years, the availability of low cost and more interactive digital multimedia hardware such as web cam, digital camera, surveillance camera and mobile phones etc. have made it easy to capture instances at any time. With the proliferation of such digital contents, multimedia editing software (Adobe Photoshop, Avid, Audacity etc.) allow manipulations in it even with little effort. These manipulations/modifications can be performed perfectly such that it looks like original content. As a result, digital contents should not be blindly accepted. Due to potential alteration, it has become sparingly difficult to judge the authenticity of a given multimedia content by naked eye. Thus, there is an urgent need of such a tool that can assure the authenticity and originality of altered contents.

A lot work has already been reported in image forgery detection. In recent years, many cases regarding sting of famous personalities (political, actor or social activist) are reported and telecasted by television media in India. These stings (Video/Audio) affect beliefs of viewers and change their psychology. A long manual procedure in examination of such controversial video or audio tapes cannot return faith of innocent people. So there is an urgent need of such tools which can check the originality and authenticity of such contents.

© Institute for Computer Sciences, Social Informatics and Telecommunications Engineering 2015
J.I. James and F. Breitinger (Eds.): ICDF2C 2015, LNICST 157, pp. 29–38, 2015.
DOI: 10.1007/978-3-319-25512-5_3

Therefore, it is necessary to develop tools to detect any type of forgery if exists. In present work, we have focused a particular type of video forgery detection. Before getting into video forgery detection techniques, a small description of digital video is given below.

"Videos refer to pictorial (Visual) information, including still images and time-varying images. A still image is a spatial distribution of intensity that is constant with respect to time. In time varying image (video) visual pattern changes image by image."

Video is a sequence of images (frames). Fraudsters attempt to change the information contained within these sequence of frames thus changing the content of the original video. These changes can either be in spatial information within a frame in temporal information between two frames. Thus, video forgeries can be of various types depending upon the way in which information is tampered in a video sequence.

A most popular type of forgery is frame duplication. In such forgery, some sequence of frames are copied and pasted elsewhere in the same video sequence. This type of forgery is performed either to hide any particular information or to insert any false information in the video sequence. Duplicating a group of frame in a video sequence is an easy task. As a result of frame duplication, particular information can be hide as shown in Fig. 1.

Fig. 1. Example of frame duplication [1]

Another type of duplication is to duplicate a specific region in the video sequence. This type of tampering can duplicate a motion of the same object elsewhere in the same video sequence.

Our focus is to detect frame duplication type of forgery. Various researchers have already contributed to detect frame duplication. Most relevant researches are discussed here to detect frame duplication type of forgery.

Wang and Farid [1] have explained a duplication type of video forgery with the example shown in Fig. 1. To hide a particular person from the sequence 4–6 (left), frames 1–3 is copied and then pasted at the place of frame 4–6(right). This kind of forgery is generally known as frame duplication. A common technique is to compare correlation of the two consecutive frames. This technique is computationally high. Wang and Farid [1] have proposed a method in which video is split in group of frames, and correlation coefficients are computed. For similarity check, these coefficients are compared and highlighted where found similar. Results are good up to 90 % of accuracy. The given method was good for stationary camera and robust to MPEG compression.

Kobayashi et al. [2] proposed a powerful method to detect a duplicated region in the video based on noise characteristics. With the help of inherent parameters of a camera, result found was more accurate and reliable. Consistency of noise level function in each frame is sufficient to differentiate between attacked and original region. However, this method is good only for static camera and performance dramatically decreases as the compression is performed on the videos.

Hsu et al. [3] adopt a method using noise residue between two consecutive frames for frame duplications. Parameters of GMM are used to lower down the complexity. The results are accurate for stationary camera but not good for compressed videos.

Lin et al. [4] proposed a method to detect and localize the duplicated frames. Method uses histogram difference of RGB values and takes the correlation of histogram differences of adjacent frames between query and test clip. Based on threshold value candidate clips are selected for further analysis. Once candidate clips are selected, block wise of histogram of luminance values of blocks are calculated and if difference between query and test frame is below threshold the blocks are similar. Process is applied on all blocks of all frames between test and query frame. Finally a frame duplication classification scheme is used that uses the number of matching blocks between frames of query clip and test clip to classify them into duplicated or not duplicated frames.

Milani et al. [5] propose a method to detect spatio-temporal forgeries by analyzing left footprints. Method deals with spatio-temporal region copy paste either, by part of group of frames, or by repeated slice of single image. For the image based attack they take residue of adjacent frames for all frames. A 3D residual matrix is calculated. Small regions with zero residues are eliminated using the morphological erosion operation. A coarse-to-fine or big to small scheme iterations are performed on the morphed residual matrix, to find the duplicated 3D spatio-temporal slices. For image based attack true positive, false negative, true negative and false positives are 62 %, 38 %, 93.8, and 6 %. For video based attack detection rate is 88 %.

Mondaini et al. [6] proposed a method to detect whole frame duplication and for object insertion. Authors used camera sensor pattern noise as a characteristic of a camera. Presented work also claims to be robust to some level of invariance to MPEG compression.

2   Proposed Methodology

The Frame duplication is one of the major attacks performed on videos because it is easy to perform in comparison with other types of attack. Hence a need of efficient, fast and reliable algorithm arises to detect frame duplication. In this type of attack some sequence of frames are replaced with some other sequence of frames from the same video sequence.

A novel method is presented through this paper to detect frame duplication. After performing a number of experiments on any raw video (even with static scene), it is concluded that there is very less probability to have two or more frames exactly same on the basis of intensity values. The reason behind such result is noise caused during acquisition time. We tested it with different quality camcorders and for the different scene with different light intensities even though results are same.

Proposed algorithm is able to identify and localize the frame duplication forgery in targeted video sequences $f(x, y, t_i)$.

If $i = M$, we assume that there are M instances of frames.

Let us assume that a group of frames (i = 1 to k) is duplicated at any other place in the same video sequence. The one very obvious approach is to perform an exact match between all possible pairs of frames to detect duplication. Such type of detection is computationally very high and never should be adapted for detection. Therefore, we present a novel method which is not only computational efficient but also robust to compression artifacts. Figure 2, shows the block diagram of proposed method.

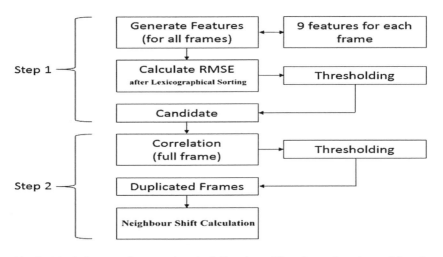

Fig. 2. Block diagram of proposed method. Step 1 candidate frame detection and Step 2 duplicated frame detection.

2.1   Feature Calculation

In spite of comparing intensity values of each pixel as a feature to match two frames, we have chosen nine symmetrical features [7] for each frame. After a lot experiments on our duplicated frame data, we found these features are strong enough to detect duplicated frames. To calculate features each frames are divide into four sub blocks (B_1, B_2, B_3, B_4) as shown in Fig. 3. Features are discussed in following sub-sections.

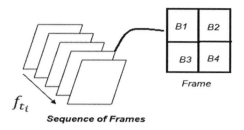

Fig. 3. Sub-blocking of frames

Features are calculated as follows:-

1. **Mean of Block:** *One feature is extracted for each frame.* Mean of a frame is calculated as shown in (1).

$$\mu = 1/MN \sum_{i=0}^{i=M} \sum_{j=0}^{i=N} X(i,j) \tag{1}$$

Where X(i, j) is the set of intensities in each frames. M, N is the dimension of frame. Hence for k number of frames, we will get k means.

2. **Ratio for each Sub Block:** This will result in *four identical features for each frame.* Mean of intensities of each sub block is divided by mean of respective frame one by one as shown in (2). Hence for four different sub blocks of a particular frame, four new features are derived.

$$r_i = \frac{4 \sum B_i}{\sum B} \ for \ (i = 1, 2, 3, 4) \tag{2}$$

3. **Residue for each Sub Block:** *Four features are extracted for each frames.* Formula given below (3) is used to get residual feature of each of the frame.

$$e_i = \sum B - 4 \sum B_i \, for \, (i = 1, 2, 3, 4) \tag{3}$$

For four sub block of a particular frame, four new features are derived again. Hence, we get nine features for each frame f_i. Maintain a feature vector for each of the frames. $f_i = \{\mu, r_1, r_2, r_3, r_4, e_1, e_2, e_3, e_4\}$, where i is the number of frames in video sequence. Therefore, we get above similar feature set for each frame.

2.2   Lexicographical Sorting

For each frames, we get nine features as f_i. For l no of frames, there will be l feature vectors. Let v1, v2, ..., vl be the feature vectors corresponding to these l frames. To perform lexicographical sorting on these vectors of size 9, we regard each of them as a

9-digit number with each digit ranging from 0 to 255. Each vector is assigned with the position of the frame in targeted video. After sorting, likely similar frames are grouped together. It should be ensured that each feature vector (vi) contains its actual position even after sorting.

2.3   Calculation of RMSE and Suspected Frame Detection

RMSE (Root Mean Square Error) is calculated between the feature vectors of adjacent frames after sorting.

$$RMSE = \sqrt{\left(f_i^{\mu,r,e} - f_{i+1}^{\mu,r,e}\right)^2} \quad for \ i = 1l - 1$$

If RMSE is found more than threshold then discards such frames and rest of the frames are marked as suspected frames. We set the threshold value little bigger in order to detect suspected frames in compressed videos.

2.4   Detection of Duplicated Frames

Finally, we get a list of frames that are suspected frames according to their RMSE. These frames are regarded as candidate frames. For exact match, we used correlation between each frames listed in the candidate list.

$$r_{xy} = \frac{\sum_{i=1}^{n}(x_i - x')(y_i - y')}{(n-1)s_x s_y} = \frac{\sum_{i=1}^{n}(x_i - x')(y_i - y')}{\sqrt{\sum_{i=1}^{n}(x_i - x')^2 \sum_{i=1}^{n}(y_i - y')^2}}$$

If the correlation between pair of frames is very high (nearly 1) that frames are marked as duplicated. This is assumed that a fraudster duplicates more than five consecutive frames in order to cheat human eyes because single frame duplication can not affect original meaning of video. Therefore, if two frames are found duplicated after correlation matching, very next four consecutive frames of these two frames are also compared as above. Frames are declared duplicated only if such group of frames is found duplicated with another group of frames. Alternatively, we can discard isolated frame matches. Single frame duplication does not have any significance for the fraudsters.

3   Results

The snapshot of the implementation result on self made video is given in Fig. 4. Column 1 is the result of the candidate selection and Column 2 is the result of the duplicated frames. First, second, third and fourth value in detected results are indicating the serial number, first frame sequence number, second frame sequence number and mean square error between their features respectively. At the bottom of column 2 localization results are given. This is clear in the snap shot that thirty frames are copied and pasted elsewhere in the same video sequence. Results are also depicting copied frames as well as the result.

Checking for frame duplication...

Candidate Duplicated Frames:			
1.0000	355.0000	385.0000	2.4057
2.0000	356.0000	386.0000	2.3997
3.0000	359.0000	389.0000	2.9248
4.0000	360.0000	390.0000	2.4226
5.0000	361.0000	391.0000	2.3996
6.0000	364.0000	394.0000	2.3244
7.0000	365.0000	395.0000	1.0324
8.0000	366.0000	396.0000	1.1729
9.0000	367.0000	397.0000	2.8981
10.0000	368.0000	398.0000	1.8974
11.0000	369.0000	399.0000	1.2184
12.0000	370.0000	400.0000	1.6664
13.0000	371.0000	401.0000	1.3284
14.0000	372.0000	402.0000	2.6695
15.0000	373.0000	403.0000	1.8024
16.0000	374.0000	404.0000	1.6727
17.0000	375.0000	405.0000	2.3556
18.0000	376.0000	406.0000	0.7273
19.0000	377.0000	407.0000	1.7541
20.0000	378.0000	408.0000	2.4911
21.0000	379.0000	409.0000	0.8475
22.0000	380.0000	410.0000	0.8275
23.0000	381.0000	411.0000	0.5174
24.0000	382.0000	412.0000	2.0826
25.0000	383.0000	413.0000	2.3776
26.0000	384.0000	414.0000	1.6985

Duplicated Frames:			
1.0000	355.0000	385.0000	2.4057
2.0000	356.0000	386.0000	2.3997
3.0000	359.0000	389.0000	2.9248
4.0000	360.0000	390.0000	2.4226
5.0000	361.0000	391.0000	2.3996
6.0000	364.0000	394.0000	2.3244
7.0000	365.0000	395.0000	1.0324
8.0000	366.0000	396.0000	1.1729
9.0000	367.0000	397.0000	2.8981
10.0000	368.0000	398.0000	1.8974
11.0000	369.0000	399.0000	1.2184
12.0000	370.0000	400.0000	1.6664
13.0000	371.0000	401.0000	1.3284
14.0000	372.0000	402.0000	2.6695
15.0000	373.0000	403.0000	1.8024
16.0000	374.0000	404.0000	1.6727
17.0000	375.0000	405.0000	2.3556
18.0000	376.0000	406.0000	0.7273
19.0000	377.0000	407.0000	1.7541
20.0000	378.0000	408.0000	2.4911
21.0000	379.0000	409.0000	0.8475
22.0000	380.0000	410.0000	0.8275
23.0000	381.0000	411.0000	0.5174
24.0000	382.0000	412.0000	2.0826
25.0000	383.0000	413.0000	2.3776
26.0000	384.0000	414.0000	1.6985

Localizing Results...
30 Frames are duplicated.
From:355-384 To:385-414
Time taken:30.893 Seconds

Column 1   Column 2

Fig. 4. Sub-blocking of frames

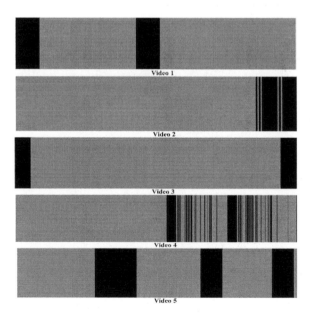

Video 1

Video 2

Video 3

Video 4

Video 5

Fig. 5. Duplicate frames detected in Videos 1, 2, 3, 4 and 5

Results of method applied on five videos (as shown in Table 2) are represented in the Fig. 5. Black regions indicate duplicated frame(s) and the gray regions indicate the non-duplicated frames. Results shown in Fig. 5 are in time domain. X axis of each Video Sequence is plotted with respect to time. Hence, a black patch is representing a group of adjacent frames which are detected as a duplicate group of frames.

4   Discussions and Performance Measurement

We have performed experiment on both compressed and uncompressed forged videos with different frame rates. Experiments on our database show accuracy approximately 98.1 % in detection of duplicated frames. False positives found in such exercise were approximately 1 %. Interestingly, In the case of moving camera 99.5 % of duplicated frames were detected. The reason behind this significant improved accuracy is least probability of occurrence of static frames in the moving camera. Accuracy is summarized in following Table 1.

Table 1. Accuracy for stationary camera and moving camera videos

Compressed video (source)	Detection accuracy	Detection time (fixed length video)
Stationary camera	98.1 %	7.96 s (For 9 s Clip)
Moving camera	99.5 %	20 s

For performance measure, we compute the following measures on the entire database:

T-P (true positive): forged frames declared forged.; F-P (false positive): genuine frames declared forged.; T-N (true negative): genuine frames declared genuine.; F-N (false positive): forged frames declared genuine. Thereafter calculating these quantities, results can be given in terms of sensitivity (Sn), specificity (Sp) and accuracy (Ac).

Sensitivity or true positive rate (TPR)

$$TPR = \frac{TP}{P} = \frac{TP}{TP + FN}$$

Specificity (SPC) or True Negative Rate (TNR)

$$SPC = \frac{TN}{N} = \frac{TN}{TN + FP}$$

Fall-out or false positive rate (FPR)

$$FPR = \frac{FP}{N} = \frac{FP}{TN + FP} = 1 - SPC$$

Accuracy *(ACC)*

$$ACC = \frac{TP + TN}{P + N}$$

Performance thus calculated shows a prominent result. Video 1, 2 and 3 from Table 2 shows a highest sensitivity as shown in Table 3. To get all the duplicated frames in forged video is still a point to concern about. Overall presented method is perfect in deciding a forged video with frame duplication. Due to lack of any global database, a comparison with other techniques could not be presented. With our database, better results are found in comparison to other techniques in reference.

Table 2. Different properties of the videos.

Properties → Test Videos ↓	Total frames (count)	Time length (s)	Resolution (Pixels)	Bitrate (kbps)	Detection time (s)
Video 1	465	15	1080 × 1920	37428	43
Video 2	414	13	1080 × 1920	34052	36
Video 3	353	11	1080 × 1920	44048	30
Video 4	469	15	240 × 320	3330	17
Video 5	274	9	240 × 320	3905	8

Table 3. Different detection measures.

	TPR or sensitivity	TNR or specificity	FPR or fallout	Accuracy
Video 1	1.0	1.0	0.0	1.0
Video 2	0.86	1.0	0.0	0.990
Video 3	1.0	1.0	0.0	1.0
Video 4	0.35	0.994	0.005	0.838
Video 5	1	0.995	0.004	0.996

5   Conclusions

A new approach to detect duplicated frames is proposed in this paper. Few frames are copied from the video clip and pasted within the same video in order to manipulate the story in video. Similarity between frames is computed to decide a duplicated frame present in the video sequence. To find out duplicated frames, nine features for each frame are calculated and compared with each other. These features make our proposed algorithm fast and more accurate than earlier such methods. Based on this analysis, we can determine and localize the duplicated frames. The result is prominent even for compressed videos. The proposed scheme exhibits simpler design and implementation. The experimental results have validated the efficiency of our video forgery detection technique.

Acknowledgments. This work is supported by Tata Consultancy Service under RSP scheme.

References

1. Wang, W., Farid, H.: Exposing digital forgeries in video by detecting duplication. In: Proceedings of ACM 9th Workshop on Multimedia and Security, pp. 35–42 (2007)
2. Kobayashi, M., Okabe, T., Sato, Y.: Detecting video forgeries based on noise characteristics. In: Wada, T., Huang, F., Lin, S. (eds.) PSIVT 2009. LNCS, vol. 5414, pp. 306–317. Springer, Heidelberg (2009)
3. Hsu, C.-C., Hung, T.-Y., Lin, C.-W., Hsu, C.-T.: Video forgery detection using correlation of noise residue. In: Proceedings of IEEE 10th Workshop on Multimedia Signal Processing, pp. 170–174 (2008)
4. Lin, G.S., Chang, J.F., Chuang, C.H.: Detecting frame duplication based on spatial and temporal analyses. In: Proceedings of IEEE Conference on Computer Science and Education, pp. 1396–1399 (2011)
5. Bestagini, P., Milani, S., Tagliasacchi, M., Tubaro, S.: Local tampering detection in video sequences. In: IEEE International Workshop on Multimedia Signal Processing, pp. 488–493 (2013)
6. Mondaini, N., Caldelli, R., Piva, A., Barni, M., Cappellini, V.: Detection of malevolent changes in digital video for forensic applications. In: Proceedings of SPIE, Security, Steganography, and Watermarking of Multimedia Contents IX, vol. 6505 (2007)
7. Tripathi, R.C., Singh, V.K.: Fast and efficient region duplication detection in digital images using sub-blocking method. Int. J. Adv. Sci. Technol. **35**, 93–102 (2011)

How Cuckoo Filter Can Improve Existing Approximate Matching Techniques

Vikas Gupta[1] and Frank Breitinger[2]([⊠])

[1] Netskope, Inc., Los Altos, USA
vikasgupta.nit@gmail.com
[2] Cyber Forensics Research and Education Group (UNHcFREG),
Tagliatela College of Engineering University of New Haven,
West Haven, CT 06516, USA
fbreitinger@newhaven.edu

Abstract. In recent years, approximate matching algorithms have become an important component in digital forensic research and have been adopted in some other working areas as well. Currently there are several approaches, but sdhash and mrsh-v2 especially attract the attention of the community because of their good overall performance (runtime, compression and detection rates). Although both approaches have quite a different proceeding, their final output (the similarity digest) is very similar as both utilize Bloom filters. This data structure was presented in 1970 and thus has been used for a while. Recently, a new data structure was proposed which claimed to be faster and have a smaller memory footprint than Bloom filter – *Cuckoo filter* .

In this paper we analyze the feasibility of Cuckoo filter for approximate matching algorithms and present a prototype implementation called mrsh-cf which is based on a special version of mrsh-v2 called mrsh-net. We demonstrate that by using Cuckoo filter there is a runtime improvement of approximately 37 % and also a significantly better false positive rate. The memory footprint of mrsh-cf is 8 times smaller than mrsh-net, while the compression rate is twice than Bloom filter based fingerprint.

Keywords: Approximate matching · Similarity hashing · Bloom filter · Cuckoo filter · Fuzzy hashing · Similarity hashing · mrsh-v2 · mrsh-net

1 Introduction

Approximate matching (a.k.a. similarity hashing or fuzzy hashing) is a technology to identify similarities among digital artifacts and can be seen as a counterpart to traditional (cryptographic) hash functions. According to the definition of Breitinger et al. [7], approximate matching algorithms can not only be used to detect similarities among objects, but also to detect embedded objects or fragments of objects.

Within the last decade, the community has proposed several approximate matching algorithms starting with ssdeep by Kornblum [14]. Four years later,

© Institute for Computer Sciences, Social Informatics and Telecommunications Engineering 2015
J.I. James and F. Breitinger (Eds.): ICDF2C 2015, LNICST 157, pp. 39–52, 2015.
DOI: 10.1007/978-3-319-25512-5_4

Roussev presented a new algorithm called sdhash [21] which outperforms ssdeep with respect to precision and recall but was slightly slower. Therefore, Breitinger et. al. combined both implementations and published mrsh-v2 [5]. Compared to sdhash, this new algorithm had less complexity and thus significant advantage with respect to runtime efficiency, however sdhash remained slightly more accurate [8].

One of the main working fields of approximate matching is digital forensics where investigators use it to reduce the amount of data automatically, e.g., filter out non-relevant data like OS-files and highlight suspect files. Since a single case can consist of several hundreds of gigabytes, it is important to have fast and reliable algorithms. Due to the continuous improvements over recent years, these algorithms have gotten very powerful and been applied in further areas, e.g., deep network packet analysis and detecting known file fragments in packets [4, 13] or in biometrics and iris recognition [20].

From a high level perspective ssdeep, sdhash and mrsh-v2 work similarly. They all use some intermediary logic to extract features from the given input, compress these features and finally print out a similarity digest a.k.a. fingerprint. Accordingly, in order to find similar objects, we compare fingerprints instead of comparing complete objects. Depending on the overlap of the fingerprints, a similarity score is returned. While ssdeep uses a Base64 encoded sequence to represent the fingerprint, both of the other algorithms utilize Bloom filters [2]. A Bloom filter is an excellent data structure for set-membership queries, offers great memory efficiency (compression) and has been studied extensively (more details are given in Sect. 2.1).

Recently, Fan et. al. [10] have proposed a new data structure for set-membership queries, called *Cuckoo filter*. A "Cuckoo filter is a compact variant of cuckoo hash table [18] that stores only *fingerprints* – a bit string derived from the item using a hash function – for each item inserted, instead of key-value pairs". The authors demonstrate that a Cuckoo filter is practically better than Bloom filters in terms of performance and space overhead.

In this paper we explore the possibility of using Cuckoo filter for approximate matching. We build a new version of mrsh-net (which is a fork of mrsh-v2) that uses Cuckoo filter and demonstrate in our evaluation section that there is a practical performance improvement compared to the Bloom filter version. Note that we only manipulate and evaluate the fingerprint representation of the approximate matching algorithm which means other existing algorithms (e.g., sdhash) could profit from our findings, too. The technical contribution of this paper include:

- Exploring the feasibility of Cuckoo filter as a more efficient alternative to Bloom filter.
- Developing a prototype by implementing mrsh-net with Cuckoo filter, called mrsh-cf.
- Analyzing some key performance parameters like runtime efficiency, memory usage and compression.

We want to point out that this is the first paper trying to use a new fingerprint representation. Prior to this work, no one has attempted to enhance approximate matching algorithms by using alternative data structures to the widely used Bloom filter.

The rest of the paper is organized as follows: In Sect. 2, we discuss the related work which includes Bloom filter, `mrsh-v2` and its branch `mrsh-net`. Next, in Sect. 3, we briefly mention cuckoo hashing which is the basis of Cuckoo filter followed by a comprehensive description of Cuckoo filter, e.g., workflow of insertions and lookups. In Sect. 4 we present our assessment and experimental results. Section 5 concludes this paper.

2   Background and Related Work

The introduction briefly mentioned the three most popular approximate matching algorithms. However, for the remainder of this paper we focus on `mrsh-v2`, since `ssdeep` can be overcome by an active adversary [1] and `sdhash` is rather complex which makes it harder to integrate our changes.

In the following subsections, we first explain Bloom filter in Sect. 2.1 followed by an overview of `mrsh-v2` including its branch `mrsh-net`.

2.1   Bloom filter

A Bloom filter is a probabilistic data structure used to test the membership of an element against a given set and was introduced by Burton H. Bloom [2]. Since then, it has found use in different applications like networks [9] and approximate matching (`mrsh-v2` and `sdhash`) algorithms.

From a programming perspective, a Bloom filter is a bit array of length m (all set to zero), that provides a compact representation of a set S, containing $|S|$ elements. Normally it supports two operations: *insert* and *lookup*.

In order to perform an operation, we need k independent hash functions that output values in the range of $0 \leq h(s) \leq m - 1$ for all $s \in S$. To *insert* s into a Bloom filter, the item is hashed using k different hash functions and the corresponding bits in the Bloom filter are set to one. The *lookup* is performed in a similar manner, the element is hashed using the k hash functions and the corresponding bits are checked, if all bits are set to one, the query returns true; otherwise returns a false.

Thus, a query to a Bloom filter returns either 'definitely no' or 'probably yes' (bits might be set to one but by different elements). The probability of being wrong ϵ (i.e. the false positive rate) is tunable and given by Eq. 1

$$\epsilon \approx (1 - e^{-kn/m})^k \tag{1}$$

where, k is the number of hash functions and n is the number of elements added to the Bloom filter. The lower the value of ϵ, the larger the bit-size m of the Bloom filter.

Bloom filter is a very space-efficient approach to represent a set of digital objects. The space used by Bloom filter is much less than compared to the space occupied by the original set. Over the years, many extensions/mutations of Bloom filter were presented like the counting Bloom filter [11], blocked Bloom filter [19] or d-left counting Bloom filter [3]. However, for the remainder of the paper any further reference to Bloom filter is with respect to standard Bloom filter.

As argued by Pagh et. al. [17], there are more efficient ways to represent $|S|$ than Bloom filters. For a false positive rate ϵ, a space-optimized Bloom filter uses $k = \log_2(1/\epsilon)$ hash functions. As per information-theory, minimum $\log_2(1/\epsilon)$ bits are required per item, while Bloom filter uses $1.44 \cdot \log_2(1/\epsilon)$ bits. The number of bits per item is dependent on ϵ, rather than item size or total number of items.

2.2 mrsh-v2 and mrsh-net

As aforementioned, mrsh-v2 is a very straightforward algorithm that was proposed by Breitinger et. al. [5]. Its proceeding is quite simple. mrsh-v2 identifies trigger points in any given byte sequence (e.g., a file or a device), that are used to divide it into chunks of approximately bs bytes. Next, each chunk is hashed using FNV [16]. In order to insert a 64 bit FNV chunk hash into a $m = 2048 = 2^{11}$ bits Bloom filter, mrsh-v2 builds five 11-bit sub-hashes based on the least significant 55 bits of the FNV hash. Finally, each sub-hash sets one bit within the Bloom filter. Note, instead of inserting complete files into the Bloom filter (as explained in Sect. 2.1), we insert chunks which then allow the similarity identification.

mrsh-v2 allows a maximum of 160 chunks per Bloom filter. If this limit is reached a new Bloom filter is created. Hence, the final fingerprint for an input can be a sequence of multiple Bloom filters. As a consequence, we have variable fingerprint lengths in contrast to the traditional definition of hash functions where we have fixed output lengths [15]. Comparing two fingerprints is a comparison of all Bloom filters of fingerprint A against all Bloom filters of fingerprint B with respect to the Hamming distance as metric.

Despite all the benefits offered by Bloom filters, there is one major issue – the database lookup complexity. Currently there is no technique to sort/order Bloom filter based similarity digests and thus comparing a single digest against a database containing x entries requires an 'against-all' comparison – a complexity of $O(x)$. In contrast, cryptographic digests can be stored in binary trees or organized in hash tables having a lookup complexity of $O(\log_2(x))$ or $O(1)$, respectively. The impact is best demonstrated on an example: comparing 1.8 GB of data with itself (the t5-corpus[1] containing 4457 files), mrsh-v2 takes over 21 min, which is too slow for practical usage.

mrsh-net. To overcome this drawback, Breitinger et. al. [6] suggested a different strategy resulting in a complexity of $O(1)$. The idea is simple: instead of having multiple small Bloom filters, they recommended having a single large Bloom

---

[1] http://roussev.net/t5/t5.html (last accessed 2015-04-10).

filter that contains all files (actually all chunks of all files). While this reduces the lookup times significantly, it loses information about successful matches. While the original implementation was a fingerprint vs. fingerprint comparison, `mrsh-net` is a fingerprint vs. set comparison. In other words, a query only returns *true* or *false*, but does not return the file that it is matched to.

3   Cuckoo Filter

The overall idea of this paper is to demonstrate the feasibility and improvements of using *Cuckoo filter* instead of Bloom filters for approximate matching. This section explains the details about the concept. If you are already familiar with Cuckoo filter, you may skip this section.

The idea of Cuckoo filter originated from Cuckoo hashing, which was proposed by Pagh et. al. [18] and is comparable to a *dictionary* data structure, i.e., there are keys and values. Usually the key is generated out of the value and has extremely fast access time. However, unlike a traditional dictionary structure, Cuckoo hashing utilizes *two* hash functions and therefore utilizes two keys and two tables. Accordingly, each lookup has a constant lookup time of 2 queries and expected constant amortized[2] time for updates[3]. Explaining Cuckoo hashing in detail is beyond the scope of this paper, however. We will focus on Cuckoo filter in the subsequent paper.

Fan et. al. in [10] modified Cuckoo hashing so that it could handle set-membership queries and called it Cuckoo filter. In their paper they demonstrated that when compared to Bloom filter, Cuckoo filter

- has a better lookup performance (with respect to runtime),
- has a better space efficiency for applications requiring low false positive rates ($\epsilon < 3\%$) and
- supports deleting items dynamically (this property is irrelevant for us).

Generally speaking, a Cuckoo filter consists of a Cuckoo hash table and three hash functions named h_1, h_2 and f_h, where each position in the hash table is called a *bucket* and can store multiple *entries*. The three hash functions are used as follows: h_1 and h_2 identify the correct buckets for insertion or lookup (identify the position), and f_h is used to compress the item (to save memory space, a Cuckoo filter does not store the items themselves but a constant-sized hash of the items). For the remainder of this paper, the following terminology is used:

m - the size of a Cuckoo filter, i.e., number of buckets.
b - the bucket size, i.e. the number of *entries* each bucket can have.
h_1, h_2 - the hash functions to obtain the positions in the Cuckoo filter for a given item.
f_h - the hash function used to obtain a tag for an item (compresses the item), where $|f_h|$ is the bit length of the hash value.

---

[2] https://en.wikipedia.org/wiki/Amortized_analysis (last accessed 2015-04-10).
[3] I.e, this overcomes chained hash table where worst case time for lookup will be linear $O(n)$.

3.1 Insert

The insertion process is best described by the example given in Fig. 1, where we have a Cuckoo filter with $m = 8$ and $b = 1$. For completeness, we printed the pseudo code in the Appendix under Algorithm 1. As shown in the figure, there are three possibilities:

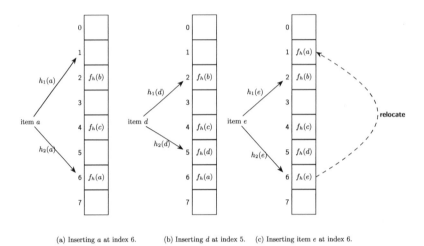

(a) Inserting a at index 6.   (b) Inserting d at index 5.   (c) Inserting item e at index 6.

Fig. 1. Illustration of Cuckoo Filter where hash functions h_1 and h_2 are used for determining buckets for an item's insertion and f_h to get a constant-sized hash of the item to be inserted. Initial setup (a): the items b and c are already in the Cuckoo filter while item a is processed.

- **Both buckets are empty**: In Fig. 1(a), item a can be inserted in bucket 1 or 6. Since both the buckets are empty, the final bucket for insertion is determined randomly (ensures buckets fill up equally). In the example, a is inserted into bucket 6.
- **One bucket is full**: In Fig. 1(b), item d can go in bucket 2 or 5. Since, bucket 2 is already occupied, d is inserted into bucket 5.
- **Both buckets are full**: In Fig. 1(c), item e can go in bucket 2 or 6. However, both buckets are occupied, which requires relocation of entries.

Relocation. The idea of relocation is to move an existing entry to its alternate bucket. For instance, in Fig. 1(a), we randomly inserted a into bucket 6, while bucket 1 remained empty. On relocation (Fig. 1(c)), we now move a from 6 to 1, which allows us to insert e into 6.[4]

---

[4] Since Cuckoo filter only store the hash of an item (the entry) and not the item itself, it is not possible to rehash an item and identify the other bucket. Therefore, the authors implemented the location hash functions (h_1 and h_2) in a manner allowing them to be derived from the current location and the entry: $h_1(x) = hash(x)$ and $h_2(x) = h_1(x) \oplus hash(f_h(x))$ where $hash$ is any hash function.

The relocation-process can carry on until a vacant bucket is found, or the maximum number of relocations is reached (500 in present implementation). In the latter case, the table is considered to be full.

Identical tags. By design Cuckoo filter allows identical tags in buckets (e.g., the same item is inserted multiple times), which allows that those items can be deleted. In theory, the same tag cannot be entered more than $2b$ times, as then both buckets are full and cannot be relocated (= full Cuckoo filter). Since, our approach does not require deleting entries, we only insert unique tags and ignore duplicates.

3.2   Lookup

The lookup process of a Cuckoo filter is fairly straightforward. For querying an item x, firstly $h_1(x)$ and $h_2(x)$ are calculated and then both buckets are checked for the presence of the $f_h(x)$. If the tag is present in either of the buckets, Cuckoo filter returns *true* or *false*.

3.3   False Positive Rate of a Cuckoo filter

As discussed in [10], the false positive rate ϵ for a Cuckoo filter depends on the bucket size b and on the tag size $|f_h|$. Since ϵ is usually a system requirement, we can estimate $|f_h|$ by:

$$|f_h| \geq \lceil log_2(2b/\epsilon) \rceil = \lceil log_2(1/\epsilon) + log_2(2b) \rceil \text{ bits.} \qquad (2)$$

If the total size of the Cuckoo filter is kept constant, b influences the length as follows:

- **A larger b improves table occupancy:** A larger b reduces the chance to get a full Cuckoo filter and hence a higher load factor α can be achieved, where α is the ratio of number of entries made (total insertions made) divided by total number of entries possible. An overview is given in Table 1.
- **A larger b requires a larger tag size to retain the same false positive rate:** A larger b increases the chance of collisions, as for each lookup more entries are checked. By increasing the tag size, the chances of having similar entries is reduced. Figure 2 shows the relation between bits/item used and false positive rate achieved for various bucket sizes.

To conclude, a Bloom filter requires approximately 10 bits per item to achieve $\epsilon = 1\%$, regardless of whether one thousand, one million, or billion items are stored. In contrast Cuckoo filters require bigger tag size to retain the same high space efficiency of their hash tables, but lower false positive rates are achieved accordingly [10].

By considering Table 1 and Fig. 2, a high space efficiency and low false positive rate can be achieved by using $b = 4$. Hence, we will use (2,4)-Cuckoo filter, i.e., each item has two candidate buckets and each bucket has up to four entries.

Table 1. Correlation between bucket size and load factor in a Cuckoo filter [10].

Bucket size b	Load factor α
1	50 %
2	84 %
4	95 %
8	98 %

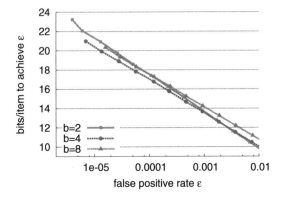

Fig. 2. Amortized space cost per item vs. measured false positive rate, with different bucket size b = 2,4,8 [10].

3.4   Number of Memory Access

For a Bloom filter with k hash functions, a positive query must read k bits from the bit array where ideally $k = log_2(1/\epsilon)$. As ϵ gets smaller, positive queries require to probe more bits and are likely to incur more cache line misses when reading each bit. In the case of a negative query, half of k bits are read before a false is returned. Contrastingly, for a Cuckoo filter, for both positive or negative queries, it requires a fixed number of reads, resulting in at most two cache line misses. Note, the authors assume that memory access is expensive while comparing is cheap [10].

3.5   Construction Rate

As discussed in [10], given the same false positive rate for both Bloom filter and Cuckoo filter and both filters configured to use same size of 192 MB, the construction rate of Cuckoo filter is higher than Bloom filter. 5.00 million keys/sec can be added to Cuckoo filter, as opposed to only 3.13 million keys/sec. This gives a clear indication of performance gains one can achieve by using Cuckoo filter over Bloom filter.

It is important to note that Cuckoo filter is a fairly new data structure and many of its characteristics have not been studied in detail. Several theoretical questions, however, remain open for future study - a couple being providing bounds on the cost of inserting a new item and studying how much independence is required of the hash functions. But as we will see in Sect. 4, Cuckoo filters do increase the performance of `mrsh-net` and any further improvement in Cuckoo filter will further enhance the performance of `mrsh-net`.

4 Assessment and Experimental Results

This section firstly gives some implementation details (Sect. 4.1) and describes the comparison criteria (Sect. 4.2). Next, we explain our experimental setup in Sect. 4.3 which is followed by a discussion about the false positives and further results in Sect. 4.4 and in Sect. 4.5, respectively.

4.1 Implementation Details

While `mrsh-net` is implemented in C, we programed our reference implementation in C++. In order to integrate Cuckoo filter, we included the library[5] provided by Fan et. al. [10]. The chunk size of `mrsh-net` is set to $bs = 320$.

It is important to note that we are no experts in writing fully optimized C/C++ programs but we tried our best to make both implementations as optimized as possible. Our prototype of `mrsh-cf` is released and can be downloaded from our website[6].

The default implementation of Cuckoo filter uses SHA-1 [12] and a variant of Austin Appleby's MurmurHash2[7] for hashing tasks. When an item x is inserted in a Cuckoo filter, it is first hashed using SHA-1. The first part of the hash obtained acts as $h_1(x)$, while the second part represents $f_h(x)$ (the tag of x). To calculate $h_2(x)$, a variant of MurmurHash2 is used.

4.2 Comparison Parameters

In [8] several criteria were proposed to compare approximate matching algorithms, which can be categorized into:

- Efficiency: includes runtime efficiency and compression rate.
- Sensitivity & robustness: includes random-noise-resistance, alignment robustness, fragment detection, and file correlation.

For this article we focus on the first category while "sensitivity &robustness" remains for future work. Apart from the above discussed parameters, the two versions are also compared by memory usage.

---

[5] https://github.com/efficient/cuckoofilter (last accessed 2015-04-10).
[6] http://www.fbreitinger.de/?page_id=218 (last accessed 2015-04-10).
[7] https://code.google.com/p/smhasher/wiki/MurmurHash2
(last accessed 2015-04-10).

4.3   Experimental Setup

The development and testing was done on a machine with an Intel Core i5 1.80 GHz quad-core processor with 8 GB RAM and 3 MB L3 cache (Linux kernel 3.16). Both, `mrsh-net` and `mrsh-cf` were compiled using GCC 4.9 with highest possible compiler optimization -O3. The program's execution time and memory usage were recorded using the GNU `time`-command[8]. For certain cases, C/C++ header *time.h* was also used to determine execution time.

We decided to run our tests on the t5-corpus which consisted of 4457 files [22]. This set is widely used within the field of digital forensics and includes many common file types like html, jpg or doc. The main facts are given in Table 2.

Table 2. Statistics of t5-corpus.

Number of files	4457
Total size	1.8 GB
Minimum file size	4.0 KB
Maximum file size	17.4 MB
Average file size	428.72 KB
Number of file types	8

Also, each test ran 10 times for computing various performance parameters for both the versions.

4.4   False Positive Rate

`mrsh-net` aims for a false positive rate of $\epsilon = 6.33 \cdot 10^{-5}$. According to Eq. 2 and setting the bucket size to $b = 4$, this requires a tag size of $|f_h| \geq 17$ bits.

However, as outlined by Table 3, $|f_h|$ does not affect the actual runtime efficiency by much (the max RSS column is discussed in Sect. 4.5). The table shows the runtime for $2 \leq |f_h| \leq 32$.

Using $|f_h| = 32$ improves the false positive rate to approximately $\epsilon \approx 10^{-9}$, but also increases the total memory footprint. We accept this disadvantage to attain a better false positive rate. As shown later, `mrsh-cf` is still more space efficient than `mrsh-net`.

4.5   Testing Results

As concluded in the last section, all the results were computed with Cuckoo filter configuration of tag size $|f_h| = 32$ bits and bucket size $b = 4$. Number of buckets m for the Cuckoo filter was obtained by dividing input object size by chunk size bs in bytes. The comparison of `mrsh-cf` against `mrsh-net` with respect to various parameters is presented below:

---

[8] http://man7.org/linux/man-pages/man1/time.1.html (last accessed 2015-04-10).

Table 3. Execution time (in seconds) and memory usage (in KB) for `mrsh-net` and various configurations of `mrsh-cf`. The version corresponds to 'mrsh-cf-b-$|f_h|$', e.g., `mrsh-cf`-4-2 means `mrsh-cf` having $b = 4$ and $|f_h| = 2$.

Version	Exec. time (sec)	Maximum RSS (KB)
mrsh-net	65.84	401396
mrsh-cf-4-2	40.03	35912
mrsh-cf-4-4	40.35	36844
mrsh-cf-4-8	40.28	38692
mrsh-cf-4-12	40.13	40944
mrsh-cf-4-16	40.06	42824
mrsh-cf-4-32	41.47	51165
mrsh-cf-8-16	39.69	51024
mrsh-cf-8-32	40.01	67452

Time Efficiency. To determine the runtime efficiency, we measured the execution time for three scenarios. First, the time to generate the Cuckoo filter for t5-corpus. Next, to compare t5-corpus against a pre-generated Cuckoo filter. Finally, the time taken to perform an all-against-all comparison. This last scenario should be approximately the same as the sum of the two previous tests. Results are presented in Table 4.

Table 4. Comparison between `mrsh-cf` and `mrsh-net` on various performance parameters.

Parameters	mrsh-cf	mrsh-net
Cuckoo filter generation time (sec)	19.74	32.90
Comparison time (sec)	21.17	33.09
Against-all comparison time (sec)	41.47	65.84
Maximum RSS (KB)	51165	401396
Fingerprint size (MB)	16	32

As can be seen, `mrsh-cf` outperforms the original implementation in all categories. For instance, generating the filter takes 19.74 s and 32.90 s, respectively, which is a time difference of about 40 %.

With respect to the all-against-all comparison, the Cuckoo filter for the complete t5-corpus was generated and then each file in the corpus was compared against this filter. The test showed that `mrsh-cf` requires 41.47 s while `mrsh-net` needed 65.84 s. To conclude, `mrsh-cf` has a significant performance gain of approximately 37 %.

Compression. Traditional cryptographic hash functions return a hash value of constant size. On the other hand, approximate matching algorithms return digests of variable length. As digests are typically stored within a database, preferably short fingerprints are desirable. Therefore, compression measures the ratio between input and output size of an algorithm [8].

$$compression = \frac{output\ length}{input\ length} \cdot 100 \ . \tag{3}$$

With `mrsh-cf`, the filter for t5-corpus has a size 16 MB, while `mrsh-net` results in a filter size of 32 MB. Accordingly, the compression for `mrsh-cf` is superior since it only needs half the size. Considering both kinds of filters, it can be safely concluded that the loading time for `mrsh-cf` will be faster than `mrsh-net`.

Memory Usage. Memory usage is calculated by determining *Maximum Resident Set Size* of a process using GNU `time`-command. 'Resident set size' (RSS) of a process represents the amount of non-swapped memory the kernel has already allocated to the process. This does not include the swapped out portion of the memory. As indicated by the name, maximum RSS is the maximum memory assigned to a process during its lifetime.

The results are shown in Table 3. The maximum RSS for `mrsh-cf` relies on the configuration. However, in all used configurations it was much smaller than `mrsh-net`. Note, this can provide a significant performance advantage when handling huge data sets as the majority of the filters will be present in memory.

5   Conclusion

In this paper, we demonstrated that Cuckoo filters have significant benefits over Bloom filters within the area of approximate matching, which is an important technology for digital forensics. While all previous work tried to improve the algorithms themselves, this is the first identification of an alternative fingerprint / similarity digest representation scheme.

Our results show that Cuckoo filters provide two major improvements over Bloom filters: (1) better lookup performance; and (2) better space efficiency for applications requiring a low false positive rate ($\epsilon \geq 3\%$). We concluded that Cuckoo filters are a superior compared to Bloom filters in approximate matching algorithms.

Furthermore, we released a prototype named `mrsh-cf` that is based on `mrsh-net` and Cuckoo filter library. This prototype outperformed its predecessor in all considered parameters. For example, the runtime efficiency was about 37 % faster while using 8 times less memory. The size of the filter generated using `mrsh-cf` was only half the size of the `mrsh-net` filter.

Although there are several benefits of using Cuckoo filter, we also face new challenges. Comparing two Cuckoo filter-based fingerprints is not as straightforward as using traditional Bloom filter fingerprints. However, the initial tests from this current work show promising (but not perfect) results.

Appendix

Algorithm 1. Pseudo code for insertion copied from [10] and slightly modified x.

1: $f = fingerprint(x)$;
2: /* this is h_1 */
3: $i_1 = hash(x)$;
4: /* this is h_2 */
5: $i_2 = i_1 \oplus hash(f)$;
6: **if** bucket$[i_1]$ or bucket$[i_2]$ has an empty entry **then**
7:     add f to that bucket;
8:     **return** Done;
9:
10: /* must relocate existing items */
11: i = randomly pick i_1 or i_2;
12: **for** $n = 0$; $n <$ MaxNumKicks; $n + +$ **do**
13:     randomly select an entry e from bucket$[i]$;
14:     swap f and the fingerprint stored in entry e;
15:     $i = i \oplus hash(f)$;
16:     **if** bucket$[i]$ has an empty entry **then**
17:         add f to bucket$[i]$;
18:         **return** Done;
19:
20: /* Hashtable is considered full */
21: **return** Failure;

References

1. Baier, H., Breitinger, F.: Security aspects of piecewise hashing in computer forensics. In: IT Security Incident Management & IT Forensics (IMF), pp. 21–36, May 2011
2. Bloom, B.H.: Space/time trade-offs in hash coding with allowable errors. Commun. ACM **13**(7), 422–426 (1970)
3. Bonomi, F., Mitzenmacher, M., Panigrahy, R., Singh, S., Varghese, G.: An improved construction for counting bloom filters. In: Azar, Y., Erlebach, T. (eds.) ESA 2006. LNCS, vol. 4168, pp. 684–695. Springer, Heidelberg (2006)
4. Breitinger, F., Baggili, I.: File detection on network traffic using approximate matching. J. Digit. Forensics Secur. Law (JDFSL) **9**(2), 23–36 (2014)
5. Breitinger, F., Baier, H.: Similarity preserving hashing: eligible properties and a new algorithm MRSH-v2. In: Rogers, M., Seigfried-Spellar, K.C. (eds.) ICDF2C 2012. LNICST, vol. 114, pp. 167–182. Springer, Heidelberg (2013)
6. Breitinger, F., Baier, H., White, D.: On the database lookup problem of approximate matching. Digital Invest. **11**, S1–S9 (2014)

7. Breitinger, F., Guttman, B., McCarrin, M., Roussev, V., White, D.: Approximate matching: Definition and terminology. Special publication 800–168. National Institute of Standards and Technologies, May 2014
8. Breitinger, F., Stivaktakis, G., Baier, H.: Frash: a framework to test algorithms of similarity hashing. Digit. Investig. **10**, S50–S58 (2013)
9. Broder, A., Mitzenmacher, M.: Network applications of bloom filters: a survey. Internet Math. **1**(4), 485–509 (2004)
10. Fan, B., Andersen, D.G., Kaminsky, M., Mitzenmacher, M.D.: Cuckoo filter: practically better than bloom. In: Proceedings of the 10th ACM International on Conference on emerging Networking Experiments and Technologies, pp. 75–88. ACM (2014)
11. Fan, L., Cao, P., Almeida, J., Broder, A.Z.: Summary cache: a scalable wide-area web cache sharing protocol. IEEE/ACM Trans. Networking (TON) **8**(3), 281–293 (2000)
12. Gallagher, P., Director, A.: Secure Hash Standard (SHS). Technical report, National Institute of Standards and Technologies, Federal Information Processing Standards Publication 180–1 (1995)
13. Gupta, V.: File detection in network traffic using approximate matching. Master's thesis, Technical University of Denmark, Copenhagen, Denmark (2013)
14. Kornblum, J.: Identifying almost identical files using context triggered piecewise hashing. Digital Invest. **3**, 91–97 (2006)
15. Menezes, A.J., van Oorschot, P.C., Vanstone, S.A.: Handbook of Applied Cryptography, vol. 5. CRC Press, August 2001
16. Landon Curt Noll. Fnv hash (1994–2012). http://www.isthe.com/chongo/tech/comp/fnv/index.html
17. Pagh, A., Pagh, R., Rao, S.S.: An optimal bloom filter replacement. In: Proceedings of the sixteenth annual ACM-SIAM symposium on Discrete algorithms, pp. 823–829. Society for Industrial and Applied Mathematics (2005)
18. Pagh, R.: Cuckoo hashing. J. Algorithms **51**(2), 122–144 (2004)
19. Putze, F., Sanders, P., Singler, J.: Cache-, hash- and space-efficient bloom filters. In: Demetrescu, C. (ed.) WEA 2007. LNCS, vol. 4525, pp. 108–121. Springer, Heidelberg (2007)
20. Rathgeb, C., Breitinger, F., Busch, C., Baier, H.: On application of bloom filters to iris biometrics. Biometrics, IET **3**(4), 207–218 (2014)
21. Roussev, V.: Data fingerprinting with similarity digests. In: Chow, K.-P., Shenoi, S. (eds.) Advances in Digital Forensics VI. IFIP Advances in Information and Communication Technology, vol. 337, pp. 207–226. Springer, Heidelberg (2010)
22. Roussev, V.: An evaluation of forensic similarity hashes. Digital Invest. **8**, 34–41 (2011)

Forensically Sound Retrieval and Recovery of Images from GPU Memory

Yulong Zhang[(✉)], Baijian Yang, Marcus Rogers, and Raymond A. Hansen

Department of Computer and Information Technology, Purdue University,
West Lafayette 47907, USA
{zhan1621,byang,rogersmk,hansenr}@purdue.edu

Abstract. This paper adopts a method to retrieve graphic data stored in the global memory of an NVIDIA GPU. Experimentation shows that a 24-bit TIFF formatted graphic can be retrieved from the GPU in a forensically sound manner. However, like other types of Random Access Memory, acquired data cannot be verified due to the volatile nature of the GPU memory. In this work a Color Pattern Map Test is proposed to reveal the relationship between a graphic and its GPU memory organization. The mapping arrays derived from such testing can be used to visually restore graphics stored in the GPU memory. Described 'photo tests' and 'redo tests' demonstrate that it is possible to visually restore a graphic from the data stored in GPU memory. While initial results are promising, more work is still needed to determine if such methods of data acquisition within GPU memory can be considered forensically sound.

Keywords: GPU forensics · Graphic recovery · Volatile memory acquisition

1 Introduction

With the advances of Graphics Processing Units (GPUs) technology and GPU-accelerated computing, many software applications begin to outsource matrix related computations to GPUs to facilitate operations such as graphic and image rendering and data analytics [16]. For example, WinZip began support of GPU computing beginning in version 16.5 and experienced significant performance gains in version 18.0 by leveraging OpenCL technology [4, 9, 10].

On the other hand, the increased utilization of the GPU has introduced some serious security vulnerabilities. As of March 2015, the memory size of a GPU can reach as large as 16 GB, potentially opening the door to information hiding [14]. Some malware and worms have also utilized the GPUs as their secret hideout to obscure themselves from anti-virus and anti-malware programs [22]. Even worse, malicious software can also be designed to steal sensitive information from other processes by accessing unauthorized data stored in GPU memory [12].

While GPUs have become toys for cyber criminals, not much work has been done in the field of GPU forensics. It is therefore the purpose of this study to (1) propose a method to retrieve graphic data stored in GPUs main memory (usually 2 GB or more) and visually reconstruct the graphic from the retrieved data; and (2) prove or disprove

© Institute for Computer Sciences, Social Informatics and Telecommunications Engineering 2015
J.I. James and F. Breitinger (Eds.): ICDF2C 2015, LNICST 157, pp. 53–66, 2015.
DOI: 10.1007/978-3-319-25512-5_5

the method is forensically sound. Though the experiments are limited to the Windows Photo Viewer application and NVIDIA GeForce GPUs, the methodology proposed here could be extended to general GPU forensics.

The paper is organized as follows: In Sect. 2, related work is introduced followed by our proposed research method in Sect. 3. Experiments and collected data are discussed in Sect. 4. And finally, conclusions are presented in Sect. 5.

2   Literature Review

This section reviews volatile forensics, GPU fundamentals, and related work on retrieving data from GPUs.

2.1   Volatile Forensics Status and Trends

Volatile data, such as system memory, "provides a great deal of information about the system's runtime status at the time of, or just after, an incident" [20]. These include network connections and configuration, running processes, open files, login sessions, and operating system time [13]. *Volatile forensics* is, therefore, important because it has the potential to reveal critical information about criminal activities, such as passwords used for encryption, indications of anti-forensic techniques, and residual memory of a malware application that would go unnoticed otherwise. In addition, volatile forensics is often recommended over hard drive forensics to save time and cost [2].

Conventional practices fail to protect volatile data as potential digital evidence, as investigators are advised to shut down and unplug the compromised computer when the evidence located in hard drive are retrieved [8, 19]. However, sufficient progress has been made in the field with volatile forensics so that it has been accepted in court [3]. Ring and Cole [18] first wrote a paper and developed software to address the issue of capturing data located in system RAM for forensic purposes. Additional tools were developed and evaluated in [7, 20, 21] on forensics of system RAM.

One of the key challenges in volatile forensics is that not all forensically sound principles defined in [1] can be satisfied without effort. There is the potential for these principles to be violated because data is volatile and operations may not be repeatable within the investigation [11]. As a result, no independent third party can retrieve the same results after the incident. Therefore, this principle should be changed as follows: An audit trail or other record of all processes applied to computer-based electronic evidence should be created and preserved. An independent third party should be able to check and review those documents and data preserved and agree that the evidence is not contaminated, and remains forensically sound [1]. This suggests that there will be an additional burden of proof on maintaining the chain of custody [5], and additional caution should be taken to prevent the evidence being tainted by the acquisition process(es), the audit process, or any anti-forensics tools [23].

It should be noted that existing techniques and tools on volatile forensics typically do not apply to GPU forensics. This is due to there being no defined file system within the GPU's RAM. Which means, where and how the graphic data is stored and organized in the GPU memory (not the System RAM) are often elusive to the OS and other applications. Existing volatile forensics approaches and tools on CPUs, coprocessors, and system RAM are not able to reveal any information stored inside the memory space of GPUs. In addition, metadata, such as the header information of a graphic file may not exist or is difficult to locate inside the GPU memory, making the investigation even more challenging.

2.2   GPU Structure and Memory Management

A typical GPU is made up of a control component, a cache component, an Arithmetic Logic Unit (ALU) and a memory component. An ALU in the GPU is often called a Stream Multiprocessor (SM), which contains multiple Stream Processors (SP). The memory component of a GPU, like that of a CPU, has different parts operating at different speeds. For example, an NIVIDIA GPU usually contains five types of memory. From the slowest and largest to the fastest and smallest, they are: global memory, constant memory, texture memory, shared memory, and registers memory. Global memory is the only type of memory that is accessible to both the GPU and the CPU and it is also the type of memory examined in this research.

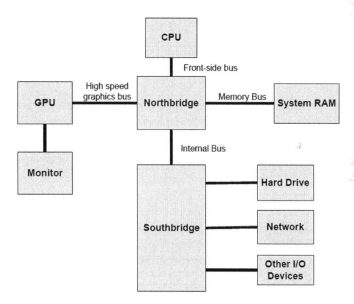

Fig. 1. Illustration of hardware connections used to transfer data from a hard disk to System RAM to Global GPU Memory

Figure 1 describes how components inside a PC are connected. The GPU is connected to and controlled by the CPU via Northbridge. In the case of NVIDIA, the GPU can be manipulated by CUDA commands. The GPU is also directly connected to the monitor via the external bus. When an application needs to utilize the GPU for processing:

1. Image data is located on the hard drive and copied to system RAM
2. Data is then copied to the GPU memory (often in different format)
3. GPU performs the computation and places the results into global memory
4. Data is displayed on monitor or placed in system RAM

For example, OpenGL will always send the data to the monitor without transmitting it back to system RAM. This indicates that forensics of system RAM alone will *not* be sufficient to capture all the live evidence because not all the data will be stored in system RAM.

2.3 Retrieving Data from GPU

Breß et al. [6] and Lee et al. [14] have both attempted to retrieve data from an NVIDIA GPU memory. They determined that it is not possible to access a certain memory space via the physical memory address where it is located. The methods they proposed were similar and described as follows:

1. Get GPU memory space information using `cudaMemGetInfo()`
2. Get access to the data of closed programs and the location it was freed from by allocating the entire memory space using `cudaMalloc()`
3. Copy all the data in GPU global memory using the `cudaMemcpy()`
4. Free the memory space allocated by using the `cudaFree()`

According to CUDA documentation, the four API methods listed above do not modify the content stored in GPU. This process is therefore believed to be able to copy data from GPU memory without contaminating it [6].

Since there is the potential that the process of retrieving GPU data could contaminate evidence stored in system RAM, it is suggested that forensic analysis of the GPU should be done only after forensic analysis of system RAM.

3 Methodology

The research question of this investigation is to explore whether it is possible to use forensically sound methods to recover the graphic data produced by the Windows Photo Viewer and captured from an NVIDIA GPU memory space.

This study breaks the question into three phases. Phase I demonstrates a forensically sound method exists to capture GPU data. Phase 2 illustrates how a graphic can be restored from the GPU data. And Phase 3 tests the validity of method.

The study used the Windows 8 Windows Photo Viewer to generate the data in the GPU global memory. An NVIDIA GeForce 650 was chosen as the testing hardware simply because it was the GPU available in the laboratory environment. A GPU memory-dump application was also developed to test the functionality and validity of the recovery process.

3.1   A Forensically Sound Method to Collect Evidence from GPU

This research adopted the method from [6, 14] to retrieve data that is buffered text data or rendered graphics data from a GPU. However, changes were made to prove that known evidence could be captured in a forensically sound manner.

The first step was to prove that graphics data from the GPU memory could be captured directly. To do so, a graphic was opened from Windows Photo Viewer and then closed with no modifications or alterations. Because Windows Photo Viewer uses GPU acceleration, the graphic data was temporarily stored in the global memory of the GPU. Then, the four CUDA APIs described in Sect. 2.3 were called to copy the GPU memory content to the system RAM, and then saved to the external storage as the evidence.

When a GPU-accelerated application is closed, the data stored in the GPU global memory is not reset. Rather, the corresponding memory space is labeled as free and will be allocated to other running processes. As a result, a simple memory dump of everything in the GPU is not effective nor efficient because it contains a mixture of data from applications that are currently executing, as well as recently closed, while the focus of this work is to prove the evidence of a single application can be captured reliably, in a forensically sound manner. To avoid unnecessary work of identifying which data (and memory locations) belongs to which process, the global memory space is first 'cleaned' before the Windows Photo Viewer is launched, as shown in Fig. 2. The cuda-MemSet() API was used to reset the contents of GPU global memory to 0. Note that the 'cleaning' stage will change GPU data and it is only needed in the lab environment to simplify the analyses. This step should *not* be performed in the actual live capturing process.

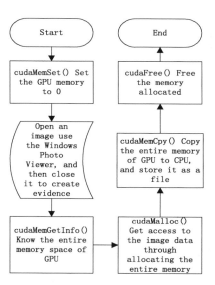

Fig. 2. Process model used to test the collection of graphic data from GPU memory

The basic process that guides the investigators on how to collect the evidence from the GPU's global memory has been introduced by both the [6, 14]. In this research, two changes were made in order to provide forensic reliability to the results. These differences are: (1) create known images before the experiment and use them as evidence; (2) clean memory and collect the evidence immediately after cleaning process to identify the relationship between the original graphics and the evidence.

To prove that data produced in Windows Photo Viewer are captured in GPU memory, a simple square test was designed. The square test draws three squares in 24-bit TIFF format with a different number of pixels. If the number of pixels captured matched with the number of the pixels in the original graphics, it meant the evidence had been captured correctly. If it did not match, further analysis was needed.

To prove the integrity and the reliability of the method, a test was designed to capture two graphics in three different format: jpg, bmp, and TIFF. The number of pixels, and the MD5 hash value of the captured data was studied to test if consistent results can be achieved repeatedly. The testing flow is described in Fig. 3.

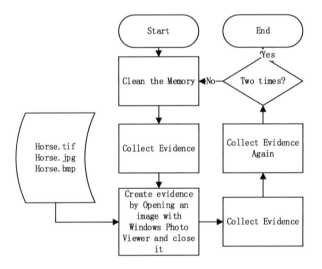

Fig. 3. Process model used to test the consistency of GPU memory capture

3.2   Recover TIFF Graphic from GPU Data

Both Windows Photo Viewer and CUDA APIs are proprietary applications. No public information is found on how graphic data are stored in the global memory of NVIDIA GPUs. To determine the memory allocation processes, Color Test, Line Test and the Color Map Pattern Test were designed. The lossless TIFF format was chosen because it is one of the popular formats that support raster graphics image and lossless compression.

In Color Tests, RGB values of 000000, 0000FF, 00FF00, 00FFFF, FF0000, FF00FF, FFFF00, and FFFFFF are used in the original graphics to compare with the captured

GPU data. In Line Tests, lines of different lengths, widths, and colors were used to relate how pixels are organized in GPU memory.

To better discover the patterns, a more sophisticated Color Map Pattern test were designed. In this test, a TIFF-format square with varying RGB color values was created (e.g. a 200 × 200 pixels square with RGB value incremented from 0 to 39999). It was opened in Windows Photo Viewer and the graphic data was retrieved from GPU global memory. If the graphic itself and the captured data can both be described in matrix arrays, then the transforming pattern can also be described in a matrix array. The Color Map Pattern procedures are illustrated in Fig. 4. Each mapping matrix is calculated as follows:

Let Evi[] denote the sequential RGB value of original graphic, Ch[] denote the sequential RGB value retrieved from GPU global memory and Patn[] denote a mapping array. For each pixel, i, $(0 \le i \le 39999)$, there is Ch[patn[i]] = Evi[i]. In the designed experiment, both Ch[] and Evi[] are known, so each pixel of a mapping pattern can be calculated from the Eq. (1):

$$\text{patn}[i] = \text{Ch-1}[\text{Evi}[i]]. \tag{1}$$

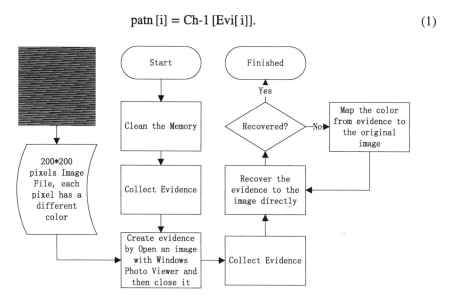

Fig. 4. Procedures used to implement proposed Color Map Pattern Test to discover mapping matrices

3.3 Validity of the Method

A series of experiments were designed to validate the graphic recovery process. The first experiment was a Photo Test where the data of images retrieved from the GPU were displayed on screen and compared against the original images. If they were visually identical, then the recovery approach was deemed correct. Otherwise it is not correct. The second experiment was the Redo Test where the operations were conducted on a different computer and then verified to determine if the same results were obtained.

4   Results and Discussions

This section describes the results of the experiments. The hardware platform is Intel Core i7- 3630QM CPU @ 2.4 GHz, 12.0 G DDR3 System RAM, NVIDIA GeForce 650 GPU. The OS running the application is 64-bit Windows 8.1 Enterprise.

In the reliability test, the experiments were conducted two times. Each time, the number of pixels of the graphic equaled the number of pixels in the evidence captured from GPU, as listed in Table 1.

Table 1. Results of Square Tests show #pixels in the evidence are idential to #pixels in the original graphic

Time	FileName	Size	#Pixels_Orig	#Pixels_Evi	Yes/No
1	Red_tif_24_100w100h.tif	100 * 100	10000	10000	Yes
1	Red_tif_24_200w200h.tif	200 * 200	40000	40000	Yes
1	Red_tif_24_300w300h.tif	300 * 300	90000	90000	Yes
2	Red_tif_24_100w100h.tif	100 * 100	10000	10000	Yes
2	Red_tif_24_200w200h.tif	200 * 200	40000	40000	Yes
2	Red_tif_24_300w300h.tif	300 * 300	90000	90000	Yes

From Table 1, column Time represents the sequence of the experiments. FileName shows basic image attributes. For example, the first file named Red_tif_24_100w100h.tif is a 24-bit TIFF image that is red and has a size of 100 pixels width and 100 pixels height. Size shows the size of the images, #Pixels_Orig shows the number of pixels in the original image, and #Pixels_Evi shows the number of pixels in the evidence. Yes/No column shows whether or not the original pixels number equals the evidence pixels number.

From Table 1, it is observed that in each experiment, the number of pixels in the graphic equals the number of pixels in the evidence, as it is clear that in each time of the experiment, the #Pixels_Orig value equals the value of #Pixels_Evi.

From the data collected from the GPU, it is also observed that each pixel in the evidence will store its graphic data in a totally different sequence when it is compared to how the data is stored in the original image. This allocation process was also observed in Color Test as well.

In the integrity and reliability experiments, two different experiments were conducted. In each experiment, graphic data was retrieved three times. The MD5 hash value of captured GPU memory data were calculated and recorded in Table 2.

Table 2. Results of Integrity and Reliability Test show MD5 hashvalue of the evidence are identical within the same experiments and are different between each experiments.

Time	FileName	Format	OrgPixel	HashValue (MD5)
1	Horse	jpg	1024 * 706	2D6A2CBC0F319AEFCA612BBC0893C68F
1	horse_bmp_24	bmp	1024 * 706	2DB6AEECC32D9F3180C03FDA438C6029
1	horse_tif_24	tiff	1024 * 706	D8D437C7F2FFD79CA03618C4033D4059
1	Horse	jpg	1024 * 706	2D6A2CBC0F319AEFCA612BBC0893C68F
1	horse_bmp_24	bmp	1024 * 706	2DB6AEECC32D9F3180C03FDA438C6029
1	horse_tif_24	tiff	1024 * 706	D8D437C7F2FFD79CA03618C4033D4059
2	Horse	jpg	1024 * 706	B90596F6DFD288C3E0A949412F985DB1
2	horse_bmp_24	bmp	1024 * 706	95377AB8EC6ECE4CBD4A0F18A36AD490
2	horse_tif_24	tiff	1024 * 706	2ACD1A88AD8F21C3956084AE5A67D529
2	Horse	jpg	1024 * 706	B90596F6DFD288C3E0A949412F985DB1
2	horse_bmp_24	bmp	1024 * 706	95377AB8EC6ECE4CBD4A0F18A36AD490
2	horse_tif_24	tiff	1024 * 706	2ACD1A88AD8F21C3956084AE5A67D529

Column Time in Table 2 shows the sequence of the experiments. FileName demonstrates name of the file. Format shows the graphics format, OrgPixel demonstrates the sizes of the graphics, and HashValue (MD5) column shows the MD5 hash value of the evidence.

The results show that the hash values of the same digital GPU evidence were always consistent in all three captures. This means the integrity of the GPU data is preserved. However, the results are *not* repeatable: the same pictures will be mapped to different locations of GPU memory space with different patterns in a different test, and therefore produce totally different hash values. This is significant to understand that the same image data may be loaded into different memory locations on different systems. Additionally, it is likely that the image data may be loaded into different memory locations on the same system if the tests were run later. In both instances, new MD5 values should be calculated for those instances.

The summarized results of Color Test are shown in Table 3. The RGB values were stored differently in GPU memory. The findings suggest the color values are stored in the format of BGR(FF), as opposed to RGB. The individual color values maintain endianness.

In the Table 3, the Num represents the sequence of the experiments; Color column shows how the tested original 24-bit TIFF file stored the color information; Clean(Y/N) column shows whether or not the environment was cleaned before the evidence is produced and put into the GPU memory; and Description column demonstrates how the graphics pixel information was stored in the GPU main memory.

Table 3. Results of Color Test show RGB values were stored differently in GPU memory

Num	Color	Clean (Y/N)	Description
1	000000	Y	000000FF
2	0000FF	Y	FF0000FF
3	00FF00	Y	00FF00FF
4	00FFFF	Y	FFFF00FF
5	FF0000	Y	0000FFFF
6	FF00FF	Y	FF00FFFF
7	FFFF00	Y	00FFFFFF
8	FFFFFF	Y	FFFFFFFF

Based on the findings of Color Test, every pixel occupies 32 bits of space in the global memory of an NIVIDIA GPU. The first 24 bits represent the RGB values in the order of Blue, Green, and Red, and the last eight bits were padded with 1 s. However, each pixel of a graphic is not stored sequentially in the GPU memory. Figure 5 illustrates a typical scenario where recovering a graphic by sequentially reading the GPU memory data rendered a totally different graphic.

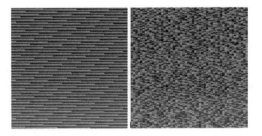

Fig. 5. Comparison between the original graphic (left) and the recovered graphic (right) by sequentially reading GPU memory data directly.

Many experiments were designed and tested to determine how the graphic data were organized in GPU memory. However, a well-defined simple rule may not exist, or at least was not easily found, to map the pixels of a graphic to their location in the global memory of a GPU. To overcome the barriers set by the unknown implementation details of both Windows Photo Viewer and CUDA APIs, the Color Map Patterns Tests were implemented to enumerate all the possible conversions. Specifically, a graphic with the same size as the evidence graphic was constructed. Each pixel of the testing graphic was given a unique RGB value so that it could be identified in the GPU memory dump. The test was conducted repeatedly and the conversion matrices were computed. If a new conversion matrix was found, it was recorded as a candidate for the conversion. Due to time constraints, the test stopped when ten possible conversions were found.

Then a TIFF-formatted Photo was opened from Windows Photo Viewer and collected from the GPU. The test was conducted four times. Each time, the memory dump was manipulated by one of those ten possible conversions. The results showed that in tests 2, 3, and 4, one of the discovered conversions were able to completely restore the graphic. However, test 1 was not successful, indicating a different conversion matrix was used and was not yet found in the Color Map Pattern Test. Figure 6 shows the conversion results of the second photo test. Pattern A5 was able to completely restore the photo. Comparing with the original photo, the recovered photo was visually identical.

Fig. 6. Results of restored graphics after applying all 10 potential matching matrices (Test 2)

A5 pattern is one of the common patterns that was identified through the Color Map Pattern Test. What we have to mention is that this recovery process can only be done through visual selection at this time. More practical methods need to be discovered in the further research. However, to the author's opinion, this process can be used in NVIDIA GPU no matter how the series change. Windows Photo Viewer was selected only because we observed that the Windows Photo Viewer can produce evidence in the GPU memory. The author believes that investigators can use a similar method to recover any graphic data that is produced by a different application.

The Color Map Pattern Tests and the Photo Tests were conducted on a different computer with a similar NVIDIA GPU. The results showed a similar trend where three out of four Photo Tests could recover an image from one of those ten discovered conversion matrices.

The findings from all the experiments are listed as follows:

1. In Square Test and Color Test, the number of pixels captured from GPU memory space equals the number of pixels of the original TIFF graphic. And the pictures were identical between the original graphic and captured graphic. The only caveat is that the RGB value of a pixel will be reordered to BGR and padded with 8 bits of

1 s. This suggests that a 24-bit TIFF formatted evidence can be retrieved from GPU memory without any loss. It also suggests that a graphic takes a different form when stored in hard drive than stored in GPU memory. GPU forensic should not aim to prove two forms of data are binary identical, but instead, to prove the data captured is not contaminated and is visually identical. Additional tests are needed to verify if the same properties hold for pictures with different formats or of extremely large sizes.

2. Results obtained from the Integrity and Reliability Test showed that the GPU memory dump approach always generates identical MD5 hash values in the same experiment (repeatedly read GPU containing the same content). But the MD5 hash values are always different among experiments (repeatedly read GPU containing the same graphic by re-open it from Windows Photo Viewer). On the positive side, the results showed the proposed method is forensically sound and reliable in the same test. The results also showed the non-repeatability feature of volatile forensics.

3. The Color Map Pattern Test proved to be an effective technique at recovering a graphic from GPU memory dump. It was especially valuable when the mapping between a graphic and its GPU memory organization is unknown and difficult to discover. With the help of this test, potential transformation matrices were enumerated. The more transformation matrices, the more likely a graphic can be restored. If we further assume that the graphic evidence is a visually meaningful picture and no two potential conversions produce visually meaningful pictures, and then the proposed work can recover a graphic from GPU memory in a forensically sound manner.

5   Conclusions

In this work, we first explained the need of GPU forensics. Since it is possible for data stored in GPU to bypass System RAM and flow directly to the display devices, GPU forensics cannot be replaced by System RAM forensics. Existing work [6, 14] illustrated a process to retrieve data from GPU global memory but it was not thoroughly examined if it is forensically sound. A series of experiments were constructed in our work and proved that evidence opened by Windows Photo Viewer can be retrieved in a forensically sound manner in the same experiment. The method however is not repeatable by re-opening the same graphic as the hash values vary based on memory allocation determined at the time the application loads the image. The reliability within each experiment, however, holds true. That is, the hash values matched within each experiment, but not between experiments. The experiments also showed the graphic data stored in GPU memory is different from the format it is stored on the hard drive in terms of both color representations and order of the pixels.

Our analyses and experiments demonstrated that no simple and clear rules can be easily found between a graphic and how it is mapped to the global memory of a GPU. In an effort to visually restore the graphic data retrieved from GPU memory, a novel Color Depth Map Test was designed in our work. The test produced a number of conversion matrices by constructing a graphic that all the pixels can be uniquely identified. The tests also showed that it is possible that a graphic can be visually recovered from one of the conversion matrices discovered from the Color Depth Map Test. The restoring method, as of right now, is not reliable and cannot be labeled as forensically sound yet due to the visual matching only. However, by trying more conversion patterns and conducting additional carefully designed experiments to prove its reliability, we are confident that the proposed method points the researchers in the right direction for discovering a forensically sound method to visually restore a graphic hiding in the GPU memory.

It should be noted that there may be limitations of these experiments due to the image files were only 200px × 200px 24-bit TIFF files. It is intended that future work will investigate this further, both in terms of image sizes as well as image formats. Since a TIFF is a raster format image, it is expected that other lossless raster image formats will have similar findings to these results. However, again, further work is needed to verify this supposition. Additionally, work should be done with lossy formats as well as vector-based graphic formats to identify the forensically sound recovery methods.

References

1. ACPO E-Crime Working Group: Good practice guide for computer-based electronic evidence. In: 7safe Information Security Website (2011)
2. Adelstein, F.: Live forensics: diagnosing your system without killing it first. Commun. ACM **49**(2), 63–66 (2006)
3. Aljaedi, A., Lindskog, D., Zavarsky, P., Ruhl, R., Almari, F.: Comparative analysis of volatile memory forensics: live response vs. memory imaging. In: Privacy, Security, Risk and Trust (Passat) and 2011 IEEE Third International Conference on Social Computing (Socialcom), pp. 1253–1258. IEEE Press, New York (2011)
4. AMD.   http://web.amd.com/assets/customerreferenceprogrampackage2012/CRP%20Oct%202013%20WinZip%20Case%20Study.pdf
5. Bilby, D.: Low down and dirty: anti-forensic rootkits. In: Proceedings of Ruxcon (2006)
6. Breß, S., Kiltz, S., Schaler, M.: Forensics on GPU co-processing in databases research challenges, first experiments, and countermeasures. In: BTW Workshops (2013)
7. Campbell, W.: Volatile memory acquisition tools-a comparison across taint and correctness (2013). http://ro.ecu.edu.au/adf/115/
8. Center, C.C.: Steps for Recovering from a Unix or NT system compromise. Technical report, Software Engineer Institute (2001)
9. Claricesimmons. http://community.amd.com/community/amd-blogs/amd/blog/2013/10/30/the-new-winzip-18-with-accelerated-performance-for-amd-apus-and-gpus
10. Geeks3D. http://www.geeks3d.com/20111217/winzip-16-5-will-support-opencl-for-ultra-fast-compression-and-decompression/
11. Hay, B., Bishop, M., Nance, K.: Live analysis: progress and challenges. Secur. Priv. **7**(2), 30–37 (2009)
12. Jang, K., Han, S., Han, S., Moon, S.B., Park, K.: Sslshader: cheap SSL acceleration with commodity processors. In: Nsdi (2011)
13. Kent, K., Chevalier, S., Grance, T., Dang, H.: Guide to Integrating Forensic Techniques into Incident Response. NIST Special Publication, 800-86 (2006)
14. Lee, S., Kim, Y., Kim, J., Kim, J.: Stealing Webpages rendered on your browser by exploiting GPU vulnerabilities. In: 2014 IEEE Symposium on Security and Privacy, pp. 19–33. IEEE Press, New York (2014)

15. McKemmish, R.: When is digital evidence forensically sound? In: Ray, I., Shenoi, S., (eds.) Advances in Digital Forensics IV. Springer (2008)
16. NVIDIA.   http://www.nvidia.com/object/what-is-gpu-computing.html#sthash.fYjRi2ZR. dpuf
17. Palmer, G.: A road map for digital forensic research. In: First Digital Forensic Research Workshop, pp. 27–30, Utica, New York (2001)
18. Ring, S., Cole, E.: Volatile memory computer forensics to detect kernel level compromise. In: López, J., Qing, S., Okamoto, E. (eds.) ICICS 2004. LNCS, vol. 3269, pp. 158–170. Springer, Heidelberg (2004)
19. Service U.S. S.: Best practices for seizing electronic evidence (2007). http://www.treas.gov/ usss/electronic_evidence.shtml
20. Sutherland, I., Evans, J., Tryfonas, T., Blyth, A.: Acquiring volatile operating system data tools and techniques. ACM SIGOPS Operating Syst. Rev. **42**(3), 65–73 (2008)
21. Urrea, J.M.: An analysis of Linux RAM forensics. Unpublished Doctoral Dissertation, Monterey, California, Naval Postgraduate School (2006)
22. Vasiliadis, G., Polychronakis, M., Ioannidis, S.: GPU-Assisted Malware. Int. J. Inf. Secur. **14**(3), 289–297 (2010). http://dl.acm.org/citation.cfm?id=2777077
23. Wang, L., Zhang, R., Zhang, S.: A model of computer live forensics based on physical memory analysis. In: 2009 1st International Conference on Information Science and Engineering, pp. 4647–4649. IEEE Press, Nanjing (2009)

Network and Cloud Forensics

Advanced Techniques for Reconstruction of Incomplete Network Data

Petr Matoušek[(✉)], Jan Pluskal, Ondřej Ryšavý, Vladimír Veselý,
Martin Kmeť, Filip Karpíšek, and Martin Vymlátil

Brno University of Technology, Božetěchova 2, Brno, Czech Republic
{matousp,ipluskal,rysavy,ivesely,ikmet,ikarpisek}@fit.vutbr.cz,
xvymla01@stud.fit.vutbr.cz
http://www.fit.vutbr.cz

Abstract. Network forensics is a method of obtaining and analyzing digital evidences from network sources. Network forensics includes data acquisition, selection, processing, analysis and presentation to investigators. Due to high volumes of transmitted data the acquired information can be incomplete, corrupted, or disordered which makes further reconstruction difficult. In this paper, we address the issue of advanced parsing and reconstruction of incomplete, corrupted, or disordered data packets. We introduce a technique that recovers TCP or UDP conversations so they could be further analyzed by application parsers. Presented technique is implemented in a new network forensic tool called Netfox Detective. We also discuss current challenges in parsing web mail communication, SSL decryption and Bitcoins detection.

Keywords: Network forensic tools · TCP reassembling · Traffic reconstruction · Web mail · Bitcoin · SSL encryption

1 Introduction

Network forensics is an emerging area of digital forensics connected with the rapid network development. Many services and digital transactions are transmitted over the Internet where criminal activities and security incidents also occur. Network forensics provides post-mortem investigation of unlawful behavior using special tools that reconstruct a sequence of events occurred at the time of the attack. This reconstruction depends only on a captured network data. In some cases, these data are incomplete, corrupted, or out of order. In order to analyze the original communication using an incompletely captured data, advanced techniques of reconstruction and communication recovery are needed. Reconstruction of TCP streams is essential for any network forensic tool [1]. If the TCP reassembling fails, application data cannot be properly analyzed.

Recovery of incomplete data in network forensics is a similar task to data recovery from damaged media, e.g., hard drives, CDs, or DVDs. If some data are missing, it can be either replaced by empty data units or approximated

© Institute for Computer Sciences, Social Informatics and Telecommunications Engineering 2015
J.I. James and F. Breitinger (Eds.): ICDF2C 2015, LNICST 157, pp. 69–84, 2015.
DOI: 10.1007/978-3-319-25512-5_6

from known data. The goal is to provide enough data enabling reconstruction of the original content. To guarantee an admissibility of forensic results newly introduced data must be unambiguously distinguished from the original ones.

In this work, we deal with the analysis and reconstruction of incomplete or damaged network data. Our research includes the development of heuristic techniques that can detect incomplete or corrupted data on network and transport layer and restore original sessions that can be further analyzed using usual application parsers. The proposed technique was implemented in a new network forensic tool *Netfox Detective*.

1.1 Contribution

The main contribution of this paper addresses practical issues connected with network data reconstruction and proposes advanced techniques for parsing and recovery of network conversations. These techniques in combination with advanced application recognition methods increase the accuracy of content reconstruction. We also explain several issues connected with application analysis, especially with web mail services, SSL communication and Bitcoin transactions. We evaluate the implementation of proposed methods and compare them with other tools.

The paper is organized as follows: section two surveys current approaches and results in the domain of network forensic tools; section three examines issues related to network data parsing and reconstruction with focus on TCP reassembling and Layer 7 (L7, application) data reconstruction; section four deals with application detection and content analysis, which is demonstrated using examples of reconstruction of web mail, SSL traffic, and bitcoin transactions.

2 Related Work

There is a wide range of tools for network monitoring and forensics, i.e., Network Security and Monitoring tools (NSMs) and Network Forensic Analysis Tools (NFATs). NSMs include network analyzers (Wireshark, tcpdump), IDS systems (snort, Bro), fingerprinting tools (nmap, p0f), and others [2]. NFATs have similar functionality as NSMs, in addition, they also assist in a network crime investigation. They capture an entire network traffic and allow an investigator to analyze it and reconstruct the original communication. Most of the NFAT tools are proprietary, nevertheless, open source NFATs also exist, e.g., PyFlag, Network Miner, or Xplico.

In theory, parsing the network communication is straightforward. However, incompleteness and corruption of communication requires new methods involving robust parsers and complex recovery procedures. Surveys of different network forensic frameworks can be found in [2,3]. These papers discuss various approaches to network forensics, major challenges, and list available tools. In our paper, we mostly focus on techniques of network data parsing and recovery.

There are not many published works describing techniques incorporated in NFAT implementations, partly due to the protection of intellectual properties of the tools. An exception is Cohen [1] that describes several challenges connected with the stream reassembling (termination of streams, out of sequence packets, missed packets) and the combination of streams into conversations. In our work, we deeply examine issues that are essential for every network forensic tool. In addition to [1], we present an algorithm that deals with these issues, and also works with sequence number overflow, which is not discussed by other authors. A detailed description of TCP reassembling is analyzed by Paxson in [4]. However, Paxson focuses on robustness of TCP reassembling in the presence of adversaries that is out of the interest of this paper.

3 Data Parsing and Reconstruction

NFATs are designed to parse captured data, process packet headers and reconstruct high-level protocol units. Application data are regularly transmitted using TCP or UDP protocols over IP networks. By definition, IP communication does not provide reliable data exchange [5]. Application data are segmented into TCP packets and encapsulated into IP datagrams. Furthermore, IP datagrams can be fragmented into smaller IP datagrams when required by an underlying link-layer technology. The main goal of an NFAT is to extract and reconstruct original application data from possibly incomplete captured collection of IP datagrams. The method for assembling IP packet-based communications into conversations is based on the following assumptions:

- An application conversation is distinguished by a pair of IP addresses, transport ports and a protocol type. The conversation consists of a pair of flows because the most of sessions are bi-directional.
- The beginning of a TCP session is identified by a synchronization TCP segment (SYN flag). A TCP segment with FIN/PSH/RST flag closes the session.
- A TCP session consists of a collection of TCP segments each associated with a sequence number. A sequence number determines an offset of the segment content in the TCP stream [6].
- An application message can be transmitted in one or more TCP segments. Receiver must reassemble several TCP segments to obtain the original message.
- The IP fragmentation happens independently on the TCP segmentation. The IP defragmentation has to be accomplished before the application content reassembling.

3.1 Challenges in TCP Reassembling

During our research of network data analysis, following challenges connected with reassembling of TCP sessions have been identified:

– *Missing FIN packets or overlapping of TCP conversations.*
Regularly, ephemeral source ports are dynamically assigned by OS to clients whenever a communication socket is created [7, p. 99]. It helps to distinguish several TCP sessions originating from the same node and targeting the same remote process. When the client finishes communication, these ports can be reused. Usually, the port number is not reused until the pool of ephemeral ports is exhausted. NFAT can exploit this behavior to recognize different TCP sessions safely. However, if there is a NAT translation along the communication path observable port numbers can be reused quickly. In such case, different TCP sessions can receive the same key fields within a relatively short period. While end systems and NAT can accurately track the use of port numbers, for NFAT system it may pose a problem as there is a very short interval between two TCP sessions with the same identification. NFAT can proceed as follows:
1. FIN segment can determine closing of the first session segment while SYN segment defines a new TCP session;
2. if these segments are missing in a captured collection, a flow needs to be detected by analyzing sequence numbers;
3. if sequence numbers of two sessions overlap, the analysis of timestamps of expected L4 packets have to be carried out.
– *Combination of two L7 flows into a L7 conversation.*
NFATs try to reconstruct original bi-directional communication between applications. If more TCP conversations use the same IP addresses and ports (see NAT problem above), these ports are not sufficient to unambiguously combine corresponding L7 flows into a whole L7 conversation. The proposed solution suggests considering initial TCP sequence numbers. TCP three-way hand-shake starts with sending three synchronization segments between a sender and a receiver. The sender sends a SYN segment with his initial, randomly chosen, sequence number. The receiver replies with an SYN+ACK segment transmitting receiver's initial sequence number and sender's next sequence number. Based on hand-shake analysis, we can match initial TCP sequence numbers of every L7 flow and its opposite L7 flow, which is necessary to create bi-directional L7 conversation based on L4 header data only. If the hand-shake is not captured, L7 flows are considered as one-directional L7 conversations.
– *TCP sequence number overflow.*
Network data parsing and analysis is mostly based on a chronological order of packets in the flow using their sequence numbers. According to RFC 793 [6], sequence numbers occupy space up to $2^{32} - 1$ Bytes, which gives possibility to transmit maximum 4.29 GB data. This value seems large enough to avoid sequence number overflow. However, since initial sequence numbers are generated randomly, maximum data size is lower than this theoretical value. Figure 1 shows a snapshot of the distribution of maximum TCP message sizes based on randomly generated initial sequence numbers as observed on 14,000 TCP sessions. The picture does not show full distribution range. TCP sessions with possible payload greater than 500 MB are excluded, because of their irrelevance for our study. However, these data show that TCP sequence

number overflow should be taken seriously. For example, we can see that the sequence number would overflow in 0,12 % of TCP sessions with payload up to 5 MB. This situation can be solved by multi-pass processing of an L4 conversation and matching incomplete TCP sessions without SYNs when their initial sequence numbers are closed to 2^{32}.

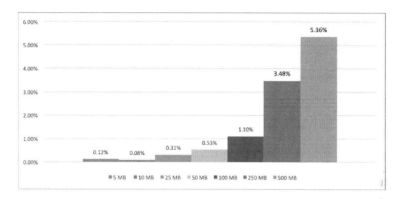

Fig. 1. Probability of TCP Seq numbers overflow related to maximal L7 payload size.

3.2 Building L7 PDUs from the PCAP File

The process of network data parsing starts with the tracking of L3 conversations based on sender's and receiver's IP addresses, see Fig. 2. Further, L4 conversations are identified using port numbers and L4 protocol type, than L7 conversations are created. In case of UDP protocol, two UDP sessions running between the same pair of ports cannot be distinguished. For example, SIP applications regularly employ the same source and destination ports, e.g., 5060, for all SIP conversations. Therefore, a L4 UDP conversation is considered to be a L7 conversation.

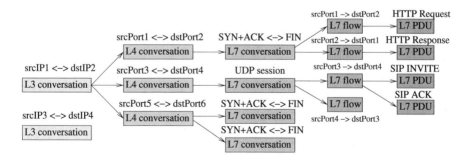

Fig. 2. Extraction of L7 PDUs from input packets.

In case of TCP protocol, the TCP reassembling is the key element in recon-struction. If all data have been properly captured, TCP reassembling is a simple task that involves port numbers, TCP sequence and acknowledgment numbers. If some packets are missing, a following procedure implementing our heuristic method can be applied to any network data. The procedure uses three heuris-tic parameters: *MaxLost*, which represents the maximal length of missing data that can be restored, *MaxTime*, describing the maximal permitted time delay between two consequent packets using timestamps, and *MaxPayload*, represent-ing the maximum payload size in a TCP packet. Based on our experience, we use $MaxLost = 4kB$ and $MaxTime = 600\ sec$[1]. *MaxPayload* is computed on-the-fly as the length of the TCP packet with the maximal size of a payload in the L7 flow. Thus, application messages are built from captured data using the following steps:

1. Select L4 flows and sort packets using their sequence numbers.
2. Process each L4 flow and create L7 flows using TCP handshake. Start with the first SYN packet.
   (a) Create a new L7 PDU if does not exist or if a previous L7 PDU was closed.
   (b) Check packet sequence number Seq_{i+1}.
   (c) If $Seq_{i+1} \neq Seq_i + PS_i$ (PS stands for a payload size obtained from the packet header), i.e., the expected packet is missing, check timestamps TS and sequence numbers Seq as follows:
      i. If $TS_{i+1} - TS_i \leq MaxTime$ and $Seq_{i+1} - Seq_i \leq MaxLost$ then a virtual packet will be created to replace the missing packet.
      ii. If $TS_{i+1} - TS_i \geq MaxTime$ and $Seq_{i+1} - Seq_i \leq MaxLost$ then there is an overlapping of TCP sessions because $i+1$ packet belongs to a different L7 flow. Skip this packet and proceed with the next one.
      iii. If $Seq_{i+1} - Seq_i \geq MaxLost$ then there are too many missing data. The flow cannot be fully restored. Close it and proceed with next SYN packet.
   (d) If $Seq_{i+1} = Seq_i + PS_i$ the expected packet is present, add it into the L7 PDU.
   (e) If FIN/RST/PSH flag is found or $PS = MaxPayload$, close the L7 PDU.
   (f) GOTO 2a.
3. Process remaining packets without SYNs. Create new L7 flows using timestamps and sequence numbers only.
4. Process every L7 flow and create L7 PDUs using TCP reassembling

---

[1] *MaxLost* was experimentally set to 4 kB, which is more than two times greater than maximal Ethernet PDU size, i.e., 1500 Bytes. *MaxTime* is six times greater than recommended TCP connection failure timeout as defined in RFC 1122. These values say that packet loss longer than 600 secs or missing 4 kB cannot be successfully recovered.

  - Add every packet of the L7 flow into the L7 PDU until FIN/RST/PSH or
    $PS = MaxPayload$. Then close the L7 PDU and create new one for new
    packets.
5. Combine opposite L7 flows into a L7 conversation using corresponding SYN
   and ACK numbers.

The main benefit of this approach is the reconstruction of original UDP/TCP
sessions even if some important packets are missing. Based on TCP initial Seq
numbers, the algorithm combines two flows into a conversation. The algorithm
deals with missing SYNs, FINs, overlapping sessions, or TCP numbers overflow-
ing. As the result, we have L7 PDU objects that can be processed on L7.

Table 1 compares our approach with a few available NSMs or NFATs. For our
study, we have chosen Wireshark, Microsoft Network Monitor, NetWitness and
Network Miner. In the first test we used an artificially arranged dataset with
(i) one FIN packet missing, (ii) one SYN packet missing, and (iii) two SYNs
missing. Original 650 kB PCAP file contained 19 conversions. Further analysis
showed that in case of missing SYNs and the same port numbers, Wireshark
joins two conversations into one. MS Network Monitor works well with missing
SYNs, but it is not able to properly close communication if a FIN is missing.
In such case, it combines two conversations into one. NetWitness also joins two
conversations into one. Network Miner works similarly to Wireshark.

Table 1. Detection of network conversation when missing SYN/FIN packets.

File	NFX Det	Wireshark	MS Monitor	NetWitness	Net Miner
One FIN missing	19	19	18	17	19
One SYN missing	19	18	19	17	18
Two SYNs missing	19	17	19	17	17

The second test used 8 MB PCAP file with some packets randomly deleted.
Table 2 shows results when 0 %, 1 %, 5 %, or 10 % of packets were removed.
Original file contained 126 conversations. Netfox Detective shows number of L7
conversations.

Table 2. Detection of network conversations when some data are deleted.

File	NFX Det	Wireshark	MS Monitor	NetWitness	Net Miner
0 % missing	126	126	132	128	76
1 % missing	126	126	132	128	75
5 % missing	129	125	129	127	71
10 % missing	131	125	129	127	66

The table shows that Netfox Detective finds more L7 conversations than originally stored in the in-corrupted file. The reason is that when some packets are missing, a corrupted L7 conversation is divided into several L7 conversation due to the large number of missing packets or large timestamp difference, see Fig. 3. Wireshark and NetWitness also miss a conversation. However, since they consider all packets between the same src/dst ports as one conversation, missing packets usually did not reduce number of all conversations. MS Network Monitor also shows stable results. The results of Network Miner are very different but we are not able to say why.

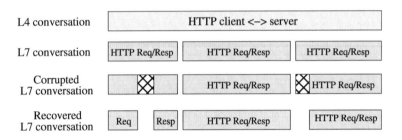

Fig. 3. Recovery of corrupted conversations.

3.3 Application Protocol Identification

The result of previously described reconstruction methods are L7 PDUs that represent L7 objects (payloads) prepared for L7 parsing. Before L7 parsing, L7 protocol should be identified in order to choose the right L7 parser. There are many methods for application protocol identification. The easiest method is based on well-known port numbers assigned by Internet Assigned Numbers Authority (IANA). Unfortunately, this method does not work well with applications using dynamic ports, peer-to-peer communication, video streaming, etc. More advanced methods use payload inspection that is suitable for protocols that can be recognized by some characteristic patterns either in a header or payload. There are also methods based on protocol fingerprinting or statistical data. In our approach, we combine several methods for application protocol identification.

1. *Identification using extended IANA database.*
   The first algorithm matches port numbers with extended IANA database of well-known ports. Our database extends IANA data by similarities, i.e., one input port number can match more applications. For example, Dropbox file hosting service can work on ports 80, 443, or 17500. Based on given application tags, L7 parser is chosen. Currently, our database can identify 1058 different application protocols.

2. *RTP Fingerprinting.*
    If there is no match on input ports, RTP fingerprinting method is applied [8].
    This method uses a multi-stage classifier that observes minimal RTP header
    length, RTP version number, and RTP payload type number. If a packet
    successfully passes this filtering, per-flow checking is applied using minimal
    number of packets in an RTP flow to reduce false positives.
3. *Statistical Protocol Identification (SPID).*
    This method developed by Erik Hjelmvik [9] is based on supervised learn-
    ing using pre-classified samples of captured network traffic where application
    protocols are correctly annotated. The algorithm generates protocol model
    database that stores application fingerprints. Currently, our database can
    identify 20 protocols with an ability to add new protocols.

4   Application Parsing

After building L7 PDUs and successful L7 protocol identification, application
data can be processed by L7 parsers. As mentioned in Chap. 3, TCP/UDP
streams are reconstructed without any knowledge of higher layers. This helps
in case when an application parser is not implemented for a specific protocol. In
that case application data can also be extracted from communication.

Main goal of our approach is to augment the reconstruction process when
some data are missing. As mentioned earlier if only a few data is missing, lost
packets can be replaced by new packets with empty payload. If more packets are
lost, an original stream will be recovered as a collection of shorter streams that
formed the original stream.

In this section, we will discuss how data reconstruction influences L7 processing and data presentation in case of incomplete data. For demonstration, we
choose three areas that build challenges for common network parsers: web mail
communication, SSL/TLS encrypted traffic, and bitcoin transactions.

4.1   Web Mail Analysis

Web mail communication is very popular today. Web mail servers employ HTTP
protocol to encapsulate transactions between a user web browser and a web
mail server. Mail exchange between web mail servers is mostly provided using
SMTP protocol. Forensic analysis of web mail services is different from common web browsing. Many web mail servers utilize advanced web technologies
like JavaScript, AJAX, JSON that dynamically create web pages. Analysis and
interpretation of captured web mail data are limited due to the usage of web
browser caches that store frequently used HTTP objects. These objects are not
present in captured traffic, therefore, they are unavailable for forensic analysis.

The web mail analysis includes two phases: (i) the identification of web mail
data between other HTTP traffic and (ii) the analysis of captured web mail
data. In addition, most of web mail transmissions are SSL/TLS encrypted, so
SSL/TLS decryption is required if possible (see Sect. 4.2). If encrypted, web

mail traffic can be identified using a name or IP address of a particular web mail server, see Table 3. If not encrypted, a pattern matching on URLs can be applied.

Table 3. Identification of web mail services during SSL/TLS handshake.

Web mail service	Server name	Encoding
seznam.cz, email.cz	email.seznam.cz	FastRPC
Gmail	mail-attachment.googleusercontent.com	application/x-www-form-urlencoded ;charset=utf-8
Yahoo	mail.yahoo.cz	application/json multipart/form-data-incl JSON
MS Live	*various*	application/x-www-form-urlencoded
Centrum/Atlas	mail.centrum.cz	application/x-www-form-urlencoded
Roundcube	*private service hostname*	application/x-www-form-urlencoded
Horde	*private service hostname*	multipart/form-data

For processing of a captured web mail data, following observations were made:

- Web mail messages transmitted over HTTP can be detected using URL patterns: */mail/.** for Gmail, *o1/mail.fpp* for MS Live Mail, *appid=YahooMailNeo* for Yahoo, etc. However, these patterns usually change with a new version of the server.
- The communication from a user towards the server is transmitted via POST method of HTTP protocol [10]. GET method is employed for listing mail folders.
- Web mail messages are mostly encoded using simple *key=value* pairs in the URL. There are several types of actions that can be identified in a *key* field: *compose-message, send-message, save-draft, get-inbox, delete-message.* Each web mail service uses different names for these actions, so data analysis should be performed for every new web mail protocol.
- Some web mail objects can be transmitted as JSON objects in MIME structure, XML-RPC objects, etc.
- Because of dynamic web programming and client-based technologies (i.e., JavaScript), forensic page rendering of web mail is difficult and cannot be fully accomplished without having contents of web caches. Practically, investigator's view is limited to a simple textual form of analyzed data.

4.2   SSL/TLS Detection and Encryption

The SSL/TLS encryption is a big challenge for current NFAT tools because it completely hides the contents of the network communication. It forms a modular framework that combines various cryptography mechanisms defined by a cipher suite [11]. Clients and servers can negotiate cipher suites to meet specific security and administrative policies during initial SSL/TLS handshake. The cipher suite defines following mechanisms:

- *A key exchange algorithm.* General goal of the key exchange process is to create a pre-master secret known to the communicating parties that is used to generate the master secret. Using master secret encryption keys and MAC keys are generated. Most common key exchange algorithms are RSA, Diffie-Hellman, ECDH, etc.
- *A peer authentication.* TLS supports authentication of both peers, the server authentication with an unauthenticated client, and total anonymity. Whenever the server is authenticated, the channel is secure against man-in-the-middle attacks. Server authentication mostly requires a RSA or DSA certificate to prove an authenticity of the server side.
- *Message integrity.* Message integrity is ensured using Message Authentication Code (MAC) algorithms like MD5, SHA1, or SHA256. A cryptographic hash (often called message digest) is computed using these algorithms and added to the end of each block.
- *A bulk cipher algorithm.* This algorithm is used for a message encryption. The specification includes the cipher type (stream, block, AEAD [12]), the key size, the block size of the cipher (applied only to block ciphers), and the length of initialization vectors (or nonces). Common bulk ciphers are RC4, 3DES, AES, IDEA, or Camellia.

There are two basic approaches for SSL/TLS decryption [13]:

- *A getting server private key.* This key can be used to calculate a session key that have encrypted the conversation. The session key is generated during the key exchange.
- *A MitM attack on SSL/TLS connection.* Another method to get decrypted contents is to use man-in-the-middle (MitM) attack employing a special proxy server to track the communication between the client and server. At the same time, the communication with the user node employs different TLS keys generated by the proxy server. In this case, proxy server should offer a fake certificate in order to impersonate the original server. There are several tools implementing this proxy, e.g., SSLsplit, Fidler, etc.

Bulk cipher algorithms incorporate methods of a block cipher or stream cipher encryption that defines how a block or stream of a plain text will be encrypted and how the encryption key is generated for each data block, e.g. CBC (Cipher Block Chaining), GCM (Galois/Counter).

- The Cipher Block Chaining requires complete data for successful reconstruction because of data dependency, see Fig. 4A. If data are corrupted, successful analysis can be provided until the first error occurs in the stream. In such case, only meta information about the conversation are available, e.g. TCP completeness, probable conversation length, duration, etc.

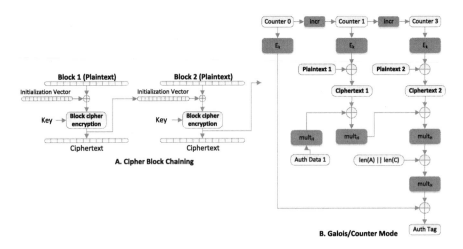

Fig. 4. CBC and GSM encryption.

- The Galois/Counter mode can be reconstructed even if some data are missing because cipher blocks are independent, see Fig. 4B.

Currently, our tool Netfox Detective supports analysis and decryption of various cipher suites, see Table 4.

Table 4. Cipher suites supported Netfox Detective.

TlsRSAWithAes128CbsSha	TlsRSAWithAes256CbsSha
TlsRSAWithAes128CbsSha256	TlsRSAWithAes256CbsSha256
TlsRSAWithAes128GcmSha256	TlsRSAWithAes256GcmSha384
TlsRSAWithRc4128Md5	TlsRSAWithRc4128Sha

If a server key is available, this communication can be decrypted as presented in Fig. 5. This picture shows a successful decryption of web mail communication encrypted using TLS.

4.3 Bitcoin Detection

Bitcoins as currency (BTC) are getting more and more popular since 2008, especially because of their anonymity. Bitcoin network is secure by design against correlating transactions with individual users. However, forensic tools can at least detect bitcoin traffic within a network.

Bitcoin operates over peer-to-peer (P2P) network consisting of two node kinds: (i) clients, which send, receive, or relay BTC transactions; and (ii) miners, which verify transactions using a special proof-of-work algorithm.

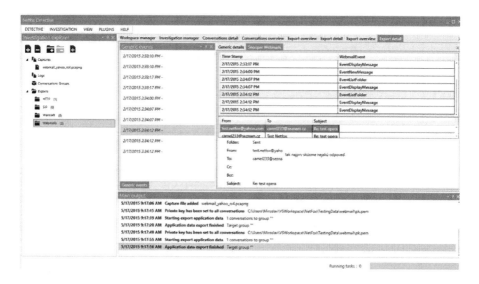

Fig. 5. Reconstruction of encrypted web mail data.

BTC uses three different protocols for its functionality where each protocol has a different value for the forensic investigation. These protocols are as follows:

1. Bitcoin v.1 protocol[2] is employed for P2P communication between peers (connected nodes). For forensic analysis, its detection can help to identify the end stations running Bitcoin client software. The protocol runs over TCP, port 8333. It transmits messages required for both a node discovery and Bitcoin transactions.

    Node discovery is provided twice in Bitcoin network:

    – Upon software start-up, a client looks for special domain names (e.g., bitcoin.sipa.be, dnsseed.bluematt.me) in DNS in order to discover initial set of peers to get connected. Usually, the client uses a list of pre-configured stable nodes of the Bitcoin network.
    – Upon successful connection to a node, the client may request a list of neighboring peers to expand its connectivity graph.

    The protocol messages that helps us to detect a communication within Bitcoin P2P network area as follows: `version` and `verack` (useful for connection initiation), `address` (to detect a communication graph and provide information of known nodes), and `ping-pong` (a keep-alive mechanism). For forensic purposes, also messages `inv`, `tx`, and `block` are important since they transmit valuable information about processed transactions. The list of all Bitcoin v.1 messages is shown in Table 5.

---

[2] See https://bitcoint.org/en/developer-documenation, June, 2015.

Table 5. Bitcoin v.1 protocol.

Messages	Description	Message	Description
version, verack	Opening messages	*tx, notfound*	Responses to *getdata*
getaddr, addr	List of known peers	*ping, pong*	Keepalive messages
inv	A new object announcement	*alert*	Broadcast notification
getdata	Request for object value	*mempool*	Retrieving a transaction
getblocks, blocks	Retrieval of a block	*filterload/add*	Bloom filter operations
getheaders, headers	Retrieval of a header	*reject*	Negative response

2. Another group of protocols (e.g., Getwork, Getworktemplate, Stratum) is used for work distribution for miners cooperating in the pool. The detection of these protocols implies an existence of bitcoin miner in the local network.
3. The last protocol group involves remote procedure call (RPC) messages that are employed for remote control of various Bitcoin related services (e.g., remote wallets controlled by a smart phone, on-line trading on Bitcoin exchanges, etc.).

Netfox Detective currently supports decoding of Bitcoin v1 protocol that helps to detect devices that run Bitcoin clients, work as Bitcoin miners, or access Bitcoin related services, see Fig. 6.

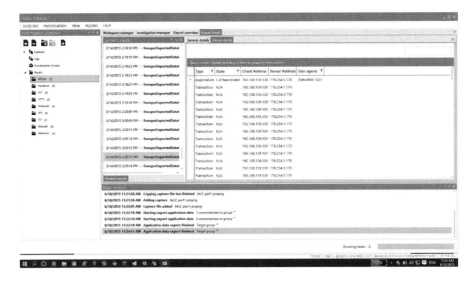

Fig. 6. Bitcoin analysis using Netfox Detective.

Based on these information, it is possible to create Bitcoin communication graphs and correlate the pool member and mining rig owner.

Captured network data can be used to provide an evidence that the seized server really conducted Bitcoin transactions, see Fig. 7.

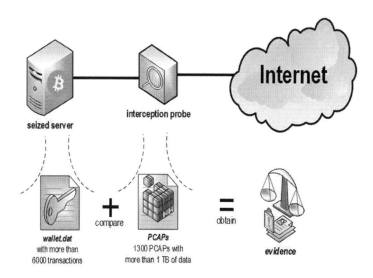

Fig. 7. Digital investigation of Bitcoin transactions.

5   Conclusion

Network forensics represent several challenges for security analysts. Network data are volatile what causes that communication traces are not captured completely. In addition, plenty of protocols are utilized in the current network communication. Many network applications also employ application-level protocol HTTP only as a data channel offering end-to-end connection. With the increased amount of traffic being encrypted, it is even complicated to recognize classes of applications in the captured communication.

In this paper, an overview of issues related to a recovery of the application content from captured traffic was presented. For identified problems, proposed methods were tested by implementing them in a novel network forensic tool. Based on the comparison to related tools, achieved results are promising for the further development of our NFAT tool.

Future work is delineated by the stated facts. Because of widely used traffic encryption, NFAT tools have to analyze meta-information associated with the traffic, e.g., recognizing events from communication, identifying end users, or approximate the meaning of information hidden in the encrypted communication. Also, the amount of communication requires NFATs to handle big data from various sources. Finally, NFATs should be extensible to deal with various classes of applications, e.g., web mail or Bitcoin traffic.

Acknowledgment. Research in this paper was supported by project "Modern Tools for Detection and Mitigation of Cyber Criminality on the New Generation Internet", no. VG20102015022 granted by Ministry of the Interior of the Czech Republic and an internal University project "Research and application of advanced methods in ICT", no. FIT-S-14-2299 granted by Brno University of Technology.

References

1. Cohen, M.I.: PyFlag - an advanced network forensic framework. Digit. Investig. **5**, 112–120 (2008)
2. Pilli, E.S., Joshi, R.C., Niyogi, R.: Network forensic frameworks: survey and research challenges. Digit. Investig. **7**, 14–27 (2010)
3. Hunt, R., Zeadally, S.: Network forensics: an analysis of techniques, tools, and trends. Computer **45**, 36–43 (2012)
4. Dharmapurikar, S., Paxson, V.: Robust TCP stream reassembly in the presence of adversaries. In: USENIX Security Symposium. (2005)
5. Postel, J.: Internet Protocol. RFC 791 (1981)
6. Postel, J.: Transmission Control Protocol. RFC 793 (1981)
7. Stevens, W., Fenner, B., Rudoff, A.M.: UNIX Network Programming: The Sockets Networking API, 3rd edn. Addison-Wesley, Reading (2004)
8. Matousek, P., Rysavy, O., Kmet, M.: Fast RTP detection and codecs classification in internet traffic. J. Digit. Forensics Secur. Law **2014**, 99–110 (2014)
9. Hjelmvik, E., John, W.: Statistical protocol identification with SPID: preliminary results. In: Swedish National Computer Networking Workshop (2009)
10. Fielding, R., Gettys, J., Mogul, J., Frystyk, H., Masinter, L., Leach, P., Barners-Lee, T.: Hypertext Transfer Protocol - HTTP/1.1. IETF RFC 2616 (1999)
11. Dierks, T., Rescorla, E.: The Transport Layer Security (TLS) Protocol Version 1.2. IETF RFC 5246 (2008)
12. McGrew, D.: An Interface and Algorithms for Authenticated Encryption. IETF RFC 5116 (2008)
13. Davidoff, S., Ham, J.: Network Forensics: Tracking Hackers through Cyberspace, 1st edn. Prentice Hall, Upper Saddle River (2012)

Forensic Analysis and Remote Evidence Recovery from Syncthing: An Open Source Decentralised File Synchronisation Utility

Conor Quinn, Mark Scanlon$^{(\boxtimes)}$, Jason Farina, and M.-Tahar Kechadi

School of Computer Science, University College Dublin, Dublin 4, Ireland
{conor.quinn,jason.farina}@ucdconnect.ie,
{mark.scanlon,tahar.kechadi}@ucd.ie

Abstract. Commercial and home Internet users are becoming increasingly concerned with data protection and privacy. Questions have been raised regarding the privacy afforded by popular cloud-based file synchronisation services such as Dropbox, OneDrive and Google Drive. A number of these services have recently been reported as sharing information with governmental security agencies without the need for warrants to be granted. As a result, many users are opting for decentralised (cloudless) file synchronisation alternatives to the aforementioned cloud solutions. This paper outlines the forensic analysis and applies remote evidence recovery techniques for one such decentralised service, Syncthing.

Keywords: Syncthing · Digital forensics · Remote forensics · Network analysis · Evidence recovery

1 Introduction

In an ever increasing mobile and connected world, the demand for end users to access their data on the go using multiple platforms and devices is higher than ever. While numerous platforms have been developed to respond to this constant information need, these platforms can give rise to data protection and privacy concerns. These concerns primarily lie with cloud-based file synchronisation services such as Dropbox, OneDrive and Google Drive. A number of these services have been leaked as sharing replicated information with government security and spying agencies without first requiring the issue of a warrant [1]. The desire for privacy has led to a rise in cloudless file synchronisation services such as BitTorrent Sync (BTSync), Syncthing and OnionShare.

One of the most popular decentralised file synchronisation services is currently BTSync, which as of August 2014 had over 10 million user installs [2]. However a significant number of these users are not comfortable with the proprietary nature of the application and its handling of their data. This has motivated a transparent alternative being developed, called Syncthing. Syncthing is an open source, cloudless file synchronisation service. Users have the ability to identify how the software finds other active nodes to sync with, transfers data

© Institute for Computer Sciences, Social Informatics and Telecommunications Engineering 2015
J.I. James and F. Breitinger (Eds.): ICDF2C 2015, LNICST 157, pp. 85–99, 2015.
DOI: 10.1007/978-3-319-25512-5_7

from node to node, and synchronises information between different devices. With BTSync emerging from beta in March 2015, limitations on how many folders can be synchronised for free have been imposed – with the free tier being limited to syncing ten folders. It is likely that the lack of transparency regarding security and privacy and these new limitations imposed on the free BTSync tier users will push many towards deploying Syncthing for their file replication needs.

Syncthing is a decentralised tool created for the purposes of data backup and synchronisation, teamwork/collaboration, data transfer between systems, etc. From a law enforcement and digital forensic perspective, an area of concern with decentralised services is the possible exploitation of the service to distribute unauthorised/illegal data: industrial espionage, copyright infringement, sharing of child exploitation material, malicious software distribution, etc. [3]. These cloudless services have no regulation by their developers and as a result are at high risk of being used for criminal activity. Syncthing has many desirable features for privacy-concerned users who wish to use file synchronisation but conscious of their data's security. Such features include [4]:

- Private – The synchronised data is never replicated anywhere else other than on devices configured.
- Encrypted Traffic – All communication between devices is secured using TLS.
- Authenticated – Every node is identified by a strong cryptographic certificate; only nodes you have explicitly allowed can connect to your cluster.
- Cost and Limitations – Most main stream cloud-based file synchronisation software give you a small storage allowance at the free tier. Syncthing is limited only by the storage available across your devices.
- Transparency – The software is open source which facilitates analysis to prove that the software is secure.

With increased privacy and security of any tool or service, there is always the contraposition of law enforcement regarding the difficulty (or possibility) of capturing evidence from these systems. At the time of writing, there are no tools available for the recovery of evidence from Syncthing.

1.1   Contribution of This Work

This paper outlines a forensic analysis of the Syncthing client, its communication protocols, its peer discovery methods, its behaviours and its data remnants of synchronised deleted files. The contribution of this work can be summarised as follows:

- An outline of the entry points to a Syncthing investigation, i.e., how to detect whether Syncthing is pertinent to an investigation.
- A description of the services network communication protocol for the purposes of building a remote evidence recovery tool.
- A proof-of-concept tool, Synchronisation Service Evidence Retrieval Tool (SSERT), has been developed for an investigation scenario outlined. The investigation is documented showing how the remote recovery of digital forensic evidence from folders shared using Syncthing might be valuable to forensic investigators.

2   Related Work

The popularity of cloudless file synchronisation services as a viable "install-and-forget" alternative to the more commonplace cloud-based solutions is a recent development. Given the relatively new provisioning of these services, there has been little time for forensic procedures and best practises to catch up. However, there has been some research conducted on the remote recovery of evidence from Syncthing's primary competitor, BTSync, as well as the cloud-based solutions. The below section outlines some of this related work.

2.1   Forensic Analysis of BitTorrent Sync

In a similar vein to the focus of this paper, there has been an investigation methodology developed for BTSync, a cloudless file synchronisation service developed by BitTorrent Inc. [5]. BTSync is a cloudless file sharing tool with the intention of providing one-to-many and many-to-many file transfers as efficiently as possible. The protocol segments a file, which enables each chunk to be managed separately. Once a part of a file is downloaded it can immediately be uploaded to a different peer who has requested that file [5]. In this fashion a file can be shared before the whole file has been downloaded. BitTorrent Sync uses the BitTorrent protocol for data transport, which is analysed in detail in [3]. One of the interesting things about BTSync is the use of keys for managing permissions between peers. Once the creation of a share a master key is constructed, this master key has read/write capabilities which allows the person who has that key to add, modify or remove contents of that share. Other, more restricted keys exist allowing a share participant to give Read Only access or enforce a window before an invitation expires [5].

2.2   Forensic Analysis of Cloud-Based File Synchronisation Services

Towards the remote recovery of evidence from cloud-based sources, a volume of work has been conducted on the recovery of evidence from file synchronisation services. Quick and Choo have analysed the data remnants of deleted files in Dropbox [6], Microsoft SkyDrive (now rebranded as OneDrive) [7], and Google Drive [8]. This volume of work outlines the processes required for the remote recovery of deleted digital evidence from a local machine. The recovery of the data from the cloud-based storage combined with data remnants discovered on the local machine can verify the recovered copy as being a true copy of the original data. The authors also proved that downloading the remote data using a browser or performing a client sync does not interfere with the hash of the recovered evidence or any associated cloud-stored metadata [9]. The work conducted by Quick and Choo on Dropbox forensics has also had similar results confirmed by Federici [10]. In this work, a Cloud Data Imager is outlined. This is a tool developed by law enforcement for the forensically sound remote recovery of evidence from Dropbox.

3   Syncthing Analysis

While Syncthing may have been inspired by BTSync, its purpose is to transparently address features that some users identified as security and privacy issues. The first of these is the fact that BTSync attempts to improve security by keeping its source code secret. This is a common tactic and is known as "security through obscurity", the effectiveness of which is questionable. BTSync also collects usage statistics on its users' activities, which the developers claim only records anonymous bandwidth and usage metrics. Some users raised concerns that were left unanswered by developers and this silence gave rise to fear that there was the possibility of more than just the metrics being stored as was first stated. That fear led to Syncthing, which attempts to assuage user security concerns through transparency in its design and protocol. Users can easily see what the application is doing and how it is doing it. This open-view approach to security risks attackers finding a vulnerability but also allows the multiple interested parties to find and fix any flaw themselves before it is exploited [11].

Syncthing makes use of Block Exchange Protocol (BEP) [12] to minimise the traffic generated by partial file updates. BEP is used between two or more devices to form a cluster. Each device has one or more folders of files described by the `local model`, containing metadata and block hashes. The `local model` containing this data is then sent to the other devices that this device has in its cluster. The combination of all files in the local models and the files selected for highest change version from the `global model`. Each device in the cluster then attempts to align all of its local folders with the global model. The device then requests missing, outdated or corrupted blocks from the other devices it has in its cluster [12]. When file data is described or transferred it is segmented as a series of blocks with each block measuring 128 kB (131072 bytes). The BEP protocol is implemented at the highest level of the stack with the lower levels providing encryption and authentication. The underlying transport protocol must be TCP using this technique [12].

3.1   Data Remnants

To detect if Syncthing is installed on a suspect's machine and to retrieve the required information for identification of remote users sharing the same content, the data remnants left on the hard drive of the machine must be discovered. Syncthing uses a single folder to store all of its configuration files, cryptography certificates and keys [13]. The default install location for this folder on Windows 7 and 8 based systems is located in `%localappdata%\Syncthing`; on Windows XP, it is located in `%AppData%\Syncthing`; on Mac OS X systems, it is located in `~/Library/Application Support/Syncthing` and on *nix systems, it is located in `~/.config/syncthing`. Alternatively, the end user can specify a different "home" directory when launching the application which facilitates a non-default location for these files. The folder contains the following files [13]:

- `cert.pem` – The device's RSA public key.
- `key.pem` – The device's RSA private key.
- `config.xml` – The application's configuration file.
- `https-cert.pem` and `https-key.pem` – The certificate and key for HTTPS GUI connections.
- `index/` – A directory containing the metadata and hashes of the files currently on the disk and available from remote peers.
- `csrftokens.txt` – A list of recently issued CSRF tokens to protect against browser cross site request forgery.
- `index/[IncrementalNumber].log` – The application's log file for all actions taken locally and outlines folders shared with remote hosts.

3.2 Peer Discovery

Each device on the network is identified by its `DeviceID`. The `DeviceID` is made up of a Base32 SHA-256 encoding of the application's public RSA key, which is created during Syncthing's initial installation [14]. When Syncthing is launched, the settings contain the global discovery server address `announce.syncthing.net` [4]. At the time of writing this resolved to the IP address `194.126.249.5`. Once the announce server address has been resolved the application queries it with a valid `DeviceID` via a `query` packet via UDP [15] and, if known and the target has registered itself as being online, a current IP address and port will be returned in an **announce** packet. The IP and port combination returned are used as the destination for the protocol's secure handshake.

As Syncthing is an open source application, users have the option to set up their own announce server to handle internal peer discovery. In this scenario, all clients would require configuration to use this custom server instead of the default one. Another option is to use the built in local peer discovery. This setting is configurable in the application's settings, but is enabled by default. Local discovery can happen in one of two ways depending on the type of network detected:

- **IPv6 Networks** – If Syncthing discovers an IPv6 network it will use Simple Service Discovery Protocol (SSDP) to send a HTTP notify packet to port 1900. Syncthing utilises the FF02::C link local address to limit notification to a network segment only. In testing Go did not support the `setsocket` operation on windows 7 systems so IPv6 beacon packets were not responded to by the clients. This notify packet will contain the same details as the **announce** packet used for global discovery.
- **IPv4 Networks** – If the application detects that IPv6 is not supported inbound, Syncthing will still announce using IPv6 if it is supported outbound. Over IPv4, the announce packet is broadcast to the network on port 21025 with a 56 byte **announce**. This local announce associates an IP:Port combination with a `DeviceID` that is cached for later use.

3.3   Block Exchange Protocol Messages

With initial discovery complete a standard TLS session is established with both parties providing certificate-based authentication. In the case of our emulated client, we present the imported certificate of the suspect system as our proof of identity. Once the secure connection has been negotiated successfully a series of messages are exchanged before any requests involving the transfer of files can be made.

Header. The messaging used by Syncthing involves specific packet types identified by a message header. This header consists of one 32 bit word indicating the message version, type and ID, followed by the length of the message itself [12]. The principal field in the header is the type field. Each message type is denoted by a different hex number as outlined below:

- (Type 0) – `Cluster Config`   - (Type 4) – `Ping`
- (Type 1) – `Index`   - (Type 5) – `Pong`
- (Type 2) – `Request`   - (Type 6) – `Index Update`
- (Type 3) – `Response`   - (Type 7) – `Close`

Also contained in the header is the version, message ID, overall message length and a flag to indicate if compression is used. Figure 1 (a) is a graphical representation of how a header message is constructed.

Cluster Configuration Message. This is the first protocol specific message Syncthing must send after a successful connection to a peer is an informational message containing details about the share topology. This message establishes the local peer's version and ClientID, the number of folders hosted and the `DeviceIDs` of peers the sender is connected to and actively synchronising with. In addition to the standard fields mentioned earlier there is an `Options` section at the end. Once a secure connection is established, a cluster configuration message must be the first packet sent, otherwise the remote peer will forcibly close the session.

Index Message. The next message that must be sent is an `index` message. There must be one `Index` message for each folder reported in the `Cluster Configuration` message and should this index message be sent in an inappropriate order, the secure connection will be dropped. The purpose of the `Index` message is to enumerate the contents of the peer's folders. An Index message with an internal structure, as shown in Fig. 1 (b), represents the current contents of the folder and supersedes any previous index that may have been sent in an earlier transmission [12].

The `Index` message contains a lot of useful forensic information. This includes the name and relative path of each file in the shared folder, the timestamp of the

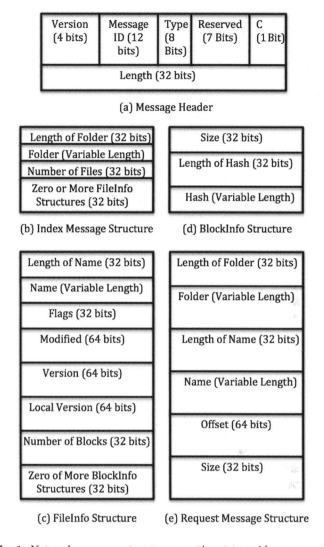

Fig. 1. Network message structures pertinent to evidence recovery

last modification date, and the BlockInfo. The BlockInfo contains the hash of each 128 kB block that constitutes each file. Syncthing uses these hashes and the modification date to minimise the number of blocks that have to be replicated to an updating peer if it already has an older version of the file. Only modified 128 kB blocks will have to be transferred. This feature also allows investigators to compare the block hash of a file recovered from a remote peer to that recorded in the suspect system's configuration files to determine if the recovered data is a forensic match of the original file [16].

Request Messages. Once the peers have determined which peer holds the most up to date version of a file, the lagging peer needs to update its version. By comparing the file `BlockInfo` the peer with the older version can determine the exact blocks it needs to make the local version of the file equal to that on the remote peer (assuming that it is the local peer that is behind). For each block identified in this manner, a `Request` message is sent to the remote peer containing the length of the folder, the name of the file containing the block being requested and the offset to the start of the block, as depicted in Fig. 1 (e). One `Request` is sent for each block required. Once a valid `Request` has been received, the remote peer responds with a `Response` message containing the requested block.

4   Investigation Methodology

Figure 2 outlines the process developed for the identification of other active nodes involved in sharing the contraband content and for the remote recovery and verification of the gathered evidence.

4.1   Security and Authentication

The entry point to a Syncthing investigation requires the recovery of the public/private RSA key pair from the suspect device. Upon initial execution, the application creates these keys, which are used to self sign certificates that are used in the TLS (Transport Layer Security) handshake. The certs provide identification to other devices when a share is initially established and are subsequently used for ongoing authentication [17]. These keys will be on the suspect device's storage as outlined above.

4.2   Remote Peer Identification

For the purposes of remote peer identification, i.e., to answer the question "What other devices are synchronising with this suspect?", the suspect machine's `*.log` file is required. This file contains a record of the folders shared with each remote peer. As can be seen in Fig. 3, the remote machine's `DeviceID` is displayed alongside some other metadata, such as the remote client version, the remote machine's hostname, and the IP address and port number of that machine at the time. The regular time-stamping used in the log file can be used to identify when that machine was online and what data has been synchronised.

Fig. 2. Process of evidence recovery for syncthing

```
[UYT2U] 17:26:31 INFO: Established secure connection to IX2735N-PPQMNFU-NQ5KLBB-
WG7WT7F-GALJHMH-EP7G2M2-TGD3UNA-F4FZTAJ at 192.168.1.3:1234-192.168.1.10:64715
[UYT2U] 17:26:31 INFO: Device IX2735N-PPQMNFU-NQ5KLBB-WG7WT7F-GALJHMH-EP7G2M2-TG
D3UNA-F4FZTAJ client is "syncthing v0.10.24"
[UYT2U] 17:26:31 INFO: Device IX2735N-PPQMNFU-NQ5KLBB-WG7WT7F-GALJHMH-EP7G2M2-TG
D3UNA-F4FZTAJ name is "Conor"
```

Fig. 3. Sample syncthing application terminal output

While this information alone might be sufficient to focus the investigation on additional devices, the logged information merely records the IP address and port of the remote device at the time. In order to check if the remote device is currently active, a request can be sent to the announce server with the persistent DeviceID. This should provide an updated IP address and port if the device has been active in the previous 30 min window.

Fig. 4. Sample records included in each *.log file

A file of significant interest to a digital investigator are the *.log files. The log file contains lists of devices the suspect system has connected to. It also contains a list of folders and corresponding files. A snapshot of a recovered log file from Syncthing can be seen in Fig. 4. In the bottom highlighted area in the figure, the DeviceIDs of remote machines can be identified. When a DeviceID is recovered, it can be used to query the global discovery server, which return the active IP address and port pair. Once the IP and port number have been identified, a secure connection can be attempted, using the already trusted device it has already been connected to. The topmost highlighted area Fig. 4 shows folder names and file names. The example log file shows the entries for the files RV.jpg, Draft.txt, ThesisReport copy.pdf, which are each contained in a folder called Test.

4.3 Remote Evidence Recovery

As part of the investigation it may become necessary to verify that the remotely device has stored a copy of the contraband data and that it is a forensically sound copy of the original on the local suspect machine. In order to perform such a task, the suspect machine's `cert.pem` and `key.pem` files are also required in order to emulate the suspect's device. As in the previous section, the current IP address and port number of the remote device can be discovered using the `announce` server. To start the remote recovery process the investigator initially requires `DeviceID` of the remote machine. The `announce` server can be queried and if has been active in the last 30 min, its IP and port will be retrieved. Subsequently, a TLS handshake is required to authenticate with the remote device.

4.4   Proof-of-Concept Tool

In order to prove the methodology outlined above, a proof-of-concept tool was created (SSERT). This tool emulates regular Syncthing client communication in order to recover evidence from one or more remote devices. The investigative process using this tool involves:

1. The investigator retrieves the pertinent public/private keypairs and application log files from a suspect device. A list of `DeviceIDs` (which the suspect device has been in communication with) can be retrieved from the application's log files.
2. The investigator provides the retrieved public/private keys and the `DeviceIDs` to the SSERT application. SSERT resolves these `DeviceIDs` to their corresponding IP address and port pairs by querying the `announce` server.
3. Using the suspect machine's credentials, a connection is made to a remote device and the TLS handshake process is completed.
4. Once a connection is established, SSERT requests a list of files available on the remote device and processes the returned `FileInfo` messages, as displayed in Fig. 1 (c).
5. The investigator then selects the file(s) of interest and the emulated synchronisation process begins. After the file is requested, the remote machine responds with N `BlockInfo` messages, as can be seen in Fig. 1 (d). N is the number of 128 KB blocks the requested file is split into for synchronisation. Each block is requested individually, downloaded and verified as a true copy from the remote machine using the supplied SHA256 hash value from the corresponding `BlockInfo` message.
6. Once the synchronisation process completes, the downloaded blocks are recompiled into the complete file. These downloaded files are verifiable as true copies against the suspect machine's local file metadata.
7. The output of SSERT includes the downloaded file(s), an audit log of the actions performed and a record of the network communication back and forth to the remote device.

5   Evaluation and Testing

5.1   Usage Scenarios

The intended usage of SSERT is in the forensic recovery of data from remote peers when the data cannot be recovered from the suspect systems due to encountering a less than ideal forensic environment. The scenarios a digital investigator might encounter whereby the methodology outlined above may prove useful are:

- **Inaccessible files** – This be either be intentional, such as deliberate secure deletion of incriminating evidence, or unintentional, such as data store volume corruption or failure. If the investigator suspects that this inaccessible shared data is pertinent to the investigation, the remote recovery of this data from another device will provide a forensically sound alternative source of evidence to the investigation.
- **Unrecoverable or destroyed external storage** – If the suspect was using a storage medium for sharing data that is not recoverable during the investigation, such as a USB flash drive, external hard drive, network attached storage (NAS), etc., the recovery of this data from a remote storage location may be the only option available to the investigator.
- **Encrypted storage containers** – If the suspect was sharing data from an encrypted container, e.g., using TrueCrypt, BitLocker or FileVault, the local recovery of this data may prove impossible without the decryption keys. In this scenario, the suspect would mount this encrypted container to facilitate synchronisation with a remote device and otherwise leave it encrypted. The forensically significant files outlined above are sufficient to prove the synchronisation of data to the local machine. The remote recovery of these files would be verifiable as true copies of those stored locally through the comparison of the file metadata contained in application log files.
- **Volatility of mobile device storage** – As with most synchronisation tools available on mobile devices, the files accessed through the mobile application are usually not stored permanently. This is typically due to local storage restrictions. Any evidence of a file's existence, e.g., artefacts left behind in slack space, are rare to find as this space is typically quickly re-allocated and re-used by another process. Syncthing's mobile application requires a user to explicitly select the file they want to synchronise to the mobile device in order to avoid accidentally filling all storage capacity by connecting to a larger remote data store. The nature of Syncthing's logging and Block Exchange Protocol means that in order for it to provide the service it offers, it must maintain extensive logs and configuration files. Recovery of these log files from any of the peers may provide enough evidence to show that a copy of the file was synchronised to a mobile device which in turn means that the user of the device had to explicitly select that file. This in turn implies knowledge and intent on the part of the device owner and may also provide evidence of usage of the mobile device based on the timestamp of the Syncthing `Index` and `Cluster Config` messaging.

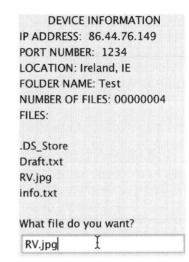

Enter Device ID

7QJ5Z-FN3G3YY-MFF6XNQ-7H4P7A2

Cancel   OK

Fig. 5. Starting point: DeviceID   **Fig. 6.** Retrieved peer information

- **Accomplice identification** – The tracking down of associates of the suspect may be a focus of the investigation, e.g., the sharing of illegal content or sensitive information with an unknown number of parties. The application's log files would show DeviceIDs along with the synchronisation timestamps with that device. This information can be used to determine which device was connected when and also whether or not they successfully received a copy of the incriminating data.

5.2   Testing

In order to test the evidence retrieval methodology and the performance of the application a test scenario was devised involving evidence of Syncthing being discovered on a suspect's system (most likely the Syncthing folder stored in the user's AppData\Local\Syncthing folder on a Windows system). Within this folder the forensic investigator can recover the public/private key-pair certificates as well as the log files. However, the folder indicated by the Index and logs is encrypted and there is no evidence of the passphrase or decryption key on the system. There is, however, a second 64 character string in the logs, which does not match the DeviceID generated for the local system.

Once the certificates have been imported into SSERT, the retrieved DeviceID of the remote machine is entered, as can be seen in Fig. 5. A query packet is sent to the announce.syncthing.net server over UDP and the server will respond with the required networking information. If the remote peer has not been online in the last 30 min, no network information will be returned and polling of the announce server is required.

Fig. 7. Original image   **Fig. 8.** Partial retrieval

When a response is received, SSERT will contact the remote peer and establish a secure connection using the imported certificates to convince the remote peer that not only is SSERT a valid Syncthing installation but also that it is the suspect system attempting to perform a routine update check. After `Cluster Configuration` and an `Index` messages are received, SSERT displays the folder and file list of items available from the remote system, as can be seen in Fig. 6.

In this test scenario, the investigator was interested in a file named `RV.jpg`, as can be seen in Fig. 7. The investigator then selects the file to recover and SSERT begins the synchronisation process by sending a series of `Request` packets (one for each 128 kb block or part thereof of the file) and listening for the `Response` messages. Once these have been saved, the `RV.jpg` image is reconstituted locally. To verify the evidence, the local copy is hashed using SHA-256 and the result compared to the hash that can be found in the suspect system's `\Index\MANIFEST` file. In one instance during testing, a disconnection occurred and a partial recovery of the remote image was gathered. Due to the JPEG compression algorithm, this partial recovery is sufficient to identify what the original image contains, as can be seen in Fig. 8, but of course the hashes cannot be verified.

6   Conclusion and Future Work

Given Syncthing's open source nature and reliable performance the protocol is likely to be used in other applications in the future. This may be either as a standalone file synchronisation utility or as the foundation for another solution. As with all hash based synchronisation utilities, it is its own activity logging and willingness to verify and check that can be used as a method of enumeration.

The location of the AppData folder provides a strong entry point to an investigation for Windows based suspect systems with a lot of potentially important information for the investigator to recover. Combined with the artefacts retrievable from this source, a strict adherence to the protocol messaging sequencing allows full client emulation including remote peer enumeration through the

announce server and full file manifest discovery through the **Config Index** trade. The open source nature of the protocol allowed the creation of SSERT proof of concept build for Syncthing evidence retrieval and in testing the application has proven to be accurate and efficient in the enumeration, recovery and verification of evidence not recoverable directly from the suspect system.

In the future, SSERT can be expanded to perform similar analysis and evidence recovery from additional synchronisation services, such as OnionShare. Combining polling and the analysis of the information available from the remote host, automated evidence downloading and metadata exporting should enable SSERT to function without manual intervention whenever an unavailable node comes online.

References

1. Greenwald, G., MacAskill, E.: NSA prism program taps in to user data of apple, google and others. Guardian **7**(6), 1–43 (2013)
2. Pounds, E.: Introducing BitTorrent Sync 1.4: An Easier Way to Share Large Files (2014). http://blog.bittorrent.com/2014/08/26/introducing-bittorrent-sync-1-4-an-easier-way-to-share-large-files/. Accessed April 2015
3. Scanlon, M., Farina, J., Le Khac, N.-A., Kechadi, M.-T.: Leveraging Decentralisation to Extend the Digital Evidence Acquisition Window: Case Study on BitTorrent Sync, pp. 85–99, September 2014
4. Borg, J.: SyncThing (2015). http://www.syncthing.net. Accessed April 2015
5. Farina, J., Scanlon, M., Kechadi, M.-T.: Bittorrent sync: first impressions and digital forensic implications. Digital Invest. **11**(Suppl. 1), S77–S86 (2014). Proceedings of the First Annual DFRWS Europe
6. Quick, D., Choo, K.-K.R.: Dropbox analysis: data remnants on user machines. Digital Invest. **10**(1), 3–18 (2013)
7. Quick, D., Choo, K.-K.R.: Digital droplets: microsoft skydrive forensic data remnants. Future Gener. Comput. Syst. **29**(6), 1378–1394 (2013). Including Special sections: High Performance Computing in the Cloud and Resource Discovery Mechanisms for P2P Systems
8. Quick, D., Choo, K.-K.R.: Google drive: forensic analysis of data remnants. J. Netw. Comput. Appl **40**, 179–193 (2013)
9. Quick, D., Choo, K.-K.R.: Forensic collection of cloud storage data: does the act of collection result in changes to the data or its metadata? Digital Invest. **10**(3), 266–277 (2013)
10. Federici, C.: Cloud data imager: a unified answer to remote acquisition of cloud storage areas. Digital Invest. **11**(1), 30–42 (2014)
11. Reddit. SyncThing: Open Source BitTorrent Sync Alternative (P2P Sync Tool) (2015). http://www.webupd8.org/2014/06/syncthing-open-source-bittorrent-sync.html. Accessed April 2015
12. Borg, J.: SyncThing: Block Exchange Protocol (2015). https://github.com/syncthing/specs/blob/master/BEPv1.md. Accessed April 2015
13. Borg, J.: SyncThing: Config File and Directory (2015). https://github.com/syncthing/syncthing/wiki/Config-File-and-Directory. Accessed April 2015
14. Borg, J.: SyncThing: Device IDs (2015). https://github.com/syncthing/syncthing/wiki/Device-IDs. Accessed April 2015

15. Borg, J.: SyncThing: Device Discovery Protocol v2 (2015). https://github.com/syncthing/specs/blob/master/DISCOVERYv2.md. Accessed April 2015
16. Garfinkel, S., Nelson, A., White, D., Roussev, V.: Using purpose-built functions and block hashes to enable small block and sub-file forensics. Digital Invest. **7**, S13–S23 (2010)
17. Paul, J.: Java Revisited: Difference Between TrustStore and KeyStore Java SSL (2015). http://javarevisited.blogspot.ie/2012/09/difference-between-truststore-vs-keyStore-Java-SSL.html. Accessed April 2015

Cooperation in Digital Investigations

A Survey of International Cooperation in Digital Investigations

Joshua I. James[1]([✉]) and Pavel Gladyshev[2]

[1] Digital Forensic Investigation Research Laboratory (DFIRE),
Hallym University, Chuncheon-si, Kangwon, South Korea
joshua@cybercrimetech.com
[2] Digital Forensic Investigation Research Laboratory (DFIRE),
University College Dublin, Belfield, Dublin 4, Ireland
pavel.gladyshev@ucd.ie

Abstract. International cooperation is becoming more important in digital investigations. This work provides a comprehensive study about Mutual Legal Assistance in relation to digital evidence. A survey of available information related to making a Mutual Legal Assistance Request is given, followed by a quantitative analysis of practitioner survey results related to making and receiving Mutual Legal Assistance Requests. The given survey is a first effort to provide data behind the challenges identified by practitioners when attempting to request Mutual Legal Assistance related to digital evidence. From this data, some justification for commonly cited challenges are found, as well as the circumstances in which these challenges arise.

Keywords: Digital evidence · Digital investigation · International cooperation · Cross-border investigation · Mutual legal assistance · Jurisdiction

1 Introduction

International cooperation in digital investigations is growing more important as relevant data is increasingly stored in multiple jurisdictions [8,13]. Many prior works have discussed the growing challenges of requesting potential evidence from foreign countries [8,9,13,17]. Specifically concerning formal international requests (Mutual Legal Assistance), the Commission on Crime Prevention and Criminal Justice [16] identified challenges with formal international requests as:

- Few states reported monitoring outgoing request to ensure proportionality
- Some states prioritize incoming requests and others don't – this causes problems when one state believes the crime 'high priority' and another state believes it is 'low priority'
- Differing income levels between countries can result in a low priority for a case even if the amount is substantial in the requesting country

© Institute for Computer Sciences, Social Informatics and Telecommunications Engineering 2015
J.I. James and F. Breitinger (Eds.): ICDF2C 2015, LNICST 157, pp. 103–114, 2015.
DOI: 10.1007/978-3-319-25512-5_8

- Multiple follow-up inquiries also take resources away from work on more urgent cases
- Several members commented that the effort for the request may be much more than the potential punishment (in the case of extradition)
- There are several states where requests for assistance in minor cases burden the Central Authority and prosecutors to the extent that they cannot focus on more serious cases.

In the author's experience, when speaking directly with cybercrime investigators, many mention a lack of international cooperation, especially timely cooperation, with some claiming that international cooperation 'never works'. From our observations, while many investigators have some complaints, the success of international cooperation appears to differ with each requesting country, and to whom the request is being made. While other works have looked at the problem of international cybercrime, and many discuss the challenges of international cooperation [12,17], to our knowledge, none have attempted to quantify formal international cooperation related to digital investigations, and attempt to identify the causes of often-mentioned challenges.

This, however, does not mean that no work is being done to solve the problem. Kent (2014) identifies a number of challenges to requesting digital evidence, especially from foreign private companies. She also provides practical and comprehensive short, medium and long term plans to improve the situation. [blinded] looks at the capacity of national and foreign organizations to deal with incoming requests for digital evidence, and proposes a national development strategy that also considers expanding capacity and capabilities in strategically important countries. To attempt to address the challenge of communication during international requests, INTERPOL is currently working on communication channels to allow the timely sending, tracking and verification of requests. Likewise, the United Nations Office on Drugs and Crime (UNODC) continues development on a 'Mutual Legal Assistance Request Writer Tool' [6] that helps to ensure that formal international requests are complete and accurate. Of course, legislation is also needed, and a number of governments and private organizations are working towards legislation to improve international cooperation [5,7].

1.1 Contribution

This work contributes to the field of digital investigation by giving a quantitative view of challenges related to international cooperation during investigations. Specifically, this work provides raw data that allows us to assess what – and when – international cooperation is working.

2   International Cooperation

International cooperation can take many forms, however, when requesting evidence from other countries that will be used in a court of law, requests normally need to be in the form of formal Mutual Legal Assistance (MLA) requests form one Central Authority (CA) to another. This study will focus on formal MLA requests.

2.1 Survey of Mutual Legal Assistance Contacts: Is Contact Information Available?

Documents specifying the requirements for mutual legal assistance requests are easily found[1] on public channels – in English – for over 100 countries (Fig. 1). Of the discovered documents, most countries had varying amounts of information available. At least contact information for a central authority was included, even with no further instructions. For G8/G20 countries, information also included general instructions for making an MLA request. The majority of documents did not contain dates or version numbers. Because of this, it is difficult assess whether the information collected is correct and up-to-date.

Fig. 1. A world map showing the countries where mutual legal assistance contact and basic required information can be easily found online in English.

The Council of Europe (CoE) maintains a website where associated countries should post their mutual legal assistance process information[2]. This information

---

[1] Easily found in this case means less than an hour searching with a public search engine using English keywords.

[2] Council of Europe. National procedures on judicial cooperation in the criminal field – Transfer of sentenced persons. http://www.coe.int/t/dghl/standardsetting/pc-oc/ Country_information3_en.asp.

specifically concerns the transfer of sentenced persons, but in many cases provides general insight into the MLA process of the country.

The Organization of American States (OAS) also maintains contact information and basic MLA requirements for its members[3]. The information contained normally describes both the legal system and the mutual legal assistance process for each member country. While not exactly comprehensive in most cases, it does provide a good starting point for making contact with the country.

2.2 Mutual Legal Assistance and Digital Evidence

Almost no documents referred to computer or digital evidence directly; however, according to [10] the language of mutual legal assistance treaties are often phrased generally, and thus is able to handle new types of evidence such as those from computer hard drives, mobile phones and other digital devices.

Three examples, are Austria [1], El Salvador [14] and New Zealand[4]. In these countries there is no specific mention of digital or computer-based evidence or information. However, the language is general enough that digital evidence could be treated the same as 'traditional' evidence.

A small number of countries, however, do specifically refer to digital or computer evidence when discussing their requirements for MLA. For example, of all the G8 countries, only France referenced "material that may be held on a computer system", specifying that more specific information may be required in the case of computer evidence [15]. Similarly, in the G20 countries both France and Japan specifically mentions material that may be held on computer systems [3]. All other countries used general language, and do not specify requirements for computer-based evidence. However, although the United Kingdom did not specify computer evidence in those documents, the U.K. provides guidelines for foreign authorities that does specify material held on a computer [4].

One of the most comprehensive documents, although not country-specific, is the UNODC's manual on mutual legal assistance and extradition [2]. In it there is discussion about the production of computer records.

3 Survey of Mutual Legal Assistance Requests

To identify challenges in international cooperation – and specifically MLA – the authors conducted a survey relating to respondents' experience writing and receiving MLA requests.

- n - is the number of elements in the sample
- p - refers to the proportion of sample elements that have a particular attribute.

---

[3] Organization of American States. Mutual Assistance in Criminal Matters and Extradition. http://www.oas.org/JURIDICO/mla/en/atg/index.html.
[4] Crown Law Office. "Making Request". http://www.crownlaw.govt.nz.

The online survey was accessed approximately 186 times resulting in 34 fully-submitted responses. Additionally, 20 hand-written surveys were submitted, making 54 submissions in total. Ideally, The survey did not collect personally identifiable information[5].

At the time of this writing, information was received from 23 countries (+2 unreported) with regional[6] distribution as follows: Africa (1), Americas (8), Asia (3), Europe (10), Oceania (1). Information was received from 4 central authorities (Ministries, etc.), 25 law enforcement personnel, 15 prosecution-related services, 5 service providers, and 5 responses claiming to not be affiliated with any of the prior groups. Survey data is made available at [blinded].

The survey was specifically targeting individuals with experience creating or receiving mutual legal assistance requests. For this reason a filter question was introduced:

> Do you have experience with either creating or responding to mutual legal assistance requests, letter rogatory or other international requests for evidence? [n = 54]
> *No (8)   *Yes (46)

Out of the sample [n = 54], only those who responded "Yes" were allowed to submit further responses. This resulted in 46 'qualified' responses. After filtering for qualified responses, the sample represents 21 countries (+1 unreported) with regional distribution as follows: Africa (0), Americas (8), Asia (3), Europe (9), Oceania (1). This distribution along with response rates is shown in Fig. 2.

Qualified responses were received from 4 central authorities (Ministries, etc.), 22 law enforcement personnel, 15 prosecution-related services, 3 service providers, and 2 responses claiming to not be affiliated with any of the prior groups. The population is summarized in Fig. 3.

85 % [n = 54] of the sample had experience with mutual legal assistance requests or international requests for evidence (any type). 72 % [n = 54] of respondents claimed to have experience specifically dealing with mutual legal assistance requests relating to cyber crime, electronic evidence or subscriber data.

3.1 Quantitative Results Overview

The first question for qualified respondents was an attempt to assess whether the sample was similar to samples from other studies. In this case, the Comprehensive Study on Cybercrime [12], question 216 was taken directly:

---

[5] This research was determined to be 'not human participant research', thus no IRB application was made.
[6] Regions are defined based on the United Nations regional groupings: "Composition of macro geographical (continental) regions, geographical sub-regions, and selected economic and other groupings". 31 Oct. 2013. http://unstats.un.org/unsd/methods/m49/m49regin.htm.

Fig. 2. World map showing countries represented in qualified responses where color denotes response rate. Red = 1 response received, and the darker the shade of green the more responses were received from the country where maximum responses <=5 (Colour figure online).

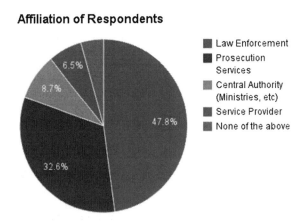

Fig. 3. The affiliation of qualified respondents by percentage of the sample [n = 46].

Does your country have legislation used as a legal basis for mutual legal assistance for cybercrime? [n = 46]
*Yes (35)   *No (8)   *Unsure (3)

According to the Comprehensive Study on Cybercrime, approximately 75 % of respondents reported the existence of national legislation applicable to cybercrime MLA matters. This study shows similar results, with the average respondents reporting the existence of national legislation applicable to cybercrime MLA matters being approximately 76 % [n = 46][7].

Fewer respondents (68 % [n = 46]) reported treaties, conventions and/or national legislation specifically relating to electronic evidence requests. Some groups reported that national legislation with specific provisions for electronic evidence were currently being implemented in their countries.

The most commonly referenced treaties, conventions or national legislation were the Palermo Convention (n = 31, p = 7), the Budapest Convention (n = 31, p = 7), and Penal (Criminal) Code (n = 31, p = 9).

Offered Services. The types of services being offered are relevant to the way requests for such services should be formed in terms of documents, information and wording. However, not all services were provided by all organizations. The most common service offered to other countries though MLA – in regards to electronic evidence – was reported to be **search and seizure**, with 91 % [n = 46, p = 42] of the respondents reporting that the service was available. This is followed by **preservation requests** (85 % [n = 46, p = 39]), **production of documents** (83 % [n = 46, p = 38]) and **taking of witness statements/evidence** (76 % [n = 46, p = 35]). Only 24 % [n = 46, p = 11] of respondents reported **temporary transfer of prisoners to give evidence** as a provided service. Further, 2 % [n = 46, p = 1] reported that **support teams** may be provided via MLA.

Best-Practice Request Writing Guides. Next was an attempt to determine what resources are commonly used to develop MLA requests. 52 % [n = 46] of respondents claimed that there is no step-by-step, best-practice guide available describing how to conduct each type of MLA request. Another 24 % were unsure if a guide existed, meaning that 76 % [n = 46] of respondents are unable to use a guide to help develop MLA requests[8]. 24 % of respondents, however, claimed that a step-by-step, best-practice guide does exist for their countries.

Best-Practice Requesting Digital Evidence. The respondents were asked about the level of standardization or best-practices related to requesting or obtaining digital evidence from foreign countries when requests are specifically about digital evidence. 61 % [n = 46] reported there were no national standards or best-practices specifically concerning digital evidence requests, and 21 % [n = 46]

---

[7] The average depends on the classification of the 'unsure' group. In this case, 'unsure' is considered a negative, or 'No' classification.

[8] Please note, in the general analysis respondent groups and countries are combined. Some respondents such as Service Providers (6 % of the population) may have no need to create mutual legal assistance request guides.

reported 'unsure' whether national standards or best-practices existed. Only, 17 % [n = 46] reported national standards or best practices existing.

Best-Practice Requesting Digital Evidence. Respondents who reported national standards or best practices exist in their countries, were asked to elaborate. Some respondents [n = 6, p = 1] reported that digital evidence is treated the same as physical evidence. Others [n = 6, p = 2] appear to say the same, citing the central authority as the point that decides the standard; however, no specific standard was given. Other respondents [n = 6, p = 2] also did not elaborate.

One response more thoroughly described the current situation, and is given below (redacted).

> "I would actually say 'kind of' not yes or no. We are supposed to make the request through the [central authority], all requests for electronic evidence go through one location...That is where the best practices ends. There is nothing else regarding formats, handling, transfer, digital verifications (hashes) etc."

In this case, there is reference to internal standards or best-practices that are followed in terms of making or receiving requests. Internally and externally, formats, handling, transfer and verification are not defined.

Information Exchange Protocols. The above is related to the state in which information or evidence is exchanged. When asked if their country has information exchange protocols in place to transfer electronic evidence internationally, 46 % [n = 46] reported no, and 26 % [n = 46] were unsure. 28 % [n = 46] claimed their country does have information exchange protocols in place to transfer electronic evidence internationally.

Information Exchange Protocols. The respondents that reported protocols exist were asked to elaborate on their protocols. INTERPOL's exchange protocol was the most commonly named, followed by Europol's protocols and the Budapest Convention. Other protocols appeared to be country-specific depending on specific treaties or memorandum of understanding (MOU) that are in place.

Request Writing Experience. To attempt to capture specific information on the MLA writing process, the respondents were asked about their experience writing MLA requests for electronic evidence. 80 % [n = 46] of respondents reported having experience writing MLA requests for digital evidence, and 20 % [n = 46] reported not having experience. Respondents with no experience writing MLA requests for digital evidence were excluded from answering the following MLA request-writing-related questions.

Request Writing Challenges. When asked about the major challenges to writing MLA requests for electronic evidence, 57 % [n = 37, p = 21] of respondents identified that the acquisition of appropriate documents from the requested country was a challenge. 51 % [n = 37, p = 19] identified "appropriately describing the required scope of digital evidence" as a challenge. Both defining the required digital evidence, and the exchange protocols for digital evidence was identified by 46 % [n = 37, p = 17,17] of respondents. Protocols for the exchange of data across borders was less of a concern, with only 30 % [n = 37, p = 11] identifying it as a challenge. Other challenges given were related to the time of the request [n = 37, p = 2].

Request Success and Failure. To assess the effectiveness of requests for digital evidence through MLA, the respondents were asked how often data was received (or not). For requests made, 30 % [n = 37, p = 11] of respondents claimed that they have never received ALL data that was requested. 38 % [n = 37, p = 14] claim that only 1 % to 25 % of their requests receive ALL data requested. The percentage of requests where ALL requested evidence was returned continues to drop, until the 75 % to 99 % range, where it slightly increases again.

For requests made, 19 % [n = 37, p = 7] of respondents claimed that they have never received SOME data that was requested. 46 % [n = 37, p = 14] claim that only 1 % to 25 % of their requests receive SOME data requested. The percentage of requests where SOME requested evidence was returned continues to drop, until the 50 % to 75 % range, where it increases again.

For requests made, 14 % [n = 37, p = 5] of respondents claimed to never receive requested electronic evidence. On the other hand, 24 % [n = 37, p = 9] of respondents claimed that at least some requested information was always returned. 35 % [n = 37, p = 13] of respondents claimed that 1 % to 25 % of their requests would result in no requested information being returned.

Request Feedback. For requests made, 38 % [n = 37, p = 14] of the respondents claimed to receive no feedback for any of their requests. 27 % [n = 37, p = 10] of respondents claimed to received feedback on 1 % to 25 % of their requests.

Most Common Requests. The most commonly-requested information is IP address and subscriber information (32 % [n = 37]). This is followed by information relating to social networks, and email (contents), equally (27 % [n = 37]). The next most commonly requested information was identified as Internet access logs and forensic imaging of devices (19 % [n = 37]). It may be possible to classify some of the remaining miscellaneous requests as one of the categories already given.

Request Preparation. The respondents were asked approximately how long it takes to prepare a MLA request for electronic evidence. 41 % [n = 37] of respondents reported that the preparation of a request takes 0 to 2 weeks, with most reporting times in days (on written surveys). 76 % [n = 37] of respondents reported that an MLA request could be prepared in 4 weeks or less.

Request Receiving Experience. To attempt to capture specific information on MLA receiving and processing, the respondents were asked about their experience receiving and processing MLA requests for electronic evidence. 59 % [n = 46] of respondents reported having experience receiving or processing MLA requests for digital evidence, and 41 % [n = 46] reported having no experience receiving or processing MLA requests for digital evidence. Respondents with no experience receiving or processing MLA requests for digital evidence were excluded from answering the following MLA request-receiving-related questions.

Required Request Information. 37 % [n = 27] of respondents reported that 75 % to 99 % of all MLA requests received contained all information necessary to process the request. 22 % [n = 27] of respondents reported that 50 % to 75 % of MLA requests received contained all information necessary to process the request, while 26 % [n = 27] of respondents claimed only 25 % to 50 % of MLA requests received contained all information necessary to process the request.

Request Denials. 48 % [n = 27] of respondents reported that 0 % to 25 % of all MLA requests received had a scope that was "too broad" or did not appear to match the reason for the request. However, 52 % [n = 27] of respondents claimed that 25 % to 99 % of all received requests had a scope that was too broad or did not appear to match the reason for the request.

Request Denials. 48 % [n = 27] of respondents reported that 0 % of requests were denied because of a lack of dual-criminality. 30 % [n = 27] of respondents reported 1 % to 25 % of requests being denied. While 22 % [n = 27] of respondents reported 25 % to 75 % of requests being denied because of a lack of dual-criminality.

Request Denials. 56 % [n = 27] of respondents reported that 0 % of requests were denied because the request may violate local rights in the requested country. 33 % [n = 27] of respondents reported 1 % to 25 % of received requests were denied because it may violate local rights in the requested country.

Request Feedback. 37 % [n = 27] of respondents reported that feedback to received requests was being given 0 % of the time. Another 37 % [n = 27] of respondents reported that feedback to received requests was being given 1 % to 25 % of the time. 11 % [n = 27] of respondents reported that feedback to received requests was being given 100 % of the time.

Request Denial. The respondents were specifically asked what the most common reason a request for electronic evidence would be denied in their country. 33 % [n = 27] of respondents reported that most requests are denied because the data no longer exists in the requested country. 15 % [n = 27] of respondents reported that requests are not denied. Other evenly-distributed reasons include the authority conducting the investigation was not clearly identified, data protection laws, requests for data were not clear, and the requested data is not normally collected by the requesting country.

Essential Information. What asked what information is essential when requesting electronic evidence from another country, the respondents gave a list of information they considered 'essential'. IP address (or IP address history) was the most commonly mentioned piece of 'essential information' [n = 24, p = 8]. Followed by 'core information about the type of data required' [n = 24, p = 7].

Most Common Requests. When asked what the most common types of electronic evidence has been requested from them, the respondents again said that

IP addresses and related information were the most commonly received requests [n = 26, p = 8]. This is followed by acquisition of hard drive / computers, data about persons, account information / subscriber information and mobile phone information, equally [n = 26, p = 5,5,5,5].

Request Language. 41 % [nv46] of respondents reported that only nationally recognized languages are accepted for MLA requests. 39 % [nv46] of respondents reported that some other foreign languages are normally accepted for MLA requests, and 20 % [n = 46] were unsure whether foreign (not nationally recognized) languages were accepted for MLA requests.

Request Point of Contact. The respondents were asked to identify the central authority responsible for sending and receiving requests for MLA involving digital evidence. The most commonly-named central authorities are the local Public Prosecutors [n = 46, p = 17], followed by the Department or Ministries of Justice and the Ministry of Foreign Affairs [n = 46, p = 9,6].

Request Creation. 54 % [n = 46, p = 25] of respondents reported that they used their own organization's internal document template to create MLA requests. 52 % [n = 46, p = 24] of respondents also reported that departments or investigators create their own MLA request documents. This is followed by 15 % [n = 46, p = 7] of respondents claiming to use request forms from INTERPOL.

Request Forms for Digital Evidence. 41 % [n = 46] of respondents reported that MLA request documents do not contain specific fields for requesting electronic evidence. 35 % [n = 46] of respondents claimed MLA request documents do contain fields specifically concerning digital evidence. 24 % [n = 46] of respondents were unsure.

Request Channels. When asked about the most commonly used channels for MLA requests, 63 % [n = 46, p = 29] of respondents reported using their national central authority. 52 % [n = 46, p = 24] of respondents reported working directly with the central authority in the requested country. 41 % [n = 46, p = 19] of respondents made requests directly with Law Enforcement organizations in the requested country, and 33 % [n = 46, p = 15] of respondents reported working directly with investigators in the requested country. This was followed by the use of the INTERPOL I24/7 network (30 % [n = 46, p = 14]).

4   Conclusions

The described survey is a first effort to provide data behind the challenges identified by practitioners when attempting to request Mutual Legal Assistance related to digital evidence. From this data, a number of weaknesses in communication and information sharing may be seen that contribute to lower quality, or even incomplete requests being made. Further, there appears to be a disconnect between the communication about the status of requests, and the status updates that are received by the requesting country. Further, more in-depth, analysis, however, is left to future work. By making this data available, this work helps to improve awareness about weaknesses of international cooperation relating to cybercrime investigations, and help describe why those weaknesses may exist.

4.1   Future Work

Future work will include a through analysis of the data beyond a superficial quantitative analysis. Further, there is much that can be said about the survey results, including which countries are 'more successful' in MLA requests, and why. We hope to use this study to develop real-world solutions that help international cooperation relating to digital evidence.

References

1. Austria national procedures for mutual legal assistance in criminal matters. Technical report
2. Manual on Mutual Legal Assistance and Extradition: Technical report. United Nations Office on Drugs and Crime, Vienna (2012)
3. Requesting Mutual Legal Assistance in Criminal Matters from G20 Countries: A step-by-step guide. Technical report, G20 (2012)
4. Requests for Mutual Legal Assistance in Criminal Matters: Guidelines for authorities outside of the United Kingdom. Technical report, Home Office (2012)
5. Internet and Jurisdiction (2015)
6. Mutual Legal Assistance Request Writer Tool (2015)
7. Mutual Legal Assistance Treaties (2015)
8. Broadhurst, R.: Developments in the global law enforcement of cyber-crime. Polic.: Int. J. Police Strat. Manage. **29**(3), 408–433 (2006)
9. Cerezo, A.I., Lopez, J., Patel, A.: International cooperation to fight transnational cybercrime. In: Proceedings of the 2nd International Annual Workshop on Digital Forensics and Incident Analysis, WDFIA 2007, pp. 13–27 (2007)
10. Chêne, M.: Mutual legal assistance treaties and money laundering. Technical report, Anti-Corruption Resource Centre (2009)
11. Gail, K.: Sharing Investigation-Specific Data With Law Enforcement - An International Approach (2014)
12. Malby, S., Mace, R., Holterhof, A., Brown, C., Kascherus, S., Ignatuschtschenko, E.: Comprehensive study on cybercrime. Technical report February, United Nations Office on Drugs and Crime (UNODC) (2014)
13. Martini, B., Choo, K.K.R.: Cloud storage forensics: OwnCloud as a case study. Digit. Inv. **10**(4), 287–299 (2013)
14. Ramirez, J.: The mutual legal assistance process in El Salvador. Technical report (2009)
15. ROMA-LYON GROUP: Requesting mutual legal assistance in criminal matters from G8 countries: A step-by-step guide. Technical report, Commission on Crime Prevention and Criminal Justice, Vienna (2011)
16. ROMA-LYON GROUP: Addressing Requests for Mutual Legal Assistance in De Minimis Cases. Technical report, G8 (2013)
17. Westmoreland, K., Gail, K.: Foreign Law Enforcement Access to User Data: A Survival Guide and Call for Action (2015)

Awareness of Scam E-Mails: An Exploratory Research Study – Part 2

Kelly A. Cole, Tejashree D. Datar$^{(\boxtimes)}$, and Marcus K. Rogers

Knoy Hall of Technology, Room # 255, 401 N. Grant Street,
West Lafayette, IN 47907, USA
{colek, tdatar, rogersmk}@purdue.edu

Abstract. This paper is the second part of an entire study conducted regarding general awareness of email scams. The goal of this particular part of research was to check the awareness level and knowledge gap among email users with respect to the actions that need to be taken in case of scam email victimization, and awareness regarding common practices that are used in identifying scam email and types of online scam media. Most common actions mentioned by respondents in case of financial scams and clicking on a malicious link were to contact their banks to close their accounts and cancel their credit cards (41.17 %) and running an anti-virus scan (20.83 %) respectively. The most frequently mentioned online scam media other than email was online ads with pop-ups, while the most common practice employed to identify email scam was to check for emails asking for or giving away money. A definite lack of awareness was found among the users with respect to the actions that need to be taken in case of financial scam victimization. In conclusion, the researchers suggest a need for formal education regarding email scam awareness and best email usage practices.

Keywords: Email scam · Financial scam · Scam victimization · Email scam awareness

1 Introduction

Worldwide spam traffic is increasing on a daily basis. Spohos's Security Threat Report 2014 mentioned that 2013 saw an increase in the spam activity level in terms of email [1]. According to Securelist [2, 3], the average worldwide spam traffic in January 2014 among all email traffic was 65.7 %, and in February 2014 was 69.9 %. In February 2014, the U.S. ranked second in the distribution of this traffic by distributing 19.1 % of the worldwide spam [3]. Increase in scam activity has increased the likelihood of a user falling victim to email scam.

With scam emails becoming more sophisticated day-by-day, it becomes harder for email users to differentiate between scam and legitimate emails. These sophisticated emails increase the chances of an individual falling prey to scam emails. This makes it imperative to examine common practices used in identifying scam emails and the awareness of required actions that need to be taken by users in case of scam email victimization. Depending on technical proficiency, various methods can be employed

© Institute for Computer Sciences, Social Informatics and Telecommunications Engineering 2015
J.I. James and F. Breitinger (Eds.): ICDF2C 2015, LNICST 157, pp. 115–125, 2015.
DOI: 10.1007/978-3-319-25512-5_9

by email users to identify a given email as scam or legitimate. Some of the common practices to identify email scams are verifying the sender, checking email headers, checking hyperlinks within the email without clicking them, checking for digital certificates, and looking for cue words in the email body (e.g., urgent, money/information request, hyperlinks, typos) [4, 5].

Various actions are advised in case of financial scam victimization, and email scam victimization. In case, and individual clicks on a malicious link, different actions need to be taken to protect the computer. Agencies such as OnGuardOnline [6, 7], Michigan State Police [8], and Microsoft [9] have stated on their respective websites that potential victims of phishing email should take the following steps in cases of financial scam victimization:

- Put fraud alert on credit cards.
- File an identity theft report with the Federal Trade Commission (FTC). The FTC will provide the complainant with an affidavit.
- Take the affidavit from the FTC and file a report with the police.

These agencies believe that victims of phishing could possibly become victims of identity theft. The Federal Bureau of Investigation asks the victims to register a compliant with the Internet Crime Complaint Center (IC3) [10]. Microsoft [9] also asks the victims to contact their bank officials, and to change passwords and PINs. In addition to following all the above actions, victims of scam emails also need to update the anti-virus software and run a scan on their computer, and change passwords to any compromised accounts [11]. In case an individual clicked on a malicious link in an email, closing the pop-up window is not a good option, as it does not ensure that the malware is removed from the browser. A safer approach is to immediately disconnect from the Internet and to reboot the machine, and perform an antivirus scan [12, 13].

Online scams take place through various media. Email scam forms a small percentage of online scams. A lot of phishing attacks take place on social networking sites [14]. The other media for online scam include social networking sites (such as quizzes, or fake messages/alerts), SMS, fake online ads (such as lotteries, tech support, money offers, investment schemes), to name a few [15–19]. It is important to examine whether users of email have awareness of other online scam media.

This paper is the second part of an entire study conducted regarding general awareness of email scams. The aim of this part of research is to understand the awareness of email users regarding actions that need to be taken if they are victimized by scam email, common practices of identifying email, and awareness of different scam media. This research is important in understanding user approach and awareness to email scam and in finding the knowledge gap of these users regarding email scam awareness. Examining the different actions taken by the users in case of scam victimization and comparing them to suggested actions discussed earlier would throw light on users' knowledge about these actions. As mentioned earlier, different users are likely to employ variety of methods to identify email scams. It is helpful in understanding the most common practices that are used in identifying email scams. These results combined with the results from the first paper of the email research series will then help determine any need for workshops related to scam emails awareness.

2   Previous Research

Several studies have been conducted in the past to check if participants are able to identify scam emails. Jakobsson et al. conducted a study to identify email scam. Participants were shown emails on a screen and were asked to verbally identify the shown emails [20]. Shannon and Bennett [21] conducted a study on a university campus where they asked 109 students to identify a single email as scam or legitimate. Wang et al. studied the indicators or visual triggers that helped individuals in identifying scam emails. They found that individual with prior knowledge of scam emails were less susceptible to phishing scams as they paid more attention to visual triggers. They also found that participant's likelihood of responding to an email was dependent on visual triggers such as typos [22].

In his paper, Freiermuth described the red flags such as convincing storyline, soliciting offers, credentials, and salutations that can be used in identifying 419 scams [23]. Ragucci and Robila conducted a study to help businesses overcome their bad business email practices by avoiding red flags in email content [24].

The previous paper in the email scam series focused on identifying variables that influenced a user's ability to identify scam email. It was found that only the Frequency of Email Usage influenced a person's ability to identify emails, while 'awareness of common practices to identify email scam' was not found to be an influencing factor towards a user's ability in email scam detection [25]. Participants were also given four emails (2 scam and 2 legitimate), and were asked to identify these emails and to point out the indicators that aided them. The most common indicators used by respondents in email identification were: requesting personal, confidential, and financial information, giving away large sum of money, embedded links, asking to log into account, sender credentials, and generic email format. It was also found that 64.5 % of respondents were correctly able to identify 3 or more emails out of the given for emails [25].

3   Methodology

The study was aimed to check the awareness level and knowledge gap among email users with respect to scam email victimization. This was done with the help of following four questions that were asked to the participants with the help of the survey:

1. Question 1: What are the possible actions that individuals will take if they fall prey to a financial email scam or clicked on a malicious link?
2. Question 2: If users were victimized by a scam email, what actions did they take?
3. Question 3: Are the participants aware of other types of online scam media apart from email?
4. Question 4: What are the common practices to identify email scams?

The first question was included so as to understand whether users had any knowledge with respect to actions that need to be taken in case they are victimized by a financial scam or clicked on a malicious link in an email. The second question was included to get an insight into the action steps that were taken by the respondents after they were actually victimized by scam email. This will prove to be of help for any future studies regarding email scam victimization by providing a gap in the knowledge as to what actions were actually taken as opposed to what actions need to be taken. The third question was included to understand if the respondents were aware of other online scam media. In the first part of scam email research study series, awareness of common practices to identify scam was used as one of the factors influencing a user's ability in email scam detection. The fourth question was included as the researchers were interested in knowing if the participants could name these common practices used to identify email scam.

A stratified random sample of N = 163 participants from Purdue University was used for the study. Researchers received approval from the Institutional Review Board (IRB) of Purdue University for administration of the survey at the university during the fall of 2011. The survey collected data for two different studies on email scam. As mentioned earlier, this research is the second between the two studies and uses a subset of the entire dataset. Participants were asked to answer a twelve-question survey as well as identify the four given emails as scam or legitimate. The survey was a combination of close-ended and open-ended questions. It asked for information such as demographics, frequency of email usage, participant's awareness of scam emails and other online scamming media apart from emails, participant's ability to identify email scam, common practices used to identify scam emails, actions taken if victimized by scam emails, and likely actions that will be taken if victimized by a financial scam. Participants had to identify four emails, two of which were scam while the remaining two were legitimate emails received by the researchers.

4   Results

The study used a sample size of N = 163, out of which 72 entries were not complete in entirety. The incomplete items included identifying the emails as scam or legitimate, common practices to identify email scams, listing other scam media, actions that were taken by victims after falling for financial scam, and possible actions that would be taken in case of financial scam of clicking on malicious link. The incomplete entries were retained in the dataset as all the research questions were independent of each other and did not necessitate a survey completed in entirety. For this particular paper only partial data from the entire data set was used. The demographics of the participants is as follows: Out of the 163 participants, 90.2 % participants were between the 18–30 years age group, 6.1 % between 31–45 years age group, and 3.7 % between 46–65 years age group. Of all the participants, 44.8 % of the participants were females, while 55.2 % were males (see Appendix, Table 5).

88.7 % of the participants replied receiving an e-mail scam, while 10.1 % replied never receiving any email scam. 1.3 % of the participants were unsure if they had ever received an e-mail scam. 90.5 % of the participants replied to never have been a scam victim, while 9.5 % replied with an affirmative (see Appendix, Table 6).

Participants took a variety of actions after receiving scam e-mail. 73.1 % replied that they deleted or ignored the e-mail, followed by 15 % of the respondents indicating that they researched online and deleted/ignored the e-mail. Only 1.9 % reported it to the authorities. Refer to Table 7 in the Appendix for a detailed list of all actions taken by respondents. 72.3 % of the respondents replied they were aware of other online scam media, 23.8 % replied in the negative, and 3.8 % were unsure (see Appendix, Table 8).

Question 1. What are the possible actions that individuals will take if they fall prey to a financial email scam or clicked on a malicious link?

A hypothetical question was asked in the questionnaire asking the participants to specify any actions they will take in either of the situations. With respect to the financial scam question, most frequently suggested action by the respondents was 'contacting the bank to cancel cards and to close accounts' (35)[1], and the action that was least frequently specified was 'running a credit score check' (1). Most common action mentioned by respondents after clicking on a malicious link was 'running an anti-virus software' (25), and the least common action mentioned was 'ignoring it' (8). For an entire list of all the actions specified by the respondents see Table 1.

Question 2. If users were victimized by a scam email, what actions did they take?

Only 9.2 % of the respondents replied to being a victim of scam email. Most common action that was taken by the respondents after being victimized by an email scam was to 'delete and/or mark the email as spam' (4), while the least common actions that were taken by the respondents after being victimized were: block the sender (1), and report it to the authorities (1) (see Table 2). Respondents did not specify which authorities were reported about the incident.

Question 3. Are the participants aware of other types of online scam media apart from email?

57.7 % of respondents replied that they were aware of other types of online scam media. Many of the respondents mentioned more than one type of scam media. Most frequently mentioned scam media was 'online ads with pop-ups' (82), while least frequently mentioned scam media was 'applications' (1). For a complete list of other online media, please refer to Table 3.

Question 4. What are the common practices to identify email scams?

52.8 % of the participants responded that they were aware of the common practices to identify email scams. Of these, many respondents mentioned more than one practice. Most frequently mentioned common practice was 'emails asking for or giving out money, emails informing about rewards, sales or business offers, or advertising emails' (44), while the least frequently mentioned common practices were: 'looking for headers and email address source' (4), and 'looking for secure sites' (4). Table 4 lists a complete list of practices employed by the respondents.

---

[1] Bracketed numbers indicate frequency.

Table 1. Frequency of the likely actions taken by respondents if they fall prey to financial scam or click on a malicious link

	Likely actions taken	Frequency
Actions for financial scam	Contact bank to cancel cards and to close account	35
	Notify the authorities	23
	Ask for help	3
	Take legal action	2
	Run a credit check	1
Actions for malicious link	Run anti-virus	25
	Close pop-up message	16
	Delete email with malicious link and change password	17
	Ask help from IT services	11
	Shut down/restart the computer and/or restore it	9
	Ignore it	8
	Delete cookies and temporary files	5
	Mark email as spam	1
	Call anti-virus company	1
	Unsubscribe	1
	Call server to cancel link	1
	No authorities to report to	1
	Irrelevant response	8
	Not sure	21
	Did not respond	26

Table 2. Actions taken after being email scam victim

Actions taken	Frequency	Valid frequency
Delete and/or mark the email as spam	4	16
Use and/or update anti-virus program	2	8
Change the password and/or email address	2	8
Block the sender	1	4
Report it to the authorities	1	4
Did not respond	7	28
Irrelevant answer	8	32
Total	25	100

5   Discussion

As students form a large part of the dataset, large number of participants from the 18–30 years age group was expected. The gender of the participants is fairly balanced with 44.8 % participants being females and 55.2 % participants being males. Majority of the participants (88.7 %) answered positive to receiving email scams. This is consistent with the figures from Spohos (2014) and Securelist (2014a, b), which were mentioned

Table 3. Other scam media apart from email

Online scam medium	Frequency
Online ads with pop-ups	82
Social media	24
Fake websites	16
Cell phone calls and/or texts	16
Hyperlinks	12
Spam and phishing	9
Online bots	4
Cookies	3
Malware/Adware and attacks	3
Unsecured login	2
Website tracking	2
Applications	1
Did not respond	37

Table 4. Common practices employed by the respondents to identify email scam

Common practices used	Frequency
Emails asking for or giving out money, emails informing about rewards, sales or business offers, or advertising emails	44
Looking for email sender either known or unknown	38
Emails asking for personal/private information such passwords, social security number, or ID number	29
Emails with hyperlinks that ask the recipient to go to a specific website	17
Typos or misspelling in the email content, bad grammar, big words in the email, emails sounding too good to be true, unknown content	15
Financial or banking information	13
Email subject heading such as heading in capital letters, generic heading, or informing about monetary gain, generic email greetings	13
Emails from Nigeria or 419 phishing emails	9
Looking for headers and email address source	4
Looking for secure sites	4
Did not respond	23
Irrelevant answer	12

at the beginning. Some participants (10.1 %) mentioned to never having received email scams, which could be due to stringent mailbox rules, extremely less email usage, or lack of awareness of scam emails. A few participants (1.3 %) were unsure if they had ever received scam email, which indicates a lack of awareness in identifying scam emails. Majority of the participants (90.5 %) who had received email scams reported of not being victimized from the scam emails. A fairly large number of participants (23.8 %) replied of not knowing any other online scam media other than email, indicating a lack of awareness of popular online scams media such as social networking sites, where a lot of phishing attacks take place (Gudkova 2014).

The first research question talked about possible actions that need to be taken in the case of financial scam victimization or clicking on a malicious link. The responses for this question (see Table 1) do not match any of the suggested actions that need to be taken in case of either financial victimization (creating a fraud alert, filing a theft report, and running a credit check) or clicking on a malicious link (rebooting the machine to clear the cache, and running an anti-virus scan for the full machine). The second research question focused on actions that were taken by the actual victims of email scams. The responses to this question (see Table 2) also do not match with the rec-ommended actions that should have been taken after falling victim to a financial scam.

The third research question focused on the knowledge of other types of scam media apart from email. None of the respondents mentioned legitimate websites such as Craigslist as one of the other scam media, while a few users mentioned options such as spam and phishing (9), cookies (3), unsecured login (2), and malware/adware attacks (3) that cannot be called as online scamming media (see Table 3). The fourth question focused on some of the common practices used to identify email scam. Participants were able to identify a number of different practices to identify scam email (see Table 4), and seemed fairly aware of the practices that should be used to check email legitimacy.

User awareness of the common practices employed in identifying scam email, but lack of awareness of different scamming media, shows a partial awareness regarding preventive measures towards email scam victimization. This lack of awareness could prove dangerous to email users; as such users will not be vigilant while using other online services and could fall victims to popular scam not implemented via email. Though the responses provided by the participants are partially correct, a huge gap in knowledge is still visible in regards with actions that need to be taken in case of financial scam victimization or clicking on a malicious link, as well as computing and different types of online scamming media. Users lacked awareness about the proper legal or safety actions that need to be taken after falling prey to an email scam. Financial scams are a popular type of scam, and the possibility of users encountering these scams is high. Lack of awareness of financial scams can lead users to lose valuable financial as well as personal information, monetary loss, and in worst cases adversely affect their financial reputation. This gap the knowledge suggests a need for some type of intervention/education to make users aware of different scamming media, and the proper legal actions that need to be taken in the unfortunate event of email scam or financial scam victimization.

6 Limitations

A reliability test for the survey was not deemed necessary due to the exploratory nature of the research. Participants did not receive any compensation for being part of the study, which resulted in participants not filling out the survey completely. As the study was conducted on a university campus, most of the data was limited to the 18–30 year age group.

7   Conclusion

There is a definite knowledge gap among the users with respect to actual actions that need to be taken after email or financial scam victimization and the actions that the users were aware of. Financial scams are one the most popular types of scam and this lack of awareness can prove dangerous to email users. The lack of knowledge gap points that users need to be educated in matters of actions that should be followed in cases of email scam victimization, or financial scam victimization. Increase of email usage is inevitable, and the recent surge in scam email traffic indicates possible future victimization of users. A formal awareness education regarding email scams and their victimizations should be developed to help users stay safe and aware while using email.

Appendix: Tables

See Tables 5, 6, 7, 8.

Table 5. Demographics of the respondents

		Frequency	Percent
Age (in years)	18–30	147	90.2
	31–45	10	6.1
	46–65	6	3.7
	Total	163	100.0
Gender	Females	73	44.8
	Males	90	55.2
	Total	163	100.0

Table 6. Frequency of receipt of scam email, and email scam victimization

		Frequency	Valid percent
Ever received scam email	Yes	141	88.7
	No	16	10.1
	Unsure	2	1.3
	Total	159	100.0
Email scam victimization	Yes	15	9.5
	No	143	90.5
	Total	158	100.0

Table 7. Frequency of actions taken after receiving a scam email

	Frequency	Valid percent
Research online if mail is scam	3	1.9
Delete it/Ignore it	117	73.1
Report to authorities	3	1.9
Research online, and Delete/Ignore it	24	15
Research online, and Report to authorities	2	1.3
Delete it/Ignore it, and Report it to authorities	4	2.5
Research online, Delete it, and Report to authorities	5	3.1
None of the above	2	1.3
Total	160	100.0

Table 8. Frequency of awareness of other scam media

	Frequency	Valid percent
Yes	4	2.5
No	5	3.1
Unsure	2	1.3
Total	160	100.0

References

1. Sophos: the security threat report 2014 (2014). http://www.sophos.com/en-us/medialibrary/PDFs/other/sophos-security-threat-report-2014.pdf
2. Securelist: spam report: January 2014 (2014). https://www.securelist.com/en/analysis/204792327/Spam_report_January_2014
3. Securelist: spam report: February 2014 (2014). https://www.securelist.com/en/analysis/204792328/Spam_report_February_2014#09
4. Office: identify fraudulent email and phishing schemes (n.d.). http://office.microsoft.com/en-us/outlook-help/identify-fraudulent-e-mail-and-phishing-schemes-HA001140002.aspx
5. Apple: identifying fraudulent "phishing" email (n.d.). http://support.apple.com/kb/ht4933
6. OnGuardOnline: identity theft. (n.d.) http://www.onguardonline.gov/articles/0005-identity-theft
7. OnGuardOnline: phishing (n.d.). http://www.onguardonline.gov/phishing#action%20steps
8. Michgan State Police: victim action steps (n.d.). http://www.michigan.gov/msp/0,4643,7-123-1589_35832_38137—,00.html
9. Microsoft: email and web scams: how to help protect yourself (n.d.). http://www.microsoft.com/en-GB/security/online-privacy/phishing-scams.aspx
10. Federal Bureau of Investigation: new e-scams and warnings (n.d.). http://www.fbi.gov/scams-safety/e-scams
11. Acohido: USA Today, 3 must-do steps to recover from a phishing scam (17 May 2013). http://www.usatoday.com/story/cybertruth/2013/05/17/phishing-scams-steps-to-recover-privacy/2193105/
12. Computer world: don't click that link, but if you do... (11 April 2014). http://blogs.computerworld.com/15907/dont_click_that_link_but_if_you_do

13. Fortinet: you clicked on that (malicious) link: from panic to peace of mind (20 April 2012). https://blog.fortinet.com/you-clicked-on-that-malicious-link-from-panic-to-peace-of-mind/

14. Gudkova, D: Kaspersky Security Bulletin. Spam evolution 2013 (2014). http://securelist.com/analysis/kaspersky-security-bulletin/58274/kaspersky-security-bulletin-spam-evolution-2013/

15. Internet crime complaint center: internet crime schemes (n.d.). http://www.ic3.gov/crimeschemes.aspx#item-17

16. Internet crime complaint center: scam alerts (March 2014). http://www.ic3.gov/media/2014/140321.aspx

17. Norton: your security resource (n.d.). http://us.norton.com/yoursecurityresource/detail.jsp?aid=social_media_scams

18. Norton: social networking scam (n.d.). http://us.norton.com/social-networking-scams/article

19. OnGuardOnline: common online scams (n.d.). https://www.onguardonline.gov/articles/0002-common-online-scams

20. Jakobsson, M., Tsow, A., Shah, A., Blevis, E., Lim, Y.-k.: What Instills trust? A qualitative study of phishing. In: Dietrich, S., Dhamija, R. (eds.) FC 2007 and USEC 2007. LNCS, vol. 4886, pp. 356–361. Springer, Heidelberg (2007)

21. Shannon, L., Bennett, J.: A case study: applying critical thinking skills to computer science and technology. In: Information Systems Educators Conference, vol. 28 (2011)

22. Wang, J., Herath, T., Chen, R., Vishwanath, A., Rao, H.R.: Phishing susceptibility: an investigation into the processing of a targeted spear phishing email. IEEE Trans. Prof. Commun. **99** (2012). doi:10.1109/TPC.2012.2208392

23. Freiermuth, M.: Text, lies and electronic bait: An analysis of email fraud and the decisions of the unsuspecting. Discourse Commun. **5**, 123–125 (2011). doi:10.1177/1750481310395448

24. Ragucci, J., Robila, S.: Societal aspects of phishing. IEEE, pp. 1–5 (2006). doi:10.1109/ISTAS.2006.4375893

25. Datar, T.D., Cole, K.A., Rogers, M.K.: Awareness of scam e-mails: an exploratory research study. In: Proceedings of the Conference on Digital Forensics, Security and Law, pp. 11–34 (May 2014)

Cyber Peacekeeping

Nikolay Akatyev[1(✉)] and Joshua I. James[2]

[1] Seoul Tech Society, Seoul, South Korea
nikolay.akatyev@gmail.com
[2] Digital Forensic Investigation Research Laboratory, Hallym University,
Chuncheon, South Korea
joshua@cybercrimetech.com

Abstract. Until now, many works have focused on attempting to define cyber warfare, as well as appropriate response leading to conflict escalation. Instead, this paper proposes a comprehensive definition of Cyber Peacekeeping motivated by prior research on peacekeeping, cyber conflict and warfare, and international relations in cyberspace. Cyber Peacekeeping works to promote online safety and security, which assists in both physical and cyber conflict cessation, and helps protect cyber civilians from becoming either victims or participants in cyber conflicts. This work defines key terms of cyber peacekeeping, as well as its scope and goals in relation to conflict prevention, mitigation, aftermath containment and cleanup. We then propose a potential organizational structure of Cyber Peace-keeping to support its defined roles and functions. Through a case study of a notable past cyber conflict, examples of practical cyber peacekeeping are shown, as well as the roles that peacekeeping could have played in such conflicts.

Keywords: Cyber peacekeeping · Cyber conflicts · Cyber war · Cyberspace safe layer · International relations in cyberspace · Stability and security · Information clearinghouse

1 Introduction

The term 'peacekeeping' was coined in the 1950s and has drastically evolved since. Conceptually, Bellamy et al. [1] defines peacekeeping as peace operations conducted by 'uniformed personnel with or without UN authorization' in order to help bring peace and stability. Until now, peacekeeping has normally referred to the physical world, using physical means against physical threats.

However, as computer systems have become a critical part of the lives of billions of people and their governments, cyber-conflict becomes more feasible, potentially more devastating, and more likely to play a role in physical world conflicts. As of yet, however, there are no examples of peacekeeping in cyberspace though some prior works have attempted to define certain aspects of what we will call 'cyber peacekeeping'.

As described by Lynn III [2] "the Pentagon formally recognized cyberspace as a new domain of warfare". Since cyberspace is being treated as a new front for warfare, both war and peace in the context of cyberspace need to be considered. However, in the past

© Institute for Computer Sciences, Social Informatics and Telecommunications Engineering 2015
J.I. James and F. Breitinger (Eds.): ICDF2C 2015, LNICST 157, pp. 126–139, 2015.
DOI: 10.1007/978-3-319-25512-5_10

several years there has been increasing discussion on cyber-warfare and cyber conflict. Melzer [3] discusses in what conditions cyber attacks can amount to "armed attack". Further Schmitt [4] in Tallinn Manual discusses options of retaliation in cyberspace. However attribution and estimation of threat are still major challenges during cyber attacks [5]. Incorrect attribution or overestimation of the force of retaliation is likely to exasperate already complicated conventional and cyber conflicts.

Nations are currently building cyber-offensive capabilities [6] resembling the so-called 'war atmosphere' described by Lynn III [2]. The result is that a cyber security framework centered on one country can more easily lead to conflict escalation because the retaliation can come directly from the victim country, not from an international organization that can attempt to assess and enact appropriate, yet peaceful, response.

Besides the mentioned academic and political discussions, real-world cases of conflict between Israel and Palestine [6] and allegedly state-sponsored attacks on Estonia [7] and Iran [8] give examples of growing insecurity and instability in cyberspace that has physical-world consequences. In these cases, physical and cyber conflicts are related, where increasing conflict in cyberspace leads to increased physical-world tensions, and vice-versa.

Cahill et al. [9] and Kleffner [10] recognized this situation. They discussed the threat of online propaganda and possibilities of escalation of physical conflicts as result of activities in cyberspace. As a solution Cahill et al. proposed the concept of 'cyber warfare peacekeeping' and Kleffner argued for the necessity of 'peace operations in cyberspace'.

However, these works heavily modeled traditional peacekeeping that has been shown to have limits [1, 11]. Cahill [9] and Kleffner [10] suggested ad-hoc solutions for cyberspace stability and security without proposing a consistent framework. Inheriting these limitations for operations in a quickly changing and globally-connected cyber-space would already inhibit any cyberspace peacekeeping initiatives.

Bellamy [1] described in detail how such a complex tool as peacekeeping suffered from ambiguous interpretation without clear definition, without a consistent framework, and without clear description of goals and functions.

Moreover we are unaware of any prior work that has addressed the problem of the aftermath of cyber-conflicts as well as the threats of re-engineered cyber weapons and consequent necessary cleaning up activities.

Instead of focusing on the appropriate escalation of cyber-conflicts or ad-hoc solutions, we propose an approach focused on a framework for cyber conflict prevention, mitigation and post-conflict containment and rehabilitation, termed *Cyber Peacekeeping*.

1.1 Contribution

In this work we propose a more comprehensive definition of Cyber Peacekeeping (CPK) and a framework describing the goals, roles and functions of CPK.

This work contributes to the area of cyber security, cyber investigation and international relations by proposing a novel approach to cyber conflict cessation known as Cyber Peacekeeping. Further, this work contributes two novel concepts: *cyberspace safe layer,* which is a classification model for critical infrastructure, and an *information clearinghouse* that attempts to provide unbiased, verified information to reduce the risk of conflict escalation.

2 Trends in Cyber Warfare

To provide a background for design and implementation of Cyber Peacekeeping the current section surveys existing organizations and their efforts in cyber security, cyber investigations and cyber conflicts.

2.1 Existing International Cyber Security Entities

ITU IMPACT [12] is an international organization affiliated with the United Nations (UN), particularly with its International Telecommunication Union (ITU). This organization recognizes specifics of cyberspace such as its global nature, difficulty of attribution and low entry barrier. It demonstrates an example of successful collaboration among public and private actors in cyberspace. Unfortunately, IMPACT focuses mostly on criminal activities and protection of commercial assets. Moreover major players like the U.S., China and Russia do not participate in the organization.

At the regional level, the NATO Cooperative Cyber Defense Centre of Excellence (CCDCOE) [13] is another example of multilateral cooperation. NATO, along with INTERPOL, the UN and international CERTs conduct training, and in some ways assist in the communication between countries during cyber attacks and investigations.

Many countries now have national CERTs as well as developing cyber policing and cyber military capabilities. These organizations, however, so far are mostly concerned with prevention, mitigation and investigation once cyber attacks occur. Currently there is some uncertainty regarding who should be a first responder to an international cyber attack. Since such attacks are normally difficult to attribute to a specific actor, it is initially unknown whether it is criminal case or a national security issue.

A common function of all existing organizations is the proposal of regulations, training and information sharing. However, cyber conflicts have fast developing active phases which need adequate reaction in a timely manner that many of these organizations do not have the capacity or capability or coordination to handle during major conflicts.

2.2 Examples of Past and Ongoing Cyber Conflicts

In 1982, the explosion of a pipeline in Siberia [14] was alleged to be the first cyber incident that also had physically destructive consequences. Allen [6] describes the alleged first major cyber conflict between Israel and Palestine, which compromised civil services and attracted volunteer cyber warriors for both sides from all around the globe.

Cyber attacks on Estonia [7] in 2007 and Korea in 2011 [8] interrupted normal operations of government services and caused a cyber arms race initiating the creation of NATO CCDCOE in Estonia and Cyber Terror Response Center (CTRC) and Cyber Command in Korea.

Stuxnet [8] was alleged to be the first full-scale state-sponsored operation which targeted and destroyed physical objects. Devastating aftermath followed where criminals reused this sophisticated cyber weapon to attack private corporations.

Continuous tension between Taiwan and China periodically lead to cyber attacks [15] which result in a buildup of cyber-offensive capabilities.

Ongoing conflict between opposition and governmental forces in Syria [16] as well as ISIS [17] have cyber-offensive capabilities. Utilizing information warfare, they attract volunteers both in cyber and physical spaces escalating the conflict.

The described cyber capabilities may be used to escalate the political situation in cyber and physical spaces, threaten critical infrastructure and consequently physical safety, leave devastating aftermath, or everything at once. However, existing organizations are not well positioned to respond to the described threats, if conflicts involve more than one country or region. International CERTs, INTERPOL, and others were unable to help defend Estonia or Korea against massive Distributed Denial of Service (DDoS) attacks. And IMPACT and related organizations could not address aftermath of Stuxnet. While humanitarian missions operate in Syria and coalitions fight ISIS in physical space, no organizations adequately address cyber elements of these conflicts.

2.3 Cyberspace Specifics

Cyberspace is overarching and fast-changing, and has a major difficulty in proper attribution [2, 6, 9]. Further, as has been shown, there is a low barrier to cyber weapon reusability.

A fast-changing and agile cyberspace means that traditional approaches are less applicable to cyberspace issues. Cyber Peacekeeping must consider above mentioned properties of cyberspace in its design and implementation.

3 Cyber Peacekeeping

This section describes a framework for Cyber Peacekeeping that includes descriptions of roles, functions and organizational structure. The goal is that the proposed framework provides a solid foundation for practical implementation of CPK, and points for future discussion of the subject.

The proposed framework is motivated by prior works and the current state of cyber warfare, discussed in sections one and two.

3.1 The Need for Cyber Peacekeeping

American adults are estimated to spend an average of approximately 6 h a day using digital devices [18]. A growing number of people, however, are spending more time with digital devices than without. Cyberspace as a new realm of human activities possesses opportunities as well as challenges. There are a number of prior works describing the benefits that digital technologies provide, such as accessible education, health care and freedom of speech. For every benefit described there are also warnings about the future of cyberspace.

Notably, governments are struggling to find a balance between openness and control of the Internet. With the absence of norms and rules to which governments are accustomed, it also becomes possible to start conducting cyber warfare related operations. If detected, victim States may escalate conflicts by retaliating disproportionately or even potentially towards mis-attributed actors. The spread of cyber weapons among volunteer cyber warriors, terrorists and criminals is another source of escalation. Amidst growing criminal and military threats, espionage will undermine the openness of cyberspace and eventually separate governmental and civil networks that would greatly slow development, as described by Kaspersky [19].

Cyber Peacekeeping is needed to protect an increasingly-connected number of people, to help prevent escalation of cyber conflicts - especially those that may lead to real-world conflict escalation - to provide knowledgeable arbitration among States, and to help build and maintain trust and openness in cyberspace.

3.2   Overview of Cyber Peacekeeping

To carry out its mission, we define goals, roles and functions for Cyber Peacekeeping as shown in Fig. 1.

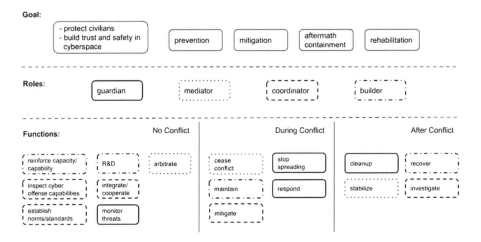

Fig. 1. Overview of the framework of CPK reflecting layers of goals, roles and functions when there is no conflict, during conflict and after conflict. Solid line, guardian role and related functions; dotted line, mediator and related functions; dashed line, coordinator and related functions; dash-dotted line, builder and related functions.

Each role of Cyber Peacekeeping can contribute to the safety and security of cyberspace at all three different stages of a conflict: no conflict, during conflict and after conflict. For example CPK as a guardian will monitor potential threats when there is no conflict. During conflict it will stop the spread of cyber attacks and involved cyber weapons responding with counterattacks as a last measure. After conflict CPK as a guardian will lead cleanup activities related to distribution and alteration of cyber weapons. In Fig. 1 relations among roles and their functions for different stages of a conflict are depicted by different types of lines: solid, dot, dash, dash-dot.

The goals of Cyber Peacekeeping are defined as:

- Protect civilians
  - The main goal of CPK is the protection of civilians. CPK must be impartial to any State independent of contributions.
- Increase trust and security in cyberspace
  - Through conflict prevention, mitigation and rehabilitation tasks, trust in cyberspace can be maintained and security increased.
- Prevention
  - Focuses on preparation for potential attacks, and preventing cyber conflict escalation when conflicts begin
- Mitigation
  - Focuses on containing conflicts and minimizing damage to infrastructure and civilians
- Aftermath Containment
  - Focuses on containment of tools and information that may be re-purposed or reused in other conflicts, as well as using collected information for prevention
- Rehabilitation
  - Focuses on rebuilding infrastructure, security and trust post-conflict

3.3   Definition of Cyber Peacekeeping

Cyber Peacekeeping is defined as *cyber conflict prevention, mitigation, aftermath containment and rehabilitation with a focus on conflict de-escalation and civilian security.*

Cyber Peacekeeping works to promote online safety and security with accordance to international laws and agreements in order to protect civilians as its main goal. CPK is a framework to maintain conditions for lasting peace in cyber and physical spaces impacted by possible threats in cyberspace. CPK defines specific roles and functions at different stages of peace conditions: no conflict, during conflict, after conflict.

3.4   Roles of Cyber Peacekeeping

As defined, the CPK's main role is the protection of civilians in relation to conflict prevention, mitigation, aftermath containment and rehabilitation. Based on this definition, CPK roles are defined as: *guardian, mediator, coordinator* and *builder*. These roles could be considered similar to departments, each with specific functions at specific stages of cyber conflicts.

3.4.1   Guardian

The guardian engages threats directly using technical, non-offensive means to protect civilians, and maintain peace in cyberspace. The guardian monitors, responds to and cleans up threats on a technical level. Functions - defined below - are related to helping prevent ongoing attacks, monitoring the decimation of threatening software and cleaning up their aftermath.

3.4.2 Mediator

The mediator engages with threats through activities involving participating actors of a conflict with a goal to reduce threats and de-escalate conflicts. The mediator's role closely models the mediator's role in traditional peacekeeping, where it engages with adversaries to establish and facilitate dialog with the purpose of conflict prevention, cessation and stabilization afterwards. In addition the mediator of cyber conflicts must take into account specifics of cyberspace in order to effectively resolve the conflicts. The mediator relies on norms and standards of relations in cyberspace when attempting to resolve a conflict.

3.4.3 Coordinator

Currently, there are no established norms and standards of international relations in cyberspace. The coordinator will work to develop these standards during peacetime and collaborate with the mediator for their promotion.

Similar to the mediator role, the coordinator functions mostly involve communication. However, while the mediator establishes communication among participating actors of a conflict, the coordinator establishes communication among as many stakeholders of cyberspace as possible including private, public and academic organizations.

Lynn III [2] emphasizes complexity and fast-changing environment of cyberspace, and explains that "U.S. Cyber Command integrates cyber defense operations across the military" for coordinated and fast response to threats. Globally, there are different international stakeholders in cyberspace with different goals and cultures. As a coordinator, the CPK becomes a communication channel for international cyber operations and boosts cooperation across diverse international actors to negotiate control of cyber offense capabilities, establishment of norms and standards. The coordinator supports all other roles facilitating international cooperation to mitigate ongoing conflicts and investigate consequences.

3.4.4 Builder

The builder consistently reinforces the capacity and capabilities of governments, private organizations and critical infrastructure during peacetime. The builder helps to secure computer systems, maintain capacity during conflict and helps recover essential services disrupted or destroyed as the result of the conflict.

3.5 Functions of Cyber Peacekeeping

Each of the above roles have specific functions categorized by the current stage of conflict; No conflict, During conflict, After conflict.

3.5.1   No Conflict

When there is no - detected - conflict in progress, CPK's main role is that of coordinator which must unite efforts to keep safety and stability and to prevent conflicts. The builder role has significant number of functions at this stage as well, including conducting research and development and reinforcing capacities and capabilities of States as well as the CPK itself. The guardian role actively monitors threats, while the mediator attempts to arbitrate any potential conflicts that could escalate.

When there is no conflict, the builder performs long-term functions such as conducting research and development and reinforcing capabilities and capacities of stakeholders in cyberspace. The CPK conducts its own R&D as well as collaborates with academia to develop up-to-date defensive and offensive tools and methods.

Together with law enforcement organizations, the builder provides training to organizations and agencies that are responsible for critical infrastructure and services directly linked to the safety of civilians.

While working with governments, the coordinator analyses trends of international relations in cyberspace in order to guide efforts establishing norms and standards. This task is supported by working with relevant organizations, such as anti-virus companies, to understand the current threat landscape.

To strengthen collaboration among diverse stakeholders the coordinator also helps coordinate cyber defensive drills among participating governments and organizations. ITU IMPACT conducts cyber security exercises aimed to strengthen collaboration among different CIRTs which serve for protection of business [11]. Cyber Commands conduct their military exercises to protect national assets [2] or show the strength of collaboration for deterrence [20]. The main goal of CPK is to protect civilians, so for this purpose the CPK unites and promotes collaboration not only among different cultures and languages but also among different entities such as private companies, national agencies and international organizations.

Further, Allen [6] compared cyber weapons to Weapons of Mass Destruction (WMD). The international community already established treaties and protocols to ensure non-proliferation of WMD. For that purpose the international community applies mechanisms of inspections and sanctions. The CPK can also unite the international community to inspect buildup of cyber offense capabilities including malware, vulnerabilities and surveillance systems.

When detected cyber threats are beginning to escalate conflict, the mediator can engage relevant stakeholders in order to arbitrate conflicting parties and prevent conflict before further escalation.

The guardian is responsible for technically monitoring the current threat landscape, and attempting to identify any stakeholder vulnerabilities and upcoming potential conflicts. Through monitoring of potential threats, the guardian can react to upcoming threats by coordinating relevant stakeholders and offering technical expertise to remove identified threats.

As a synergy of the guardian and builder roles the CPK helps to audit and protect assets identified as key resources, as well as government online services and elements of critical infrastructure. Social engineering methods [21] have been observed during conflicts between China and Taiwan [15]. The CPK audits, educates and promotes secure use of technology to the public, private organizations and governments. The guardian role is tasked with discovering new technical and social engineering methods.

The guardian independently monitors - but does not block - media outlets to identify content that may result in national or international conflicts. The guardian helps to audit the technical security of key data centers and other online-resources, and collaborates with states to ensure prevention of unauthorized cyber attacks from their infrastructure by third parties.

3.5.2   During Conflict

During a conflict the CPK actively employs its executive and diplomatic functions to stop technical attacks and establish a dialog among conflicting parties. The CPK coordinates actions of the international community to reduce the effects of ongoing attacks, and attempts to rebuild and protect identified critical services - such as health or fire emergency services - in real time.

Impartially to the side of the conflict, as the builder role the CPK must help maintain critical infrastructure and essential services even under severe attack. If a system or service is identified as critical infrastructure, the CPK should have the ability to actively configure systems to ensure their security. In case of web-services, the CPK can add additional computational resources or redirect traffic when such services are under Denial of Service (DoS) attacks.

During conflict, the coordinator must coordinate the actions of the international community to quickly reduce the negative effects of attacks against stakeholders. For example, coordinating ISPs of countries to block IP addresses involved in a DoS attack.

The main task for the CPK in the case of an ongoing cyber conflict is to stop the conflict. As a mediator the CPK can utilize mechanisms of persuasion or coercion to bring adversaries to negotiate [22]. The CPK utilizes support of the international community and stakeholders of cyberspace as a tool for mediation. Clearly established norms and standards of behaviour in cyberspace, which are developed in peacetime, would give the CPK solid ground to negotiate with adversaries.

As a guardian, the CPK actively engages threats to civilians to stop conflicts from spreading and to ensure that any response, if necessary, is legal and proportionate.

Analysis of conflicts in Syria [16] and China [21] shows that participants actively spread hacking tools in order to attract new volunteers worldwide. A key task of the guardian includes monitoring Internet activities [6] which spread malware or explicitly provide hacking tools for volunteers, like in the case of the conflict between China and Taiwan [21]. The guardian identifies and helps to block sources attempting coordinate attacks through the spread of tools or volunteer hacking [6].

During conflicts, the guardian can also provide objective and verified information in response to propaganda spread in media and social networking service. The CPK is not a censor, but instead provides a platform for the distribution of verified information, and clearly indicating what information cannot be substantiated. The CPK will use the same communications channels to attempt to distribute information provided in this verification platform.

3.5.3 After Conflict

After conflict the CPK attempts to stabilize the situation, and prevent further destruction or recurrent attacks. Little attention has been given to the problem of recovery and cleanup from the aftermath of cyber conflicts, though there are real-world examples of how cyber weapons and their descendants [8] are spread and may harm civilians, such as Stuxnet variants like Duqu and Gauss.

After conflict, the builder helps States to recover their critical infrastructure and essential services which were damaged during the conflict. The builder analyzes identified weak points in protection of critical infrastructure and services, and helps to reinforce capabilities and capacities for their protection.

Partnering with public and private actors, the coordinator collects and analyzes cyber weapon samples, and helps produce countermeasures for governments, organizations and civilians. These guidelines are also technically implemented in practice through the builder and guardian roles.

The CPK also facilitates cooperation among diverse stakeholders in cyberspace in order to find - and properly attribute - attackers, prevent further attacks and show examples of accountability. The coordinator helps to investigate cases, attribute attacks and supervise enforcement of local and international law.

Once conflict is finished there is still a high possibility that adversaries would re-engage. The mediator continues efforts to establish dialog among adversaries and to stabilize the situation with the purpose to prevent further conflict. Unlike traditional warfare with spatially localized effects, cyberspace is interconnected and the results of attacks spread globally. This means that each adversary must collaborate to eliminate consequences in cyberspace. The mediator attempts to involve past adversaries in the activities to cleanup the aftermath and control cyber offensive capabilities.

Post-conflict, the guardian's goal is monitoring and prevention of descendants of cyber weapons and viruses. The guardian is responsible for identifying what cyber weapons were used, and how. This information is used to improve threat monitoring, and building protections for systems. Further, by monitoring cyber weapons, guardians can help prepare law enforcement and private organizations for crime-related derivative malware that emerges.

3.6 Implementation of Cyber Peacekeeping

In this section we propose specific, practical functions that CPK could begin that would immediately have real-world impact. The described functions of CPK can be divided into two categories depending on whether the tasks are urgent or long-term. These categories are defined as Rapid Response Division (RRD) and Long-term Stability and Relief Division (LSRD). These divisions and their main functions are shown in Fig. 2, with functions further described in Table 1.

Table 1 categories functions of RRD and LSRD. We described all functions and their impact in the Sect. 3.5. Here we attempt to analyze how these functions can fit to the concept of immediate and long-term tasks.

Fig. 2. Overview of the structure of Cyber Peacekeeping implementation divided into Rapid Response and Long-Term Stability Divisions with their corresponding main functions.

Table 1. Rapid Response Division and Long-Term Stability and Relief Division functions lists.

Rapid Response Division functions	Long-Term Stability and Relief Division functions
• monitor threats • arbitrate potential warring parties • cease conflict • stop spreading of threats • respond to aggressors • maintain cyberspace safe layer • maintain information clearinghouse • mitigate the effect of attacks • cleanup consequences • stabilize the situation	• reinforce capacities and capabilities • conduct R&D • inspect cyber offense capabilities • establish norms and standards • unite stakeholders • monitor threats permanently • mitigate the effect of attacks by international cooperative efforts • cleanup all consequences • recover critical infrastructure and services • stabilize for lasting peace and security • investigate and attribute

3.6.1   Rapid Response Division

The RRD is a response to the described overarching specifics of cyberspace and fast-changing situations online. The RRD mostly operates in conditions of ongoing cyber conflicts which may escalate and spread quickly, making immediate response necessary.

The RRD focuses on the protection of the *cyberspace safe layer (CSL)*, which is the pre-identified, minimally-required critical infrastructure necessary for civilian safety. Prior research describes the necessity to protect critical infrastructure [23]. However, there is no mutual agreement about definition what constitutes critical infrastructure in different countries. Here, the CPK together with the international community and individual States should attempt to define minimal critical infrastructure required for civilian safety. The CSL then becomes the focus of CPK when conflicts arise in the country or region.

The guardian role of CPK provides protection of CSL when there is an ongoing conflict, meanwhile for the mediator it becomes the first goal of negotiation with warring parties in order to prevent their attacks on the CSL.

The builder must audit and improve security of the assets included in the CSL at the first place, maintain its endurance during the conflict and recover after the conflict.

The main function of the coordinator is to define minimally-required critical infrastructure among most of the stakeholders in the international community.

Another equally important part of conflict de-escalation is the management of an *information clearinghouse (ICH)* that helps to identify verified and unverified information, and distribute this information to potential actors, such as citizens that may attempt to join physical conflict based on false information. While there are many real-world examples of propaganda being used to sway opinion, such propaganda online represents a direct threat of escalation of a cyber conflict into physical violence.

The guardian will collect, analyze and publish objective information. The builder will research and develop the infrastructure to run the ICH. And the coordinator will engage the international community for the participation in the ICH.

3.6.2   Long-Term Stability and Relief Division

The LSRD acts to ensure long-lasting peace and stability. The LSRD partially inherits its structure from ITU IMPACT and CERTs together with our proposal of a monitoring and cleaning team that responds to the threats of aftermath of cyber conflicts.

The LSRD performs long-term tasks such as tier-based capacity and capability building through R&D and consulting, facilitating dialog in the international community to establish norms and standards in cyberspace, monitoring potential threats in unstable environments and monitoring threats remaining after conflicts to clean them up. Further, the LSRD coordinates training, intelligence and defense capabilities among public and private stakeholders in cyberspace.

4   Case Study

This section attempts to demonstrate how Cyber Peacekeeping may be applied to real cyber conflicts. In this example, the ongoing conflict between Taiwan and China has been chosen.

Taiwan and China have deteriorating diplomatic relations, and are periodically involved in cyber conflicts against each other [15]. These cyber conflicts attract civilian volunteers from both sides, and include attacks on government services and defacing political websites. Recent cases described by [21] involve social networks exploited to get information about military staff for malicious purposes and social engineering.

Such cyber activities reignite tensions in the physical world and stimulate a buildup of offensive cyber capabilities. As a coordinator, in the long-term, the CPK will attract attention of the international community to the problem. The CPK can engage to facilitate mutual understanding and stress the mutual - and collateral - danger when cyber weapons are used.

As a builder the CPK would monitor technical and social engineering methods from both sides in order to educate personnel of critical services, and build cyber security capacity in the cyberspace safe layer for both countries. Further having an attack on the cyberspace safe layer the guardian will protect it.

For cases involving media and social networks, an information clearinghouse as an implementation of a guardian role will provide objective and trustworthy information to attempt to reduce the attraction of volunteers, where possible.

When the cyber conflict has stabilized, as a mediator the CPK will attempt to facilitate a dialog between recently warring countries and help establish mutual agreements and collaboration to cleanup defaced websites and minimize the spread tools used during cyber attacks. As a guardian the CPK would explicitly participate cleaning up consequences of the conflict. At a global landscape, the coordinator will unite the efforts of the international community to assess consequences of the conflict and investigate its cause and aftermath.

While CPK alone is unlikely to bring peace between countries at war, this case shows that CPK can be employed at different stages of peace conditions and can be a practical tool to help with prevention of escalation of conflicts like those seen in Taiwan vs China [15] or Israel vs Palestine [6], as well as helping with the prevention of a cyber arm race which happened in South Korea [8], Estonia [7] and Taiwan [15].

5   Conclusions

Cyber Peacekeeping is a large, very difficult subject, but one that will need a practical solution as cyberspace is increasingly used for terror, espionage and war. Currently, international relations are not at a point where truly global Cyber Peacekeeping is possible. Implementation at a regional level is also undesirable since many regions already have organizations that have at least some overlap with Cyber Peacekeeping, as proposed. Instead, already established international organizations, such as INTERPOL or the United Nations, should attempt to fill the identified gaps. The challenge then would be allowing Cyber Peacekeeping to remain agile and responsive while being associated with large, notoriously slow entities.

Alternatively, some described aspects of Cyber Peacekeeping could be implemented regionally, such as the concept of a cyberspace safe layer, and information clearinghouse. If these are established regionally, or even nationally, then once a global entity for Cyber Peacekeeping does exist, current local implementations and standards could be directly applied.

5.1   Future Work

Cyber Peacekeeping is still a new, untested idea. Future work will focus on discussions and feedback from potential stakeholders as to the practicality of the roles and functions that have been identified.

Specifically, future work will continue to develop the concept of a cyberspace safe layer, possibly for national use and assessment. Likewise, the practicality of an information clearinghouse will be explored by building prototypes and assessing their performance against past conflict escalation events.

References

1. Bellamy, A.J., Williams, P.D., Griffin, S.: Understanding Peacekeeping. Polity, Cambridge (2010)
2. Lynn III, W.J.: Defending a new domain: the pentagon's cyberstrategy. Foreign Aff. **89**, 97–108 (2010)

3. Melzer, N.: Cyberwarfare and International Law. UNDIR Resources, Helgafell (2011)
4. Schmitt, M.N. (ed.): Tallinn Manual on the International Law Applicable to Cyber Warfare. Cambridge University Press, Cambridge (2013)
5. Hathaway, O.A.: The Law of Cyber-Attack. Faculty Scholarship Series. Paper 3852 (2012)
6. Allen, P.D., Demchak, C.: The Palestinian-Israeli Cyberwar. Mil. Rev. **83**, 52 (2003)
7. Rehman, S.: Estonia's Lessons in Cyberwarfare. USNews (2013)
8. Boo, H.-W., Lee, K.-K.: Cyber war and policy suggestions for South Korean planners. Int. J. Korean Unification Stud. **21**(2), 85–106 (2012)
9. Cahill, T.P., Rozinov, K., Mule, C.: Cyber warfare peacekeeping, pp. 100. In: Proceedings of the 2003 IEEE Workshop on Information Assurance (2003)
10. Kleffner, J.K.: Keeping the cyber peace: international legal aspects of cyber activities in peace operations. Int. Law Stud. **89**, 1 (2013)
11. Bayo, O.A.: The factors behind success and failures of United Nations peacekeeping missions: a case of the Democratic Republic of Congo. J. Altern. Perspect. Soc. Sci. **3**(4), 19 (2012)
12. ITU International Multilateral Partnership Against Cyber Threats. http://www.impact-alliance.org/
13. NATO Cooperative Cyber Defense Center of Excellence. https://ccdcoe.org/
14. Bronk, C.: Hacks on Gas: Energy, Cybersecurity, and U.S. Defense. Rice University, Houston (2014)
15. Chang, Y.: Cyber conflict between Taiwan and China. Strateg. Insights **10**(1), 25–35 (2011)
16. Farwell, J.P., Arakelian, D.: A Better Syria Option: Cyber War. The National Interest (2013)
17. Al-Marashi, I.: The Angel of Death is coming for you, ISIL. AlJazeera (2015)
18. Mobile Continues to Steal Share of US Adults' Daily Time Spent with Media. eMarketer (2014)
19. Eugene Kaspersky Press Club 2013. Canberra, Australia (2013). http://outsidelens.scmagazine.com/video/Eugene-Kaspersky-Press-Club-201
20. Kulikova, A.: Is a cyber arms race between the US and Russia possible? Russia Direct (2015)
21. Cole, J.M.: China's Shifting Cyber Focus on Taiwan. The Diplomat (2013)
22. Sartre, P.: Making UN Peacekeeping More Robust: Protecting the Mission, Persuading the Actors. International Peace Institute, New York (2011)
23. Das, S.K., Kant, K., Zhang, N.: Handbook on Securing Cyber-Physical Critical Infrastructure. Elsevier, Amsterdam (2012)

Social Media Investigations

Explanatory Case Study of the Authur Pendragon Cyber Threat: Socio-psychological and Communication Perspectives

Kathryn C. Seigfried-Spellar[1](✉), Ben M. Flores[2],
and Darrin J. Griffin[2]

[1] Purdue University, West Lafayette, IN 47907, USA
kspellar@purdue.edu
[2] The University of Alabama, Tuscaloosa, AL 35487, USA
bmflores@crimson.ua.edu, djgriffinl@ua.edu

Abstract. Cyber(terrorism) threats posted via social media are capable of devastating, real-world effects, including miscommunication and rumors, panic, and financial loss. This manuscript details a case study of the cyber(terrorism) threat that occurred at The University of Alabama on September 21, 2014, referred to as the Authur Pendragon incident. The Authur Pendragon threat led to a week of fear, social media hyperactivity, and the propagation of rumors, all of which reached beyond The University of Alabama campus. A timeline of the event, which includes social media posts, official University responses, and mass media coverage, are presented followed by an analysis of the case from both a socio-psychological and communications perspective. Recommendations for managing cyber threats and rumor mongering are provided as well as future research suggestions.

Keywords: Cyberterrorism · Cyber threat · Authur pendragon · Rumor mongering · Social attachment model · Affiliation

1 Introduction

According to a report released by the International Telecommunication Union, approximately 3 billion people, or 40 % of the world's population, are Internet users [1], and there are approximately 1.64 billion smartphone users worldwide [2]. In 2014, the most popular social media site was Facebook, followed by LinkedIn, Pinterest, Instagram, and Twitter [3]. Application software, known as "apps", is also a popular feature on mobile devices that are downloaded by the user to perform a particular function (e.g., sharing images/videos, communicating). There is no doubt that the globalization of technology and the popularity of digital devices have impacted the way we communicate and socially interact with others, and this impact, of course, includes the rise in social media threats.

According to Britz [4], cyberterrorism is "the premeditated, methodological, ideologically motivated dissemination of information, facilitation of communication, or, attack against physical targets, digital information, computer systems, and/or computer programs which is intended to cause social, financial, physical, or psychological harm

© Institute for Computer Sciences, Social Informatics and Telecommunications Engineering 2015
J.I. James and F. Breitinger (Eds.): ICDF2C 2015, LNICST 157, pp. 143–175, 2015.
DOI: 10.1007/978-3-319-25512-5_11

to noncombatant targets and audiences for the purpose of affecting ideological, political, or social change; or any utilization of digital communication or information which facilitates such actions directly or indirectly" (p. 197). Cyber(terrorism)[1] threats posted via social media are capable of devastating, real-world effects, including miscommunication and rumors, panic, and financial loss [4]. This manuscript details an explanatory case study of the cyber(terrorism) threat that occurred at The University of Alabama on September 21, 2014, referred to as the Authur Pendragon incident. An explanatory case study is appropriate for contemporary events that are out of the authors' control, and the goal is to identify possible explanations for a set of events [5]. The Authur Pendragon threat led to a week of fear, social media hyperactivity, and the propagation of rumors, all of which reached beyond The University of Alabama campus. A timeline of the event, which includes social media posts, official University responses, and mass media coverage, is presented followed by an analysis of the case from both a socio-psychological and communications perspective. Recommendations for managing future cyber(terrorism) threats and rumor mongering are discussed.

2 Authur Pendragon Cyber Threat

On Sunday, September 21, 2014, a threatening comment was posted following a YouTube video about "racist sororities" at The University of Alabama (UA) by the username Authur Pendragon (see Fig. 1). This post directly threatened fraternity and sorority (collectively referred to as "Greek") students at UA in response to allegations of racism. Since 2011, the University of Alabama is home to the largest fraternity and sorority community in the United States with over 9,500 undergraduate student members and 59 Greek organizations (see greekaffairs.ua.edu).

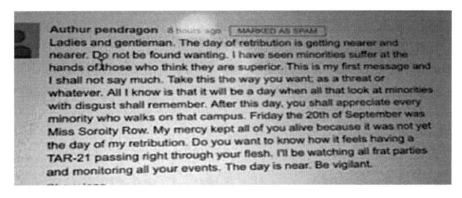

Ladies and gentleman. The day of retribution is getting nearer and nearer. Do not be found wanting. I have seen minorities suffer at the hands of those who think they are superior. This is my first message and I shall not say much. Take this the way you want; as a threat or whatever. All I know is that it will be a day when all that look at minorities with disgust shall remember. After this day, you shall appreciate every minority who walks on that campus. Friday the 20th of September was Miss Sorority Row. My mercy kept all of you alive because it was not yet the day of my retribution. Do you want to know how it feels having a TAR-21 passing right through your flesh. I'll be watching all frat parties and monitoring all your events. The day is near. Be vigilant.

Fig. 1. Original Authur Pendragon threat posted Sunday, September 21, 2014 on a YouTube video.

---

[1] There is no consensus on the definition of a cyberterrorist threat, and the authors are not arguing whether or not the case presented is a cyber threat vs. cyberterrorism threat. Therefore, the authors will use cyber (terrorism) threat to denote this distinction.

YouTube is one of the largest video hosting websites where users can post comments to videos through self-created usernames. Although the exact time of the original post could not be confirmed, by 9:30 pm that same day, Tutwiler Hall, an all female dormitory, was locked-down after a concerned parent of a student read the cyber threat online and contacted The University of Alabama Police Department (UAPD). This student claimed that there were armed gunmen in Tutwiler Hall as a result of the Authur Pendragon post. Tutwiler Hall remained under lockdown until Monday (9/22) morning shortly after midnight while The University of Alabama Police searched all 14 floors for armed gunmen (see Appendix 1 for full timeline visualization).

2.1   Social Media Communications

During the Tutwiler Lockdown, students turned to the Internet for answers, specifically social media. For example, Twitter is a popular social media site that allows users to create an account and post, or "tweet", 140 text characters or less. Students tweeted "first-hand accounts" of the Tutwiler lockdown along with pictures, videos, and news links showing UAPD's presence. When the same topic circulates on Twitter, it becomes "trending" news, and "hashtags" serve as titles or keywords making it easier to search for specific topics. Although the Authur Pendragon post was removed sometime during the Tutwiler lockdown, the image was already circulating around Twitter through the trending hash tag, #Pray4Bama. #Pray4Bama reached users across the country. For example, a Texas A&M student tweeted a comment in response to the Tutwiler lockdown at 11:35 pm Sunday night (see Appendix 2/Section 4/Image 2).

In addition, as information circulated on the Internet about the lockdown and the Authur Pendragon threat, rumors spread that individuals wearing *joker masks* were in Tutwiler Hall, *machetes* were stabbed through fraternity doors, and students were being *choked* on campus. Over the course of several days, the rumors were so prevalent that a formal email was sent to the entire campus community by UAPD directly dispelling the rumors and addressing safety concerns by students and parents. By Monday morning, faculty across campus reported a noticeable drop in student attendance. In fact, there were reports of Greek social organizations encouraging their members to not attend classes due to safety concerns.

At 10:30 am on September 22, 2014 (Tuesday), a second post by Authur Pendragon surfaced on social media via an email that was sent to Ian McDaniel (see Fig. 2). Students again reacted quickly by circulating an image/screenshot of the new message via social media.

However, the Twitter conversation moved to other channels of social media, specifically Yik Yak. Yik Yak is an app that allows users to post *anonymous* comments to people who are geographically located within a certain mile radius; these comments are cycled through quickly depending on the frequency of posts, so the more comments being posted, the faster newer comments replace older comments, which gives the sense of being a "real-time" feed of information. On Yik Yak, rumors quickly spread as well as theories and investigative strategies for locating Authur Pendragon (See Appendix 2/Section 4/Image 5). According to Baker, there has been a rise in the number of social media threats in the United States via Yik Yak [5]. Since Yik Yak's

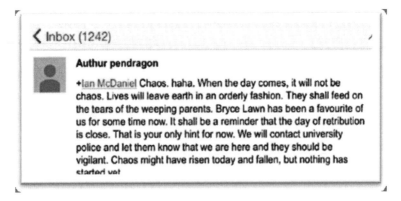

Fig. 2. Second post by Authur Pendragon on Tuesday, September 22, 2014.

creation in November 2013, several students have been arrested for posting cyber threats on Yik Yak [6, 7].

Campus not only talked about the two Authur Pendragon threats, they also discussed the appearance of suspicious text messages from a person claiming to be Authur Pendragon. Specifically, text messages were sent to Greek affiliated students telling them to hand over their fellow members in order to save their own lives. The text messages were reported to UAPD, and a suspect named Dakota John Timm was arrested the following day. However, students were skeptical, and screenshots of the threats continued to circulate on social media (see Appendix 2/Section 2/Image 1).

Although Twitter and Yik Yak were the largest social media forums during the Authur Pendragon incident, students discussed the threat via GroupMe, a group messaging app. Around midnight of Wednesday, September 23rd, a second set of text messages were sent via GroupMe from someone claiming to be Authur Pendragon. This message also demanded Greek students to turn over other Greek students as ransom (see Appendix 2/Section 2/Image 2). However, this second set of threats quickly circulated on other social media forms, including Twitter. Eventually, another student was arrested, Daniel Simmons, who confessed to UA Police that he sent the messages but only meant them as a prank; Simmons thought that his friends would know it was a joke based on his usernames, "Ray Rice/Sid the Sloth". Please see Appendix 2 (Section 2) for other examples of social media communications involving Authur Pendragon.

Finally, Reddit.com is not a social media platform; however, students used the site during the Authur Pendragon incident to generate investigative leads. Reddit has different sections, known as subreddits, which help categorize topics of interest for the Reddit community, a community made up of individuals known as Redditors [8]. In response to Authur Pendragon, Redditors actively engaged in vigilantism on two different subreddits; specifically, they researched and identified "persons of interest" and some Redditors actually contacted law enforcement, as well as one of the current authors, hoping to provide investigative leads. Please note that the Appendix does not cite or include any information from the subreddits; the current authors felt they were ethically obligated to protect the identities of the individuals discussed on the subreddits.

2.2   University Public Email Communications

The University sent the majority of its responses to the Authur Pendragon threat via campus email. For instance, UA sent its first email just after the Tutwiler Lockdown was lifted around 12:06 am on Monday, September 22nd. This email informed students that no gunmen were found in Tutwiler and the lockdown had been lifted (see Appendix 2/Section 3/Image 1). A follow-up email was sent later that morning at 9:36 am addressing the lockdown and explaining how the University was handling the situation (see Appendix 2/Section 3/Image 2). However, the University did not formally address the Authur Pendragon threat until 2 h later (i.e., Monday, September 22nd at 11:22 am). The UA Chief of Police sent out a formal email to the student body discussing the Authur Pendragon post on YouTube as well as the FBI's involvement with the case (see Appendix 2/Section 3/Image 3). The last email on Monday the 22nd at 5:10 pm from the University formally addressed several rumors circulating campus (see Appendix 2/Section 3/Image 4), including:

- There was no machete with a note on the door of a fraternity
- No one dressed as the Joker was in Tutwiler or on sorority row
- There was not a man on sorority row with a box tied to him in a threatening manner
- No one was shot and no one has been arrested, and
- No students were choked on the Quad or anywhere else.

These rumors may seem unusual; however, there were screenshots of them trending on social media, which gave the rumors a sense of legitimacy because "proof" existed.

Despite the four emails sent by UA on Monday, social media continued to buzz with rumors, and students were discouraged to attend class by concerned parents and members of the Greek system. Thus, on Tuesday, September 23rd, the University responded with more frequency by sending out multiple emails in what appears to be an attempt to stop the rumors. The first email came at 6:15 am and informed students that the Interim Vice President of Student Affairs would be available to address questions and concerns that morning (see Appendix/Section 3/Image 5). A second email was sent at 9:47 am discussing the FBI's involvement in the investigation, and it announced that the student who sent threatening text messages had been identified and arrested. This email also stated that classes were to continue as planned and directed students with concerns to contact the University's counseling center (see Appendix 2/Section 3/Image 6). At 10:24 am, another email directed parents and students with concerns to the UA call center (see Appendix 2/Section 3/Image 7). At 1:35 pm, UA urged students and parents to follow UA's official Facebook page and emails – specifically, UA stated in this email that no new prank messages had arisen despite rumors on social media (see Appendix 2/Section 3/Image 8).

By 5:08 pm, the University informed students via email that a 20-year-old student had been arrested and placed in jail under a $2,500 bond. The student was reportedly responsible for the threatening text message on the night of Monday September 22nd. However, the source of the original threat by Authur Pendragon still remained unidentified (see Appendix 2/Section 3/Image 9). At 5:35 pm, the Provost of The

University of Alabama emailed the student body informing them that they would not be penalized for missing class, but they were expected to make up the work (see Appendix 2/Section 3/Image 10). After the Provost's email, communication from the University ceased for the remainder of Tuesday.

The campus community only received one email from the University the following day (Wednesday, September 24th). This email confirmed that the University would function normally; however, students were not required to attend class if they had concerns. The email also encouraged all students to call the help lines regarding any safety concerns (see Appendix 2/Section 3/Image 11s). On the following day, Thursday, September 25th, the first email was sent at 6:05 pm with a long address from the University's President, Dr. Judy Bonner. Dr. Bonner summarized the week's events and described in great detail the level of security that the University implemented to protect its students (see Appendix 2/Section 3/Image 12). At 11:11 pm that same evening, the University addressed a rumor on social media that another person was arrested, and officers interviewed a person wearing a Halloween mask on campus (see Appendix 2/Section 3/Image 13).

On Friday, September 26th at 4:00 pm, the University sent out an email informing students that no new threatening messages had been posted, classes/attendance would resume as normal on Monday, and the University would only give updates when new information was available regarding the original threat (see Appendix 2/ Section 3/Image 14). This same email also referenced several other universities that had experienced threatening messages through social media. The last email from the University on the subject of Authur Pendragon was sent the following week on Tuesday, September 30th at 3:22 pm. It informed students that Daniel Simmons was arrested on charges of making a terrorist threat; Simmons was responsible for the threat that was posted on the fraternity GroupMe that circulated the night of Wednesday, September 24th. However, it was believed that Simmons was not responsible for the initial Authur Pendragon threat (see Appendix 2/Section 3/Image 15). After this email, communication from the University on the Authur Pendragon case ceased.

2.3   Mass Media Communications

Local, state, and national media reported on the events following the Authur Pendragon threat. The University of Alabama's newspaper, *The Crimson White*, was the first newspaper to publish an article about the lockdown at Tutwiler Hall at 9:44 pm [8]. Following *The Crimson White,* a state level newspaper, *AL.com,* posted early Monday morning an article that discussed the Tutwiler's lockdown being attributed to "social media posts" [10]. A few hours later, this story made national news with *USA Today*'s article at 3:36 am [11]. While many articles cited "social media reasons" for the lockdown, Authur Pendragon was first mentioned by local news station, *Tuscaloosa News*, on their website at 7:00 am citing the Authur Pendragon threat on YouTube [12]. While other national articles were written on the topic of social media threats and the lockdown at Tutwiler [13, 14], at 12:30 pm, Authur Pendragon finally received national mass media attention by *The Huffington Post* [15].

After September 22nd, only local and state media reported on incidents concerning the threats and The University of Alabama [16–20]. However, a few noteworthy articles should be mentioned. *AL.com* posted an article on Tuesday September 23rd about the second Authur Pendragon post [21]. Also, *Tuscaloosa News* published an article at 11:00 am about Dakota Timm's arrest for sending threatening text messages [22, 23]. Finally, the last news article was published on Tuesday, September 30th by *AL.com* addressing a second arrest of a student for sending the second set of threating texts through Group Me by Daniel Simmons. This article also summarized the week's events, including the original Authur Pendragon threat, the Tutwiler Hall Lockdown, and other related concerns [24]. Please see Appendix 1 for a detailed timeline of the events discussed.

3 Socio-psychological and Communication Studies Perspectives

Although the Authur Pendragon case remains currently inactive, it provides a unique opportunity to study a community's response to a cyber(terrorism) threat, as well as the acceleration of rumor mongering on social media. Mass-mediated fear plays a critical role in terrorism threats, specifically the fear and vulnerability that steams from the threat of physical harm [25]. However, the fear that results from a cyberterrorism threat may be in response to threats other than physical harm and violence, such as economic harm or the disruption of critical infrastructures [26]. The Internet is the perfect vehicle for terrorism, including recruitment of members, attacking computer systems, as well as, posting threatening messages, which can quickly circulate through cyberspace. In addition, the globalization of communication technology allows a cyber threat posted on a YouTube video to be capable of spreading so quickly that it outpaces rational thought – as seen with the Authur Pendragon case.

It is traditionally believed that the common response to threats of terrorism or natural disasters is mass panic. Mass panic is the "acute fear reaction marked by loss of self-control which is followed by nonsocial and nonrational flight" [27]. However, mass panic or "mass flight" is uncommon and quite rare [28, 29]. Instead, the normal reaction of "fear" (not mass panic) should be expected [30], as well as sociotropic fear, which is the general fear for society or the community [25]. As seen with the Authur Pendragon case, there was a generalized fear for The University of Alabama community, specifically the Greek system that was targeted by the message; however, there is no evidence of mass panic or uncontrollable flight – even after the explosion of rumors on social media.

Instead, the community responded according to Mawson's social attachment model of group behavior, which recognizes the more common response of affiliation [28]. Affiliation is "seeking the proximity of familiar persons and places, even thought this may involve approaching or remaining in a situation of danger" [28]. Mawson argues that the separation from an attachment figure is more stressful than being in the presence of danger [28]; whereas, mass panic implies uncontrollable flight, affiliation implies moving toward the familiar.

According to the social attachment model, there are four reactions to threats or disasters depending upon the social support available (Present vs. Absent), as well as the perceived degree of physical danger (Mild/Anxiety vs. Severe/Terror) [28]. Increased attachment (i.e., affiliation) occurs in situations where the level of physical danger is low, but causes anxiety, and attachment figures are present; however, if these attachment figures are not present, orderly flight or evacuation is likely to occur. That is to say, individuals without social support are more likely to flee a situation in search of familiar figures (i.e., fly home to parents) compared to the local residents within that community [28]. However, when the danger is high causing intense fear, individuals with familiar support are more likely to flee together as a group but again mass panic is unlikely. Finally, mass panic is most likely to occur in situations where the danger level is high and the individuals lack social support [28].

The University of Alabama's Authur Pendragon threat resulted in a low intensity "flight-and-affiliation" reaction. During the week of September 22nd, class attendance dropped, and there were reports of students traveling home to their families because they felt unsafe. In addition, many on-campus residents moved in with off-campus residents due to the perceived threat. In this way, the Authur Pendragon case appears to have resulted in increased attachment for those students with a strong, local support system, whereas those students who lacked familiar support were more likely to travel home in search of attachment figures. Although the authors are unable to ascertain which students left campus during that week, anecdotes suggest that the new freshman class and out-of-state students were more likely to travel home compared to the upperclassmen or in-state students.

Research also suggests that proximity plays a role in the way that people perceive risk and dread [31], and how they communicate information during crises [32]. Proximity to an event changes the way in which the credibility of information is processed and perceived – with those further from a risky situation/threat believing the likelihood or harm to be greater. Distance from a crisis can also alter whether someone is more likely to seek information or provide information to others. Although a negative relationship between proximity and credibility seems counterintuitive, the findings of previous research [31] may explain why some UA students fled campus. That is to say, parents of out-of-state students were more likely to label a cyber threat as real, and in response, they were more likely to encourage and enable their children to come home. However, students with families closer to campus were more likely to practice a realistic appraisal (i.e., lower perception of threat) of the events taking place on campus. Overall, the theories of proximity and social attachment appear to explain the "flight-affiliation" response by students at UA. In addition, there was no evidence of mass panic or uncontrollable flight; although, it may be argued that mass anxiety occurred thanks to the explosion of rumors on social media.

Rumors are unconfirmed or unverified information passed from one person to another, and in situations where there is ambiguity, rumors fill in that missing information [33]. Since it takes time to confirm the likelihood or existence of a threat, terror situations "provide a fertile ground for rumors if individuals do not receive the facts they desire" [34]. Researchers found that users of social media rely on recency of updates/posts for establishing credibility of messages [35]. There was a lack of trust by the students since the institution was slow to provide credible information – this lack of trust facilitated the student's reliance on social media. Research indicates that people are more likely to believe rumors when there is a lack of trust in an organization [25]. Thus, the fact that UA did not release a formal statement until 12 h after the initial Tutwiler dorm lockdown and the Authur Pendragon threat, this likely led to a substantial distrust by students, which facilitated rumor mongering.

As members of the campus community, the authors can also confidently report that the lack of credible information and slow response time by the institution led to an increase in distrust of the school by the students. In addition, rumors are more likely to be retransmitted when they are attractive (e.g., contains visuals) or sent by credible sources (e.g., popular news media, local service) [34]. The Tutwiler lockdown occurred approximately 9:30 pm and by 9:44 pm UA's student newspaper, the Crimson White, published a story online: "UAPD investigations death threat at Tutwiler Hall" [9]. This story included photos of UAPD officers and vehicles at Tutwiler during the lockdown (see Fig. 3). Also, students shared photos of themselves barricaded in their dorm rooms and bathrooms, some holding hands, which may have further facilitated rumor mongering (see Fig. 4).

Fig. 3. UAPD officers outside of Tutwiler Hall during lockdown on September 21, 2014

Fig. 4. UA students shared photos via social media during the Tutwiler lockdown. Retrieved from www.reblop.com

Finally, the rumors were easily retransmitted through the use of text messaging and social media, including Facebook, GroupMe, and Twitter, and these sources may be deemed credible if the message is sent by someone you know and trust. For instance, the sender may retransmit a message sent by someone else by taking a screen-shot of the original message. So, rather than saying "a friend told me this", the sender takes a screen shot and transmits the original message, which may suggest that this information is more than just a rumor. Traditional mass media has been referred to as the "oxygen" of terrorism [36]; however, following this analogy, social media is the uncontrollable catalyst – especially when apps, such as Yik Yak, facilitate anonymous posts, and propagate rumors and the flow of invalidated communications.

4 Practical Recommendations for Managing Cyber Threats and Rumors

Hindsight bias naturally gives people this feeling that, when looking back on a situation, the consequences or outcomes could, and should, have been predicted [37]. In addition, people are "cursed with knowledge," meaning we are unable to perceive the past from our original viewpoint, which lacked foresight [38]. Thus, it is always challenging to provide constructive recommendations due to these naturally occurring biases; however, keeping these biases in mind, the authors have carefully identified several productive recommendations for university administers as well as law enforcement.

First, new information and communication technologies have taken the place of traditional ways that people share information (e.g., social media vs. telephone hotlines). Various social media apps and platforms were utilized by the students at The University of Alabama campus (e.g., Yik Yak, Twitter, GroupMe, Reddit); however, the University administration and law enforcement provided information to students via official emails. Thus, students were receiving information quicker by social media channels, so it would benefit law enforcement to screen social media, which would facilitate earlier detection of crises and rumor mongering. By identifying the rumors earlier, formal responses could be sent containing accurate information via the same social media channels [39]. It is important for administrators and law enforcement to communicate with the public using the same channels they are receiving their information.

Second, the speed of information that is provided to people during crisis is vital. After reviewing the events that took place, it is fair to claim that the mass media, the campus police, and university administrators were slow to provide information about the specific details that led to the lockdown of the dormitory. Westerman et al. found that recency of social media updates was an integral variable in raising the credibility of information [35]. It is not clear why there was a lack of trust and credibility despite the updates provided via the school's homepage, emails, and pre-recorded voicemails; it may be the fact that the University did not address the threats and rumors until 12 h after the lockdown. By this time, social media had already exploded with rumors. However, when UAPD did formally address the rumors in an email sent Monday, September 22nd at 5:10 pm, it did appear to reduce many of the myths circulating campus. Thus, providing information immediately, even if it is simply acknowledging that law enforcement and the University are aware of the situation, may be just enough to maintain the public's trust [24]. According to Breckenridge and Zimbardo [25], the "public must have ready access to accurate information concerning threat assessment and preparedness as well as to developments and protective governmental responses" (p. 128).

Finally, institutions should immediately share information about the legal consequences for creating threats, rumors, and potential panic. Based on this case study, the potential for students to "cry wolf" or create pranks is high, as is evidence from the numerous rumors on social media and the two students arrested. Thus, university officials and law enforcement should pre-develop guidelines of communication for faculty, staff, students, and other administrators during a cyber threat or campus crisis situation. For instance, on Tuesday, September 23rd, a UA Dean notified faculty at 9:28 am that students were expected to attend class; however, the Provost directly emailed the students at 5:35 pm stating that they would not be penalized for missing class the rest of the week. In addition, the authors can anecdotally report that students were suspicious of faculty members who cancelled class during that week; specifically, there were rumors that the faculty members who cancelled class had privileged or inside information on the threats. Overall, having guidelines or protocols in place will strengthen trust in the institution because faculty and administrators will have a cohesive message for students.

5 Future Research Recommendation

Ironically, one of the authors was in the process of developing an institutional review board proposal at UA to hold focus groups about what students expect from the university and police in the event of a crisis. However, this study was abandoned as a result of the cyber threat since it became evident that students desired a prompt and consistent flow of information. Future researchers should develop institutional review board proposals on public responses to cyber threats before they begin. This tactic of preemptive data collection will be challenging, but initiating proposals before a crisis occurs will allow researchers to test theories, models, and obtain participant data more accurately – thereby removing hindsight bias and "curse of knowledge". After all, students will most likely be eager to share their personal experience during and following a cyber threat.

In conclusion, the theoretical perspectives and recommendations in this manuscript are based on the authors' first hand observations as members of The University of Alabama. However, these were anecdotal observations rather than empirical data since crises are naturally unexpected events. Future researchers should be prepared to test theories regarding the best way to transmit credible information to a community during a perceived act of cyberterrorism.

Appendix 1: Visual Timeline of Cyber Threat and Communications

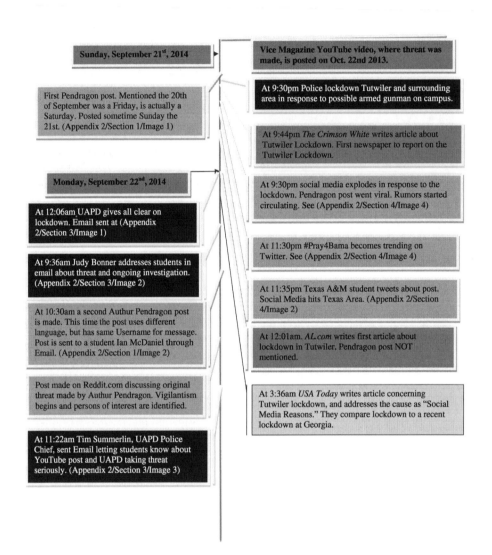

At 5:10pm UA releases email notifying all students of the dismissed rumors that circulated on social media. (Appendix 2/Section 3/Image 4)

At 9pm, threatening text messages from person claiming to be Authur Pendragon began circulating. Social media fueled images of text. (Appendix 2/Section 2/Image 1)

Tuesday, September 23rd, 2014

At 6:15am, UA email notified students that Interim Vice President of Student Affairs Dr. Hood would be available for questions from 9am to 11am. (Appendix 2/Section 3/Image 5)

Post made on Reddit.com discussed second Authur Pendragon post. Vigilantism continues.

From 9:47am, UA emailed students about the FBI's involvement and that a student who made prank messages was arrested. Also, the counseling center was available for students. (Appendix 2/Section 3/Image 6)

At 10:24am UA released email informing students about the UA Call Center in order to address concerns. (Appendix 2/Section 3/Image 7)

At 11:30am *The Washington Times* publishes an article by The Associated Press concerning Tutwiler lockdown. Lockdown reaches National News.

At 11:50am *AL.com* posts Authur Pendragon Message in article discussing Tutwiler Lockdown.

At 12:30pm *The Huffington Post* posts article on Lockdown, Pendragon post addressed. Pendragon reaches National Attention.

At 1:47pm *The New York Times* publishes an article by the Associated Press. President Bonner claims the students were not in danger, and that a parent called authorities on possible gunmen.

UAPD arrested Dakota John Timm for sending threatening text messages on Monday night. Exact time of arrest not released.

At 9:36am, *AL.com* posted article about second Authur Pendragon message; notified public that UA was aware and investigating post.

At 11am *Tuscaloosa News.com* posted article on student Dakota John Timm's arrest,. Also addressed overall concerns from students on UA's lack of communication.

At 2:25pm Yik Yak began rumors of an Authur Pendragon conspiracy, involving Autumn Equinox., which is September 23rd 2014. (Appendix 2/Section 4/Image 16)

At 1:35pm UA sent Email addressing second Pendragon message. UA referred to message as a "prank." (Appendix 2/Section 3/Image 8)

At 10:42 pm *The Crimson White* publishes article criticizing Dr. Hood's Q&A session, saying that not enough information was given to students.

At 5:08pm. UA notifies the students through Email that a student has been arrested for sending threatening messages, but they do not believe the student is connected to the first message. Link to a joint video with President Judy Bonner and Timm Summerlin is linked. (Appendix 2/Section 3/Image 9)

At 5:35pm UA Provost Joe Benson sent email letting students know that classes are not cancelled, but no student will be penalized for missing class. (Appendix 2/Section/Image 10)

Wednesday, September 24th, 2014

At12:06am and 12:57am, a second set of threatening text messages were sent through a fraternity GroupMe chat. The messages were claimed to be from Authur Pendragon, demanding Greek life students as sacrifices. (Appendix 2/Section 2/Image 2)

At 11:02am, UA sent out "Wednesday Safety Reminders" email notifying students that they were not required to go to class. (Appendix 2/Section 3/Image 11)

Conspiracy theories circulated via social media as to the motivations for the posts. (Appendix 2/Section 4/Image 5). Rumors spread that law enforcement failed to apprehend gunmen on campus. See (Appendix 2/Section 4/Image 3). Notable drop in student population on campus in response to these rumors.

At 2:00pm, *TuscaloosaNews.com* posted article that Dakota Timm was officially charged with Obstruction of an Investigation and Harassing Communications; however, the Tuscaloosa County District Attorney's office dropped the Obstruction charge.

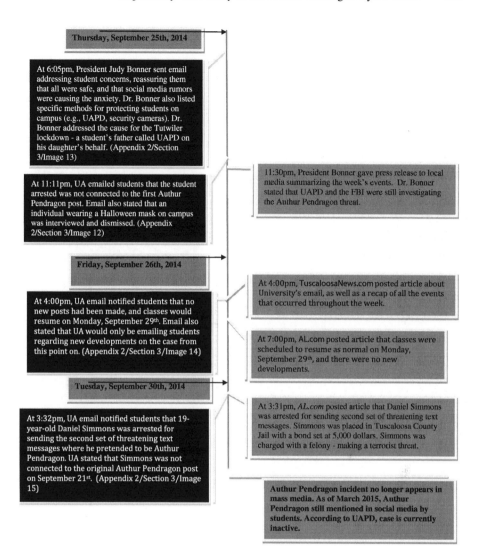

Thursday, September 25th, 2014

At 6:05pm, President Judy Bonner sent email addressing student concerns, reassuring them that all were safe, and that social media rumors were causing the anxiety. Dr. Bonner also listed specific methods for protecting students on campus (e.g., UAPD, security cameras). Dr. Bonner addressed the cause for the Tutwiler lockdown - a student's father called UAPD on his daughter's behalf. (Appendix 2/Section 3/Image 13)

11:30pm, President Bonner gave press release to local media summarizing the week's events. Dr. Bonner stated that UAPD and the FBI were still investigating the Authur Pendragon threat.

At 11:11pm, UA emailed students that the student arrested was not connected to the first Authur Pendragon post. Email also stated that an individual wearing a Halloween mask on campus was interviewed and dismissed. (Appendix 2/Section 3/Image 12)

Friday, September 26th, 2014

At 4:00pm, TuscaloosaNews.com posted article about University's email, as well as a recap of all the events that occurred throughout the week.

At 4:00pm, UA email notified students that no new posts had been made, and classes would resume on Monday, September 29th. Email also stated that UA would only be emailing students regarding new developments on the case from this point on. (Appendix 2/Section 3/Image 14)

At 7:00pm, AL.com posted article that classes were scheduled to resume as normal on Monday, September 29th, and there were no new developments.

Tuesday, September 30th, 2014

At 3:31pm, AL.com posted article that Daniel Simmons was arrested for sending second set of threatening text messages. Simmons was placed in Tuscaloosa County Jail with a bond set at 5,000 dollars. Simmons was charged with a felony - making a terrorist threat.

At 3:32pm, UA email notified students that 19-year-old Daniel Simmons was arrested for sending the second set of threatening text messages where he pretended to be Authur Pendragon. UA stated that Simmons was not connected to the original Authur Pendragon post on September 21st. (Appendix 2/Section 3/Image 15)

Authur Pendragon incident no longer appears in mass media. As of March 2015, Authur Pendragon still mentioned in social media by students. According to UAPD, case is currently inactive.

Appendix 2: Collection of Pendragon Threats and Related Texts

Section 1 Pendragon Threats

Image 1: Original Threat

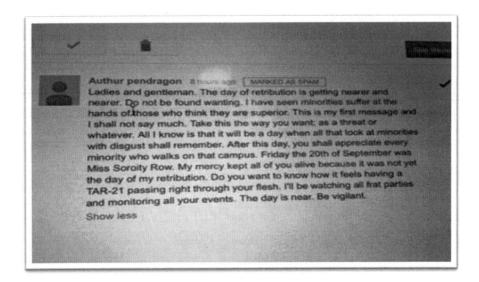

Image 2: Second Threat

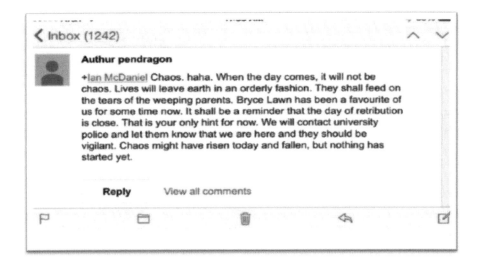

Section 2 Cell Phone Threats

Image 1: 1st Anonymous Cell Phone Threat

Image 2: 2nd Anonymous Cellphone threat

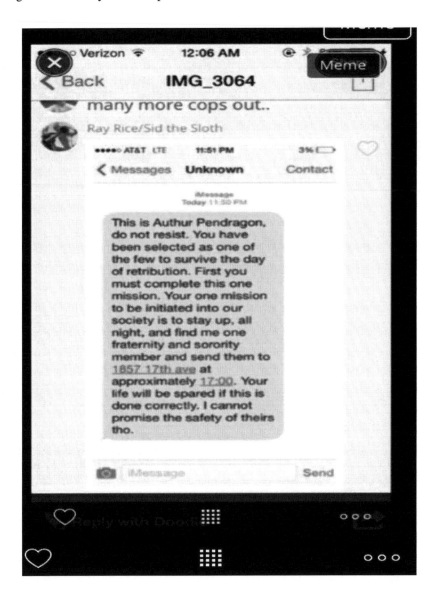

Section 3 University of Alabama Emails

Image 1

uanews <uanews@advance.ua.edu>   Mon, Sep 22, 2014 at 12:06 AM

To: STUDENTNEWS@listserv.ua.edu

UAPD responded to reports of individuals with firearms at Tutwiler. Officers thoroughly searched the building and no weapons or unauthorized persons were found. The information that was provided to UAPD and other law enforcement agencies was based on rumors and social media posts and not actual witness accounts. UAPD will continue to investigate the situation to determine where the posts originated.

Image 2

uanews <uanews@advance.ua.edu>   Mon, Sep 22, 2014 at 9:36 AM

To: STUDENTNEWS@listserv.ua.edu

Last night, The University of Alabama received an unconfirmed report of armed individuals in the vicinity of Tutwiler. The information was sent to UAPD from an external law enforcement agency who had been contacted by a parent whose daughter had heard it from multiple other students who had seen social media posts. No eye-witness or firsthand knowledge of the alleged threat was reported to UAPD or any law enforcement agency.

UAPD responded to Tutwiler within 1 minute of receiving the information, and promptly confirmed that reports of armed individuals were not accurate. However, in an abundance of caution, UAPD conducted a thorough search of Tutwiler.

Residents of Tutwiler were asked to stay in their rooms while the search was conducted. Due to the size of Tutwiler and the thoroughness of the officers' search, this process took about 45 minutes. No weapons or unauthorized individuals were found in Tutwiler or in the vicinity. Students were never in danger.

I can assure you that UA will always respond quickly and notify the campus community when you need to take immediate action. In this case, no one was in danger and immediate action was not required.

We understand that the time it took to be cautious was concerning to students and their parents, faculty and staff, and I want to reiterate that we will always put your safety and security first. UAPD will continue to investigate the situation.

Judy Bonner

President

Image 3

uanews <uanews@advance.ua.edu>   Mon, Sep 22, 2014 at 11:20 AM

To: STUDENTNEWS@listserv.ua.edu

Many of you know that an alarming comment was posted on a YouTube recruitment video over the weekend. While we have no credible information at this point to determine whether this is a legitimate threat, The University of Alabama is taking this situation very seriously. Posting a terrorist threat is a crime and will be treated as such. UAPD is aggressively investigating to identify the individual(s) involved. Among other things, we have requested search warrants and are consulting with the FBI.

This comment appears to have been the catalyst for the incident last night at Tutwiler. And the ongoing social media conversation continues to fuel rumors and speculation and generate additional inaccuracies.

I can assure you that your safety is our top priority. I encourage you to continue to go about your normal routine. If you see something suspicious, please contact UAPD immediately at 205-348-5454.

Tim Summerlin

Chief of Police

The University of Alabama

Image 4

uanews <uanews@advance.ua.edu>   Mon, Sep 22, 2014 at 5:10 PM

To: STUDENTNEWS@listserv.ua.edu

Please see the update below on the events of the last 18 hours regarding safety issues on and off campus.

•   UAPD has issued search warrants to social media sites regarding the YouTube comments. Officers continue to process and follow-up with new information and tips that have been provided.

•   Based on the information that has been evaluated to this point, classes will continue as scheduled and UA will maintain normal operations. Faculty members are encouraged to work with students who present specific or unique concerns.

•   The student in the advisory sent earlier this afternoon about the off-campus incident admitted to investigators that the incident she described did not occur. The investigation into this case has been closed.

•   The fire alarm in Presidential Village was due to sensor that was activated by a non-fire event.

•   There was no machete with a note on the door of a fraternity.

•   No shots were fired at Presidential Village.

•   The FBI is not on campus, and did not conduct a raid in Paty Hall.

•   No one dressed as the Joker was in Tutwiler or on sorority row.

•   There was not a man on sorority row with a box tied to him in a threatening manner.

•   No one was shot and no one has been arrested.

•   No students were choked on the Quad or anywhere else.

Students who have concerns about their safety are encouraged to go to myBama and to sign up for Rave Guardian, an app that will immediately alert UAPD if a student becomes concerned about his/her safety.

Additional information about safety can be found in the Safer Living Guide at http://police.ua.edu/slg.html.

Image 5

uanews <uanews@advance.ua.edu>   Tue, Sep 23, 2014 at 6:15 AM

To: STUDENTNEWS@listserv.ua.edu

Dr. Steven Hood, interim vice president of Student Affairs, and UAPD officers will be available in the living room of Tutwiler Hall on Tuesday, Sept. 23, from 9 a.m. to 11 a.m. for students who have concerns and questions.

Image 6

uanews <uanews@advance.ua.edu>   Tue, Sep 23, 2014 at 9:47 AM

To: STUDENTNEWS@listserv.ua.edu

The guiding principle at The University of Alabama is to promote the personal safety of students, faculty and staff, and UAPD continues to investigate and has been in contact with the FBI in identifying sources of the postings.

Overnight, UAPD responded to messages sent to UA students that proved to be false. UAPD was able to identify a student who sent one of the prank messages.

Although the ongoing social media conversation continues to fuel rumors and speculation and generate additional inaccuracies, the campus community is encouraged to continue its normal routine. Classes will continue as scheduled and UA will maintain normal operations. Faculty members should work with students who present concerns or fears related to these incidents.

Students who need to talk with someone should contact The UA Counseling Center at 1000 South Lawn Office Building (1101 Jackson Avenue). The Center is open Monday, Wednesday, Thursday and Friday from 8 a.m. to 5 p.m. and Tuesday from 9 a.m. to 5 p.m. The center may be reached at 205-348-3863.

Students who have concerns about their safety are encouraged to go to myBama and to sign up for Rave Guardian, an app that will immediately alert UAPD if a student becomes concerned about his/her safety. Additional information about safety can be found in the Safer Living Guide at http://police.ua.edu/slg.html.

Any suspicious activity should be reported to UAPD immediately at 205-348-5454.

Image 7

uanews <uanews@advance.ua.edu>   Tue, Sep 23, 2014 at 10:24 AM

To: STUDENTNEWS@listserv.ua.edu

Parents and students who have questions about recent events on the UA campus may contact the UA Call Center at 205348-1001 and 877-408-1001.

Image 8

uanews <uanews@advance.ua.edu>   Tue, Sep 23, 2014 at 1:35 PM

To: STUDENTNEWS@listserv.ua.edu

Despite ongoing rumors on social media, no new prank messages concerning The University of Alabama have been posted since Monday, Sept. 22, at 10:30 a.m.

Student well-being remains a high priority, and UA Provost Joe Benson has asked all faculty to work with students who have specific or unique concerns.

Parents and students are urged to continue to check the UA website and UA Facebook and Twitter pages for accurate and up-to-date information.

Also, the UA Call Center remains open. However, the volume of calls is currently high. Parents and students who have not been able to get through are asked to please keep calling 205-348-1001 or 877-408-1001. Your calls are important to us.

Image 9

uanews <uanews@advance.ua.edu>   Tue, Sep 23, 2014 at 5:08 PM

To: STUDENTNEWS@listserv.ua.edu

A 20-year-old UA student has been arrested and charged with obstructing governmental operations following an alarming message that was sent Monday night, Sept. 22. He was placed in the Tuscaloosa County Jail on a $2500 bond.

This message is not believed to be directly connected with the initial intimidating post that was sent on Sunday night, Sept. 21.

The investigation into the Sunday night post is active and ongoing, and the full force of the University's investigative resources are being directed toward it. Two search warrants have been issued and additional search warrants are being sought. Investigators continue to actively follow up on tips, leads and information.

UAPD is working collaboratively with state and federal partners, including the Federal Bureau of Investigation, to garner additional information about these posts and to identify the individual or individuals who posted them.

To view a video of UA President Judy Bonner and UAPD Chief Tim Summerlin discussing this situation, click here: https://vimeo.com/106982472.

166   K.C. Seigfried-Spellar et al.

Image 10

uanews <uanews@advance.ua.edu>   Tue, Sep 23, 2014 at 5:35 PM

To: STUDENTNEWS@listserv.ua.edu

The University of Alabama continues to deal with a good bit of misinformation regarding the operation of the institution. This is to make it clear that the University will continue to operate as usual. All classes will meet as scheduled. Any student who is uncomfortable attending class will not be penalized, but will have to make up work missed.

The Call Center will close Tuesday at 6 p.m. CST and open again at 8 a.m. CST on Wednesday. Updated and accurate information can be found at UA.EDU.

Joe Benson

Provost

Image 11

uanews <uanews@advance.ua.edu>   Wed, Sep 24, 2014 at 11:02 AM

To: STUDENTNEWS@listserv.ua.edu

Please see the information below regarding safety issues on campus.

•   The University will continue to operate as usual. All classes will meet as scheduled. Any student who is uncomfortable attending class will not be penalized, but will have to make up work missed.

•   The Call Center is open until 5 p.m. CST today. To reach the Call Center, dial 205-348-1001 or 877-408-1001.

•   Students who have concerns about their safety are encouraged to go to myBama and to sign up for Rave Guardian, an app that will immediately alert UAPD if a student becomes concerned about his/her safety.

•   Additional information about safety can be found in the Safer Living Guide at http://police.ua.edu/slg.html.

•   Students who need to talk with someone should contact The UA Counseling Center at 1000 South Lawn Office Building (1101 Jackson Avenue). The Center is open Monday, Wednesday, Thursday and Friday from 8 a.m. to 5 p.m. and Tuesday from 9 a.m. to 5 p.m. The center may be reached at 205-348-3863.

Image 12

uanews <uanews@advance.ua.edu>   Thu, Sep 25, 2014 at 6:05 PM

To: STUDENTNEWS@listserv.ua.edu

As we near the end of a very stressful week, our campus is getting back to normal. There were no new threats overnight, and we continue to pursue the identity of the individual(s) who posted the original intimidating message as aggressively today as we did when it was posted last weekend. We will continue our efforts until a resolution is achieved.

Please know that many investigative actions are occurring behind the scenes and are not visible to the general community. To protect the integrity of the investigation, specific details will not be released, since doing so could compromise the ongoing case. Investigators have spent countless hours collecting, vetting, and following up on tips, leads and information, and the social media companies involved are cooperating with UAPD on this matter. We are taking these posts with the utmost seriousness. We are collaborating with state and federal partners and are working to make sure students are reassured with a strong uniformed presence.

Through the years, we have added additional sworn officers to the University of Alabama Police Department. UAPD now has 76 sworn officers and 17 key staff. Four additional officers are currently in training. We also have a force of 49 uniformed security assistants who provide a physical presence on campus, extending the eyes and ears of the police department.

In addition to trained personnel, UA has strategically located surveillance cameras around campus. Through our internal and external PA system, our University Relations staff and UAPD can send announcements to specific buildings, to a group of buildings, to every building on campus and across the entire campus outside.

The reality is that information can now be sent via social media to hundreds of thousands of people instantly. That is what happened on Sunday evening and, because of the panic that instantly ensued, a student in Tutwiler called her dad in

Birmingham and told him that people dressed as clowns had entered Tutwiler Hall with guns. UAPD was notified at this point and responded within one minute to Tutwiler. Once UAPD had determined that this information was not true, they were able to talk directly with the student. She indicated that she saw something on social media that made her think that this had happened.

Unfortunately, the next 24 hours were full of the same type of rapidly spreading rumors and speculation. One rumor was followed by another rumor and, in the end, none of the rumors were substantiated. For our students and especially for the parents of our students, the original social media post and the subsequent flurry of rumors that circulated via social media created grave concern. I fully understand and I share the anxiety this generated.

Since Sunday evening, UA's Emergency Preparedness and Response Policy Group has met continuously to proactively manage the University's response. University Relations has communicated regularly with students, parents and the University of Alabama community. We set up a call center so parents and others could obtain information. Our interim vice president of Student Affairs and two UAPD officers met with students at Tutwiler to try to answer their questions. And, Student Affairs staff met with a variety of student groups to do the same thing. Residence hall assistants have been checking on students and helping address their concerns. The Provost's office continues to work with deans and faculty to ensure that faculty are providing support and are working with students. The president of our Faculty Senate sent an email to the faculty asking them to support students and help them use this as a learning experience.

I want to encourage students who are concerned about their safety to go to myBama and sign up for Rave Guardian, an app that will immediately alert UAPD if a student becomes concerned about his/her safety. Additional information about safety can be found in the Safer Living Guide at http://www.police.ua.edu/images/saferlivingguide.pdf.

Also, students can call the University Police directly at 205-348-5454 if they have any information pertaining to this case or during an emergency situation.

Please be assured that the safety of our community is our top priority, and we will continue to work diligently to preserve it. Thank you for your care and concern and for being a partner with us as we all work together to achieve this imperative.

Judy Bonner

Image 13

uanews <uanews@advance.ua.edu>   Thu, Sep 25, 2014 at 11:11 PM

To: STUDENTNEWS@listserv.ua.edu

Despite rumors currently circulating on social media, no arrests have been made in the initial social media post investigation. The individual whose photo appears on the Tuscaloosa County Sheriff's Office website is not connected to UAPD's investigation.

Earlier this evening, in an unrelated matter, UAPD talked to an individual who was seen wearing a Halloween mask. After interviewing this person, officers determined that the individual had no ill intent.

Image 14

uanews <uanews@advance.ua.edu>   Fri, Sep 26, 2014 at 4:00 PM

To: STUDENTNEWS@listserv.ua.edu

No new messages have been posted since Monday morning, Sept. 22. UAPD continues to aggressively investigate the original social media post.

All classes will continue as scheduled on Monday, Sept. 29. Students who missed class this week should work with their professors to make up missed work.

During the month of September, at least a dozen colleges and universities across the nation have experienced a threatening message posted on social media. While none of the threats have been credible, they have caused significant panic and uncertainty on each campus.

After today, the University will send updates only when there is new information to report. Individuals who become aware of suspicious behavior should immediately contact UAPD. In an attempt to help the campus return to normal and reduce the stresses that come from inaccurate information, we also ask all students, parents and employees to refrain from sharing rumors and speculation.

Image 15

---

uanews <uanews@advance.ua.edu>   Tue, Sep 30, 2014 at 3:22 PM

To: STUDENTNEWS@listserv.ua.edu

Daniel Evan Simmons, a 19-year-old University of Alabama student, has been arrested by UAPD and charged with making a terrorist threat. The arrest is the result of further investigation into the additional alarming messages that were sent during the early morning hours of Tuesday, Sept. 23. This message is not believed to be directly connected with the initial intimidating post that was sent on Sunday night, Sept. 21. Simmons has been placed in the Tuscaloosa County Jail on a $5,000.00 bond and has been issued an interim suspension by UA. UAPD continues to investigate the original post.

Section 4: Social Media Posts

Image 1: Crimson White First Tweet

User Actions
Following

The Crimson White@TheCrimsonWhite

BREAKING: Police have a perimeter set up outside of Tutwiler dorm following anonymous threats of gun violence.

Reply
Retweet
Favorite
More

Image 2: Texas A&M student tweet

Image 3: GroupMe social media screenshot post

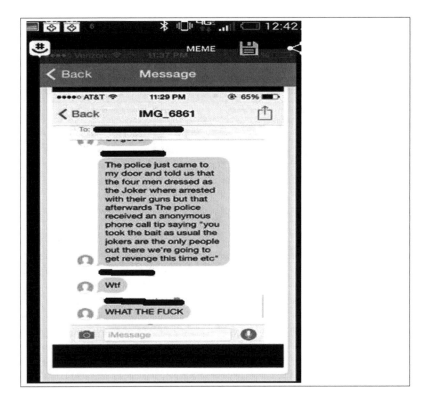

Image 4: #Pray4bama Trending on twitter

Image 4 Cont

instagram.com/p/jwKSQGP01C/
Expand Reply Retweet Favorite More

#SABANISAMIDGET @DanRayWalls · Jan 3
BREAKING NICK SABAN STATUE BEING TORN DOWN N TUSCALOOSA REMINDS ME OF WHEN THE IRAQIS TORE DOWN SADDAM'S. **#PRAY4BAMA**

Expand Reply Retweet Favorite More
Mississippi, US

Haley Hughes @haleyehughes · Nov 30
#pray4bama
Expand Reply Retweet Favorite More

J.R. Lind @jrlind · 10 Nov 2012
#pray4bama RT @ccineastnash: Bama has now lost five games in the last four years. Will the misery never end.
Expand Reply Retweet Favorite More

Khaleesi Jerron @Jerron1234 · 22 Jul 2012
@LT4BAMA @kellymonaco1. Kelly Kelly Kelly, Bama lies. Don't get your hopes up. She don't even take her medicine everyday. **#Pray4Bama**.
View conversation Reply Retweet Favorite More

Taylor McMann @Taylor_McMann · 17 Jul 2012
I'm so tired of hearing about all these on campus shootings. Who in their right mind thinks it is ok to do that? STOP. **#Pray4Bama** #Pray4AU
Expand Reply Retweet Favorite More

rae❤ @raeee21_ · 2 Mar 2012
i wouldnt know what to do if i was in a tornado & everything around me was flying everywhere... it would feel so surreal ! **#pray4bama**
Expand Reply Retweet Favorite More

rhonda burridge @RhondaBurridge · 23 Jan 2012
RT @HighlandsNews: Highlands leadership is meeting w/local officials to assess the storm impact & respond. **#pray4Bama** coth.co/hresponse
Expand Reply Retweet Favorite More

Derek ツ @DJBatts1 · 8 Dec 2011
To all followers if you are not watching the NCAA rewards then watch it now!!!!(:
#Pray4Bama(:
#Trent4Heisman(:
Expand Reply Retweet Favorite More

Image 5: Arthur Pendragon conspiracy theory on Yik Yak

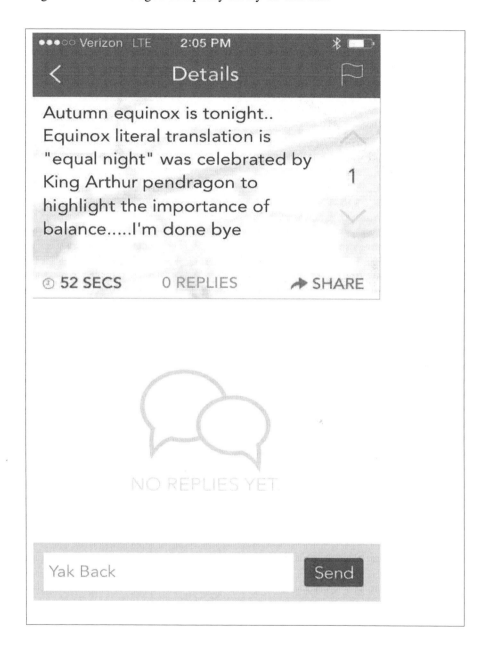

References

1. International Telecommunication Union: ITU releases 2014 ICT figures: mobile-broadband penetration approaching 32 per cent; Three billion internet users by end of this year (2014). www.itu.int/net
2. eMarketer: 2 billion consumers worldwide to get smart(phones) by 2016: over half of mobile phone users globally will have smartphones in 2018. www.emarketer.com. Accessed 11 December 2014
3. Duggan, M., Ellison, N.B., Lampe, C., Lenhart, A., Madden, M.: Social media update 2014. Pew Research Center. www.pewinternet.org. Accessed 9 January 2015
4. Britz, M.T.: Terrorism and technology: operationalizing cyberterrorism and identifying concepts. In: Holt, T.J. (ed.) Crime on-Line: Correlates, Causes, and Context, pp. 193–220. Carolina Academic Press, Raleigh (2010). (cid:E49F8381-0746-4436-94F8-9427DA094F30@home.network)
5. Yin, R.K.: Case Study Research: Design and Methods, 5th edn. Sage Publications, Thousand Oaks (2014)
6. Baker, D.: Yik Yak School threats shoot up in U.S., not just San Diego. San Diego Union-Tribune. www.utsandiego.com. Accessed 21 November 2014
7. Raleigh, L.: Yik Yak arrests – an updated timeline. Telapost (2015). www.telapost.com
8. Sporkicide: Reddit, FAQ, basics, what is Reddit? Reddit (2014). reddit.com
9. McWhorter, A.: UAPD investigates death threat at Tutwiler Hall. The Crimson White. cw.ua.edu. Accessed 21 September 2014
10. Brown, M.: University of Alabama dorm given the all clear after rumors of gun violence. al.com. Accessed 22 September 2014
11. Wolfe, J.: Lock down on Alabama dorm lifted after gun threat. USA Today. usatoday.com. Accessed 22 September 2014
12. Taylor, S.: University of Alabama police investigating threats of gun violence at Tutwiler Hall. tuscaloosanews.com. Accessed 22 September 2014
13. Associated Press: Alabama says no weapons found after dorm lockdown. The Washington Times. washingtontimes.com. Accessed 22 September 2014
14. Associated Press: President: no danger from threat at Alabama Dorm. The New York Times. nytimes.com. Accessed 22 September 2014
15. Kingkade, T.: Anonymous threat puts women's dorm at University Of Alabama on Lockdown. The Huffington Post. huffingtonpost.com. Accessed 22 September 2014
16. Dethrage, S.: 'Alarming comment' on YouTube video led to lockdown of University of Alabama women's dorm. al.com. Accessed 22 September 2014
17. Ward, K.: Questions remain after Q-and-A session. The Crimson White. cw.ua.edu. Accessed 23 September 2014
18. Enoch, E.: University of Alabama classes to continue as scheduled Monday as investigation into threat continues. tuscaloosanews.com. Accessed 26 September 2014
19. Reed, J.: University of Alabama: no new threats since Monday, classes to continue next week as scheduled. al.com. Accessed 26 September 2014
20. Roberts, K.: University of Alabama president Judy Bonner: recent threats still being investigated. tuscaloosanews.com. Accessed 25 September 2014
21. Reed, J.: University of Alabama investigating second threat made against Campus. al.com. Accessed 23 September 2014
22. Enoch, E.: University of Alabama student charged with making social media threat. tuscaloosanews.com. Accessed 23 September 2014

23. Taylor, S.: Documents say University of Alabama student sent text messages to two women. tuscaloosanews.com. Accessed 24 September 2014
24. Brown, M.: University of Alabama student arrested for 'terrorist threat', not connected to original threat. al.com. Accessed 30 September 2014
25. Breckenridge, J.N., Zimbardo, P.G.: The strategy of terrorism and the psychology of mass-mediated fear. In: Bongar, B., Brown, L.M., Beutler, L.E., Breckenridge, J.N., Zimbardo, P.G. (eds.) Psychology of Terrorism, pp. 117–131. Oxford University Press, New York City (2007)
26. Holt, T., Bossler, A., Seigfried-Spellar, K.: Cybercrime and Digital Forensics: An Introduction. Routledge, Abingdon, UK (2015)
27. Quarantelli, E.I.: The nature and conditions of panic. Am. J. Sociol. **60**, 265–275 (1954)
28. Mawson, A.R.: Understanding mass panic and other collective responses to threat and disaster. Psychiatry **68**(2), 95–113 (2005)
29. Sullivan, G.R., Bongar, B.: Psychological consequences of actual or threatened CBRNE terrorism. In: Bongar, B., Brown, L.M., Beutler, L.E., Breckenridge, J.N., Zimbardo, P.G. (eds.) Psychology of Terrorism, pp. 153–163. Oxford University Press, New York City (2007)
30. Perry, R.W., Lindell, M.K.: Understanding citizen response to disasters with implications for terrorism. J. Contingencies Crisis Manage. **11**(2), 49–60 (2003)
31. Heath, R.L., Seshadri, S., Lee, J.: Risk communication: a two-community analysis of proximity, dread, trust, involvement, uncertainty, openness/accessibility, and knowledge on support/opposition toward chemical companies. Public Relat. Res. **10**, 35–56 (1998)
32. Egnoto, M.J., Griffin, D.J., Svetieva, E., Winslow, L.: Information sharing during the University of Texas at Austin active shooter/suicide event. J. Sch. Violence, 1–19 (2014)
33. Barkan, S.E.: Collective behavior and social movements. In: Sociology: Understanding and Changing the Social World, comprehensive edition, p. 625 (2011)
34. Liu, F., Burton-Jones, A., Xu, D.: Rumors on social media in disasters: extending transmission to retransmission. In: 2014 Proceedings of Pacific Asia Conference on Information Systems (PACIS) (2014). http://aisel.aisnet.org/pacis2014
35. Westerman, D., Spence, P.R., Van Der Heide, B.: Social media as information source: recency of updates and credibility of information. J. Comput. Mediated Commun. **19**(2), 171–183 (2014)
36. Dettmer, J.: Supplying terrorists the "oxygen of publicity". In: Moghaddam, T.M., Marsella, A.J. (eds.) Understanding Terrorism: Psychosocial Roots, Consequences, and Interventions, pp. 187–207. American Psychological Association, Washington D.C. (2004)
37. Fischoff, B.: Hindsight does not equal foresight: the effect of outcome knowledge on judgment under uncertainty. J. Exp. Psychol. Hum. Percept. Perform. **1**, 288–299 (1975)
38. Birch, S.A., Bloom, P.: The curse of knowledge in reasoning about false beliefs. Psychol. Sci. **18**(5), 382–386 (2007)
39. Palen, L., Vieweg, S., Liu, S.B., Hughes, A.L.: Crisis in a networked world features of computer-mediated communication in the April 16, 2007, Virginia Tech Event. Soc. Sci. Comput. Rev. **27**(4), 467–480 (2009)

Smartphone Verification and User Profiles Linking Across Social Networks by Camera Fingerprinting

Flavio Bertini$^{(\boxtimes)}$, Rajesh Sharma, Andrea Iannì, and Danilo Montesi

Department of Computer Science and Engineering,
University of Bologna, Bologna, Italy
{flavio.bertini2,rajesh.sharma,andrea.ianni,danilo.montesi}@unibo.it

Abstract. In recent years, the spread of smartphones has attributed to changes in the user behaviour with respect to multimedia content sharing on online social networks (SNs). One noticeable behaviour is taking pictures using smartphone cameras and sharing them with friends through online social platforms. On the downside, this has contributed to the growth of the cyber crime through SNs. In this paper, we present a method to extract the characteristic fingerprint of the source camera from images being posted on SNs. We use this technique for two investigation activities (i) smartphone verification: correctly verifying if a given picture has been taken by a given smartphone and (ii) profile linking: matching user profiles belonging to different SNs. The method is robust enough to verify the smartphones in spite of the fact that the images get downgraded during the uploading/downloading process. Also, it is capable enough to compare different images belonging to different SNs without using the original images. We evaluate our process on real dataset using three different social networks and five different smartphones. The results, show smartphone verification and profile linking can provide 96.48 % and 99.49 % respectively, on an average of the three social networks, which shows the effectiveness of our approach.

Keywords: Pattern noise · Image fingerprint · Profile matching · Social network analysis · Online forensics

1 Introduction

In the last decade, many social platforms have invaded the web as well as mobile devices. These various networks model the specific needs of the users: social interactions, photo sharing, instant messaging to name a few, and users are often present across multiple social networks. Another important reason for the huge popularity of social platforms among users is the increase in usage of smartphones, which in turn has introduced changes in the user habits with respect to multimedia content on social networks [13].

An important problem across these social networks is that of fake profiles, which have seen a sharp increase in recent times. For example, *Facebook*'s most

© Institute for Computer Sciences, Social Informatics and Telecommunications Engineering 2015
J.I. James and F. Breitinger (Eds.): ICDF2C 2015, LNICST 157, pp. 176–186, 2015.
DOI: 10.1007/978-3-319-25512-5_12

recent annual report [8] has estimated that an average 8.35 % of its monthly active users are fake profiles.

In this paper, we deal with two problems (i) *smartphone verification*: the task to verify if a specific device is the source of given images and (ii) *user profiles linking*: the task to decide if a restricted set of user profiles (with different user ids or nicknames) belong to the same user. These two problems have their application in online forensics. Also, importantly, user profile linking is one of many kinds of missing data problem [14,15].

Recently, researchers exploited sensor imperfections to extract the fingerprint to identify a smartphone [2,6,7]. The concept behind a smartphone's fingerprint is similar to a human's fingerprint, which is used extensively in criminal investigations. The intuition behind the focus on smartphones are two. Firstly, smartphones are more personal than laptops or desktops, partially thanks to the hard bound phone contract. Secondly, and which is the base of our study, smartphones have various sensors, for example, camera, microphone-speaker [6], and accelerometer [7], which can be used to make a unique fingerprint of the device. Our proposed method is based on hardware imperfections of the built-in camera leveraging the fact that methods based on hardware imperfections provide better results than software imperfections [12].

We exploit the possibility of making a unique fingerprint of a smartphone based on the built-in camera imperfections, proposing a method robust enough that it does not get affected by the compression techniques used by various social networks. The smartphone camera fingerprint allows for linking different user profiles based on the pictures being posted on them, assuming the pictures have been taken with the same smartphone camera. In our experiments, we have compared the processed pictures from social networks with unprocessed ones and across social networks. The resulting method is strong enough to perform users linking from the sets of images belonging to different social networks and thus subject to different compression algorithms. In other words, it does not require original images for confirmation as original images might be difficult to obtain for various reasons such as for privacy and inaccessibility of the device. On an average of the three social networks, smartphone verification and profile linking can provide results of 96.48 % and 99.49 % respectively.

The rest of the paper is organized as follows. In Sect. 2 we briefly review the previous works related to smartphone fingerprinting techniques and forensic investigations on SNs. Section 3 describes our methodology. Section 4 presents the experiments and analyses of our results. Section 5 concludes the paper with future directions.

2   Related Works

In this section, we describe literature from three different domains, at the intersection of which our work lies. Firstly, we explain techniques to identify fingerprints of smartphone devices using various built-in sensors. Next, we describe various approaches proposed in the past for the source camera identification. In the last, we present methods to identify and match user profiles in SNs.

Fingerprinting the smartphones: Recently, researchers have proposed various techniques to fingerprint smartphones using built in sensors. For example, in [6] authors proposed a technique using speakers-microphones embedded in smartphones to uniquely fingerprint the individual devices through playback and recording of audio samples. The authors of [7] propose a method for identifying mobile phones based on the integrated accelerometers. In [2], authors exploit both (i) speakerphone-microphone and (ii) accelerometer calibration errors to de-anonymize the mobile devices.

Fingerprinting for source camera identification: Various techniques have been proposed for source camera identification. The manufacturing process of the camera introduces hardware defects. In [16] authors use the chromatic aberration to identify the source camera. In [12] it is shown that the Photo-Response Non-Uniformity (PRNU) is a unique feature of the sensor which is able to successfully distinguish between two cameras of the same brand and model. One of the main problems concerning the original Lukáš et al's algorithm presented in [12] is that it works correctly only with unscaled photos, because the footprint signal is of the same dimension of the image. To overcome this limitation, a method able to operate with different size images is proposed in [9]. To achieve our aim, that is, verifying the source camera and linking user profiles on SNs, we combine a PRNU-based method with a denoising algorithm to deal with the (unknown) compression methods of the SNs.

Identifying users in SNs: Despite SNs regulating their services very strictly, the large amount of data shared each day often includes information and content that go beyond what the law allows [18]. This has forced to increase the control and regulation of these platforms, seeing the evolution of new methods around social network forensics. In [1], authors proposed various solutions to extract information about user activities on various SNs from the smartphones. The method is made for Blackberry smartphones and cannot be used for all the devices, whereas our proposed method is device independent. There is great value in multimedia content that transits through SNs. In [10], the authors combine user ID and their tags to identify users across the social tagging system. In [11, 17] researchers extract and use information about users' identities to match profiles belonging to the same user from different social networks, without compromising the privacy of the users, but the method fails if the malicious user falsifies his/her personal information, as it usually happens. Compared to all these approaches, our method does not only rely on the SN content, it verifies the user profiles and performs user profiles linking using smartphone's camera.

3   Methodology

First, we provide a small background in image processing as it is important in understanding the reasons behind the selection of our methodology. We then describe the procedure of verifying the image source. Finally, we explain the approach to test our method with different SNs and smartphones.

Images captured by cameras (smartphone cameras in this case) have two components, namely *signal* and *noise*. Technically the *signal* represents the information carrier, while the *noise* is an unavoidable effect on the signal due to many reasons.

The *noise* component can be categorise into a random and a deterministic component: the first one is the *shot noise* (or *photonic noise*), caused by factors such as brightness, temperature, humidity; the second one is the *pattern noise* which is systematic and regular. By systematic we mean it is present in every image, and regular signifies that it is present in the same location of every image captured by the same source (camera in this case).

3.1 Pattern Noise Extraction

We exploit a PRNU-based method [12] to extract the dominant part of the *pattern noise*, which is a regular component of the image and can be identified as average of residues of a large number of pictures. In particular, denoising algorithms [3] which are usually employed to clean up the image, can be used to remove the representative component of the image and thus leaving the noise component. If I represents the original image, RN the noise residuals and d the denoising function, then formally RN can be represented as $I - d(I)$. Then, the *pattern noise* PN_k, of the camera k can be approximated as the average residual noise of n images of the camera k [12]:

$$PN_k = \frac{1}{n} \sum_{j=1}^{n} RN_j \tag{1}$$

The denoising algorithm can affect the *pattern noise* computation, since it includes high-frequency details that might belong to signal component of the image. Although these errors can be reduced by increasing the number of samples, it is not always possible to acquire new samples (images). To address this, we have chosen the Block Matching 3D (BM3D) denoising algorithm [5] able to discern among high-frequency of noise and high-frequency of details and to deal with scaled photos.

As suggested in [5], we convert the colour images into the YCbCr color space. The Y identifies the luminance, while the Cb and Cr are the blue-difference and red-difference chroma components respectively. Then we take into account only the Y component that is the carrier of all high-frequency components (known as luminance noise) useful to determine the *pattern noise*.

3.2 Source Verification

Let $\mathcal{N}_k$ represents the set of known images belonging to source k which is used for generating the PN_k (see Eq. 1 above). $\mathcal{U}_k$ defines the whole set of images taken by the source k. Also note $\mathcal{N}_k \subseteq \mathcal{U}_k$. Thus, we can define the set $\mathcal{S}$ as:

$$\mathcal{S} = \bigcup_k \mathcal{U}_k \setminus \mathcal{N}_k \tag{2}$$

The goal is to determine for each image $I \in S$ whether it has been captured by the source k or not. To achieve this, we followed a two steps process. In the **first step**, we extract the residual noise RN from each image $I \in S$, in order to apply the normalized correlation $corr(RN, PN_k)$ between each RN and PN_k as done in [12]:

$$\frac{(RN - \overline{RN})(PN_k - \overline{PN_k})}{\|(RN - \overline{RN})\|\|(PN_k - \overline{PN_k})\|} \quad (3)$$

In this way we compute the correlation between the unknown source of each image $I \in S$ and each source k. We compute for each source k the mean μ_k of the correlation values an its standard deviation σ_k, then we define the threshold $\mathcal{T}_k$ as $\mu_k + \sigma_k$. In the **second step**, we decide that the camera k is the source of those images in S for which the correlation value is greater than the threshold $\mathcal{T}_k$. The reason behind this choice is that we know that some images in S originated from the camera k, and the correlation values have a characteristic distribution, as shown in Fig. 1.

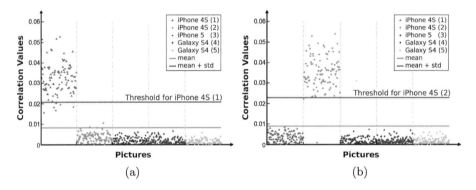

Fig. 1. Two examples of the distribution of correlation value of all the images in S using the fingerprints of two different devices. In (a) the threshold value is computed for the iPhone 4S (1) using $\mathcal{N}_1$, while in (b) for the iPhone 4S (2) using $\mathcal{N}_2$.

4   Evaluation

We describe the experimental settings and then the results of our experiments.

4.1   Experimental Setting

We choose five smartphones from two different brands, with two pairs of identical models (see Table 1). For each of these phones we have taken 200 high-resolution photographs under different conditions, in order to obtain independent samples and to reduce the random component of the noise (*shot noise*). We select three SNs: *Facebook*, *Google+* and *WhatsApp* for our analysis. Each of these SNs adopts different (unknown) compression algorithms, which lead to different characteristics in the image, summarized in Table 2. In all tests, we resize the images to compare pictures from different SNs.

Table 1. Smartphones' features.

ID	Brand	Model	Sensor	Resolution
1	Apple	iPhone 4s	CMOS	3264×2448
2	Apple	iPhone 4s	CMOS	3264×2448
3	Apple	iPhone 5	CMOS	3264×2448
4	Samsung	Galaxy S4	CMOS	4128×3096
5	Samsung	Galaxy S4	CMOS	4128×3096

Table 2. Characteristics of the SNs.

Service	Icon	Resolution	Quality
Facebook		960x720	medium
Google+		2048x1536	high
WhatsApp		800x600	low

4.2 Results

In this section, we present our results on the three tests, namely (i) original-by-original, (ii) social-by-social and (iii) cross-social. In each of these tests, to evaluate the classification process that allows to verify the source and link user profiles, we compute sensitivity (SEN) and specificity (SPE), which are well known statistical measures. In the context of this work, SEN indicates the ability of the method to correctly associate the images to the right source (i.e. smartphone or smartphone camera) and SPE as the ability to reject the other images.

Let $\mathcal{S}_k$ represents the whole set of the images which belong to the source k. Out of all the images $\mathcal{S}_k$, let $\mathcal{S}_k^+$ signify the set of images that the algorithm has successfully assigned and those that it has not recognized is represented by $\mathcal{S}_k^-$, then we can define the **sensitivity** as:

$$SEN = \frac{|\mathcal{S}_k^+|}{|\mathcal{S}_k^+ \cup \mathcal{S}_k^-|} \tag{4}$$

Let $\widehat{\mathcal{S}}_k$ represents the whole set of the images which do not belong to the source k. Out of all the images $\widehat{\mathcal{S}}_k$, let $\widehat{\mathcal{S}}_k^-$ signify the set of images that the algorithm has successfully not assigned and those that it has wrongly recognized is represented by $\widehat{\mathcal{S}}_k^+$, then we can define the **specificity** as:

$$SPE = \frac{|\widehat{\mathcal{S}}_k^-|}{|\widehat{\mathcal{S}}_k^- \cup \widehat{\mathcal{S}}_k^+|} \tag{5}$$

Test 1: original-by-original: We first verify our approach on original images, that is images directly obtained from smartphones. The test is also helpful in determining the minimum cardinality of each set $\mathcal{N}_k$, with which the *pattern noise* can be correctly extracted. Starting with a single image, the cardinality is increased, according to the following sequence: 2, 3, 4, 5, 10, 15, 20, 40, 60, 80, 100, 120 and because of resource constraints, we limit our experiments to 140. For each cardinality, we first extract the *pattern noise* and compute the threshold $\mathcal{T}$ and then compute the sensitivity and specificity for the classification result of the images (Fig. 2). This process is repeated for each smartphone.

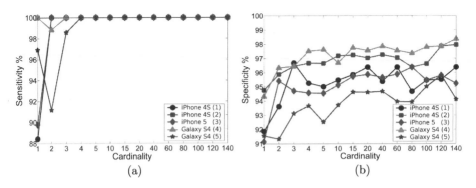

Fig. 2. The graphs represent the sensitivity (a) and the specificity (b) results for each smartphone obtained by changing the cardinality of $\mathcal{N}_k$.

Based on the results we obtained, the cardinality of the subsets $\mathcal{N}_k$ is fixed to 100 images, for the following reasons: *(i)* starting from this value, specificity index has a good stability for each source; *(ii)* we preferred a wider value to curb the inherent difficulties of the denoising function [5] in discriminating the high frequencies. The cardinality of the set $\mathcal{S}$ is of 500 images as we fixed for each device a value of 100 images.

By setting the cardinality to 100 images, we calculate the sensitivity and specificity values for each device. The result shows that for each device, the method returns 100 % of sensitivity and 95 % of specificity (Fig. 3). In other words, in our experimental setup, the method is able to perform smartphone verification with 100 % correctness and is capable of rejecting at least the 95 % of images that does not belong to the right source.

Test 2: social-by-social: In the second test, the aim is to verify the robustness of the method when it is applied to images deteriorated by the uploading and downloading process of the SNs. This feature is extremely useful to verify which smartphone has taken and uploaded the images on SNs. In this test, all the images are previously uploaded and downloaded on the same SN. In practice, we use $\mathcal{N}_k^i$ to extract the *pattern noise* for each source k so as to classify the images in $\mathcal{S}^i$, where $i \in \{Facebook, Google+, Whatsapp\}$.

Among all the SNs, *Google+* returned highest sensitivity value that is of 100 % for all devices, and also it has the best specificity index with an average value of 97.56 %. This is due to the fact that *Google+* images are least compressed compared to the other two SNs (see Table 2). Although *Facebook* compresses the images more than *Google+*, the algorithm has return an average sensitivity values of 96.92 % and an average specificity value of 91.58 %. The third social network, *WhatsApp*, has given the worst results with an average sensitivity value of 92.52 % and an average specificity value of 90.84 %. This is probably due to the fact that *Facebook* and *Google+*, whose access is mainly done using computer with large screens, are bound to keep medium/high quality definition for the

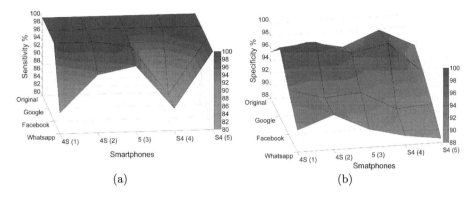

(a)   (b)

Fig. 3. Comparing the classification result values of the original images to those obtained by the downloaded images for (a) sensitivity and (b) specificity.

displayed images, while *WhatsApp*, being an application conceived for mobile devices, provides a much higher compression levels that reduces the information content of the image.

To understand the effectiveness of the algorithm, we compare the sensitivity and specificity of downloaded images with the original ones. Figure 3 shows the comparison of social-by-social with original-by-original for each device. We only show the range where is a change in values among the three SNs. On an average, our method is able to perform the smartphone verification using the images uploaded on the SNs with 96.48 % of sensitivity and 93.77 % of specificity.

Test 3: cross-social: In the final test which is the main contribution of our work, we want to demonstrate that it is possible to match a user profile on a SN using the images posted on various SNs. Moreover, it is possible to identify the source of certain images using the images posted on a user profile, the complementary of the previous test. The former case could be very useful if the smartphone is not available: the verification activity of the subject can be performed through another verified account on SN. While the latter case allows to perform a second important investigation activity, that is the ability to verify the source (smartphone) of the published images. This could be very useful to link a (fake) user profile with a smartphone. In this test, we use $\mathcal{N}_k^i$ to extract the *pattern noise* for each source k so as to classify the images in $\mathcal{S}^j$, where $i \neq j$ and $i, j \in \{Facebook, Google+, Whatsapp\}$.

We perform all the possible tests combination of the original images and the images from the SNs. The sensitivity and specificity results for each combination are shown in Fig. 4a, b, c and d. The icon in the center of the triangular histogram identifies the category from which the subset $\mathcal{N}_k$ has been selected, while the icons on the three sides represent the categories for classifying images, that is the set S.

The best results are obtained when the *pattern noise* and the relative threshold is computed starting from higher quality images as in the case of original

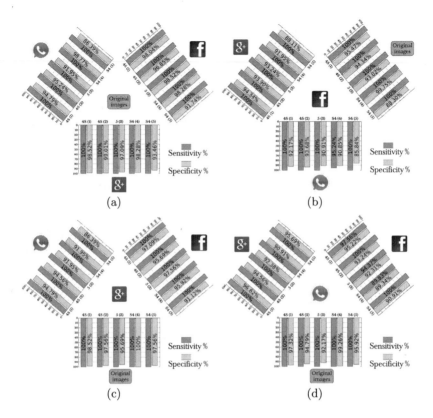

Fig. 4. Each triangular histogram shows the sensitivity and specificity results obtained. The threshold is computed using the subset $\mathcal{N}_k$ belonging to original (a), *Facebook* (b), *Google+* (c) and *WhatsApp* (d).

ones or those downloaded from *Google+*, shown in Fig. 4a and c respectively. The results are still good, even with *Facebook*, although *Facebook* reduces the image size during the uploading process: the sensitivity remains high while there is a decrease in the average specificity, see Fig. 4b. As expected, slightly worse results are obtained with *WhatsApp*. However, the method has successfully matched *WhatsApp* profiles with other SN user profiles with an average reliability of 98.78 %, as shown in Fig. 4d.

The sensitivity has a value of 100 % in all the tests, except the *Facebook – WhatsApp* combination. Although these two SNs reduce the image quality giving rise to a sensitivity degradation, the average value reaches the 99.49 %. In case of specificity, in all the categories, the average value is over 92 %. Thus, we can summarize that our method has a success rate over the 90 % for profile linking across all these three social networks.

5   Conclusions and Future Works

Social network forensic analysis, especially when coupled with smartphone devices [1], has become an important research problem. In this paper, we have presented a method by which it is possible to perform source camera verification and linking of user profiles using the images shared on social platforms. We perform our evaluation using five smartphones and three SNs with different compression characteristics of the image.

Especially given the fact that just as the uniqueness of the human fingerprints cannot be proved [4], the proposed method may fail due to the increasing number of devices and the increasing number of user profiles. To address this we plan to perform cluster based algorithm to decide if two user profiles belong to the same user. This will solve other problems, such as in classifying images of a single user profile that are taken from different sources (e.g. old or otherdevices of the user, front/rear smartphone's camera). Testing our methodology with a larger number of images, heterogeneous devices and several other SNs is another direction of our work. We also plan to test our approach on frames extracted from videos as video sharing is also a common behaviour on social platforms.

Acknowledgments. This work has been supported in part by the Italian Ministry of Education, Universities and Research IMPACT project (RBFR107725) and OPLON project (SCN_00176).

References

1. Al Mutawa, N., Baggili, I., Marrington, A.: Forensic analysis of social networking applications on mobile devices. Digit. Invest. **9**, S24–S33 (2012)
2. Bojinov, H., Michalevsky, Y., Nakibly, G., Boneh, D.: Mobile device identification via sensor fingerprinting. CoRR, abs/1408.1416 (2014)
3. Buades, A., Coll, B., Morel, J.-M.: A review of image denoising algorithms, with a new one. Multiscale Model. Simul. **4**(2), 490–530 (2005)
4. Cole, S.A.: Is fingerprint identification valid? Rhetorics of reliability in fingerprint proponents discourse. Law Policy **28**(1), 109–135 (2006)
5. Dabov, K., Foi, A., Katkovnik, V., Egiazarian, K.: Image denoising with block-matching and 3D filtering. In: Electronic Imaging 2006, p. 606414. International Society for Optics and Photonics (2006)
6. Das, A., Borisov, N., Caesar, M.: Do you hear what i hear? Fingerprinting smart devices through embedded acoustic components. In: ACM SIGSAC Conference on Computer and Communications Security, pp. 441–452 (2014)
7. Dey, S., Roy, N., Xu, W., Choudhury, R.R., Nelakuditi, S.: Accelprint: imperfections of accelerometers make smartphones trackable. In: 21st Annual Network and Distributed System Security Symposium, NDSS, vol. 2013, pp. 23–26 (2014)
8. Facebook Inc., Form 10-K Annual Report. Technical Report 001–35551, Securities and Exchange Commission, December 2013
9. Goljan, M., Fridrich, J.: Camera identification from cropped and scaled images. In: Electronic Imaging (2008)

10. Iofciu, T., Fankhauser, P., Abel, F., Bischoff, K.: Identifying users across social tagging systems. In: ICWSM (2011)
11. Liang, X., Li, X., Zhang, K., Lu, R., Lin, X., Shen, X.: Fully anonymous profile matching in mobile social networks. IEEE J. Select. Areas Commun. **31**(9), 641–655 (2013)
12. Lukas, J., Fridrich, J., Goljan, M.: Digital camera identification from sensor pattern noise. IEEE Trans. Inf. Forensics Secur. **1**(2), 205–214 (2006)
13. Salehan, M., Negahban, A.: Social networking on smartphones: when mobile phones become addictive. Computers in Human Behavior **29**(6), 2632–2639 (2013)
14. Sharma, R., Magnani, M., Montesi, D.; Missing data in multiplex networks: a preliminary study. In: International Workshop on Complex Networks and their Applications (2014)
15. Sharma, R., Magnani, M., Montesi, D.: Investigating the types and effects of missing data in multilayer networks. In: IEEE/ACM ASONAM (2015)
16. Van, L.T., Emmanuel, S., Kankanhalli, M.S.: Identifying source cell phone using chromatic aberration. In: IEEE ICME (2007)
17. Vosecky, J., Hong, D., Shen, V.Y.: User identification across multiple social networks. In: International Conference on Networked Digital Technologies (2009)
18. Ybarra, M.L., Mitchell, K.J.: How risky are social networking sites? a comparison of places online where youth sexual solicitation and harassment occurs. Pediatrics **121**(2), 350–357 (2008)

Computer and Device Forensics

Analysis of the HIKVISION DVR File System

Jaehyeok Han, Doowon Jeong, and Sangjin Lee[✉]

Center for Information Security Technologies (CIST), Korea University, Anam-Dong,
Seoungbuk-Gu, Seoul, Republic of Korea
{one01h,dwjung77,sangjin}@korea.ac.kr

Abstract. The video security market has recently seen a great expansion in addition to an increasing usage of the Digital Video Recorder (DVR), a device for storing and managing video data on a hard disk under file systems. This study first analyzes its file system for evaluating the DVR and examines the HIKVI-SION, a video surveillance product supplier, and its proprietary file system on the DVR that has yet been widely recognized by the market. Thus, this paper comprehensively analyzes the HIKVISION DVR file system and proposes a reliable method for digital forensic analyses.

Keywords: Digital forensic · File system · DVR · HIKVISION

1 Introduction

In recent years, video surveillance systems are widely used for various purposes. An embedded DVR (Digital Video Recorder), one of video surveillance systems, is used to monitor behavior, activities, or other changing information. In particular, general DVRs record video data in a digital format on a mass storage device.

Numerous DVRs use well-known file systems, such as FAT [1] and XFS [2]. However, the HIKVISION [3] products use its own file system, assumedly for increasing the efficiency of video management and copy protection. This study temporary named the system as a HIKVISION file system because it does not have an official name. The HIKVI-SION file system is a simple file system compare to other file systems; the HIKVISION file system excludes some of file operations and includes only the necessary functions. For example, in the HIKVISION file system, it is not possible to delete a file or change a file-name. Despite its high market shares, the HIKVISION has yet conducted any related digital forensic analysis. Reference [4] tried to obtain video data in the hard disk using keywords of frame, however, there is no discussion about the file system and storage mechanism.

Therefore, this study identifies the structure of a HIKVISION file system. This study uses a video file format [5] and the reverse engineer manufacturer's application software [6] to analyze the DVR hard disk storage system. The video compression format also comprises a mechanism to extract meaningful information from video data fragments [7]. After identifying the file system, this study conducts an operation test on the file system to analyze the system in detail. This study demonstrates the structure of a HIKVISION file system and proposes a reliable method to access video data and counter anti-forensic activities, such as system initialization or data overwriting.

© Institute for Computer Sciences, Social Informatics and Telecommunications Engineering 2015
J.I. James and F. Breitinger (Eds.): ICDF2C 2015, LNICST 157, pp. 189–199, 2015.
DOI: 10.1007/978-3-319-25512-5_13

2   The HIKVISION File System Structure

The basic logic of a HIKVISION file system is that each video data is allocated in the data structure, called a data block entry, which contains the time records, channels, and starting locations of the data block. A video data area is placed in data units called data blocks. If video data were to be allocated in more than one data block, other data blocks can be found by using a structure called the HIKBTREE. The HIKBTREE is used to identify the data block in a video data area, and it is also used to identify the allocation status of the data block.

The layout of a HIKVISION file system consists of four physical sections as shown in Fig. 1. The first section, the *Master Sector* has the information about the overall structure of the file system. The second section, the *System Logs* store the data regarding the events and condition of a DVR. The third section, the *Video Data Area* has numerous data blocks for storing video data. The fourth section, the *HIKBTREE* contains the metadata of video data, including the time records and others.

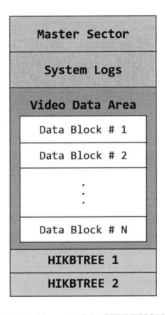

Fig. 1. The physical layout of the HIKVISION File System.

2.1   Master Sector

The Master Sector has the information about the overall structure of the file system. This area starts from the offset 0x200 and the size of master sector is 256 bytes. The signature values of the file system is 'HIKVISION@HANGZHOU (0x48 49 4B 56 49 53 49 4F 4E 40 48 41 4E 47 5A 48 4F 55)' as shown in Fig. 2. The Backup Master Sector is located next to system logs and stores exactly the same data.

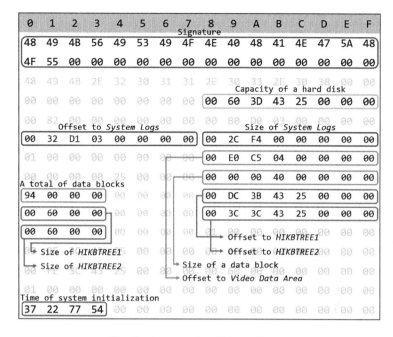

Fig. 2. An example of Master Sector.

The data in each field is stored by Little-endian systems. The Master Sector defines the followings: the capacity of a hard disk (0x25433D6000), offset and size of the system logs (0x3D13200 and 0xF42C00), offset to the video data area (0x4C5E000), size of a data block (0x400000), total number of data blocks (0x94), offset of the HIKBTREE (0x25433BDC00), size of the HIKBTREE (0x6000), time of system initialization (0x37227754), and others. The hexadecimal values in the brackets are the values of samples as shown in Fig. 2.

The *time of system initialization* in the Master Sector is referred as the last system initializes the UNIX time in the UTC. Since the DVR does not provide a delete function, new video data can only be recorded after initializing or overwriting of the system. Thus, this value could be used as an important factor as previously identified by investigators for anti-forensic usage such as in the case, where the time records are fabricated and misused as digital evidence.

2.2   System Logs

The system logs have system logs information about the events and condition of a DVR. By analyzing this, it is possible for users to discover the operation history and track the DVR performance. Offset to the system logs is defined in the Master Sector.

The system logs are classified into four types in the HIKVISION DVR and each type of the system logs also have several detail logs (Table 1).

Table 1. Types of System Logs.

Type	Value	Description
Alarm	0x01	- Start Motion Detection - Stop Motion Detection, etc.
Exception	0x02	- Video Loss Alarm - Illegal Login - HDD Full, etc.
Operation	0x03	- Power On/Local Operation Shutdown - Local Operation: Login/Logout - Local Operation: Configure Parameters - Abnormal Shutdown, etc.
Information	0x04	- Local HDD Information - HDD S.M.A.R.T - Start Recording/Stop Recording, etc.

The Fig. 3 shows the structure of a system log. Each system log starts with a constant value 'RATS (0x52 41 54 53 01 00 00 00)'. The value of the *Created time* stores the UNIX time, when a system log is generated. Next to the type, the *description for the system log* is recorded. Because this field is a variable for each system log, the size of this field is also different according to each type of a system log.

0	1	2	3	4	5	6	7	8	9	A	B	C	D	E	F
52	41	54	53	01	00	00	00	Created time				Type			
Description for a system log															

Fig. 3. Structure of a system log.

2.3 Video Data Area

The video data area stores video data in numerous data blocks. All data blocks and sizes of video data areas are defined in the Master Sector. The size of one data block is generally 1 GB (0x40000000bytes). A data block stores video data areas according to the channels and time records. In order to access the video data, the HIKBTREE should be identified first. This process is covered later in the paper.

A data block is divided into *Video data* and *IDR table*, the former occupies most of the data block and the latter is at the back of a data block (Fig. 4). Video data is encoded to H.264, so each frame is stored in a NAL (Network Abstraction Layer) unit. Each frame can be distinguished by a 1 byte NAL header (Table 2), which is used in combination with 4 bytes sequence '0x00 00 00 01' [8].

Table 2. Types of NAL header.

Type	Value	Type	Value
SEI	0x06	IDR Picture	0x65
Access Unit Delimiter	0x09	SPS	0x67
Non-IDR Picture	0x61	PPS	0x68

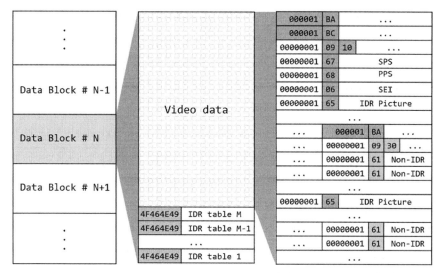

Fig. 4. Video data encoded to H.264.

In front of the NAL unit, the index of a picture is stored with one byte header '0xBA' or '0xBC', which is also used as a combination with three bytes sequence '0x00 00 01'. Due to this parts, noise occurs on the screen when playing with other players except the time when 'player.exe' is downloaded from the HIKVISION DVR.

The IDR table is created to store metadata, which contains index, channel, and time-stamp of an IDR (Instantaneous Decoding Refresh) picture. Each record of the IDR table is recorded in the direction to decrease offset from the end of a data block. It starts with a signature 'OFNI (0x4F 46 4E 49)' and is fixed to 56 bytes for each record. Through the comparison of the IDR table's timestamps as it stored in data block entries, it can be verified the time of the IDR pictures and channel. In general, a series of video data is being stored in the same data block when it is continued to record. If the DVR was being paused or the channel was being changed, other video data will be stored in one data block regardless of the condition. In this case, different video data can be extracted by comparing the timestamps of the IDR table with the recorded timestamps in data block entries.

2.4   HIKBTREE

The HIKBTREE contains the metadata of each video data in data blocks. The HIKB-TREE is a fundamental area to discover the offset to a data block, existence of video data, and other additional information of recordings. Since it has a signature value 'HIKBTREE (0x48 49 4B 42 54 52 45 45)' as shown in Fig. 5(a), the term HIKBTREE will be used. The backup HIKBTREE is located after the former one.

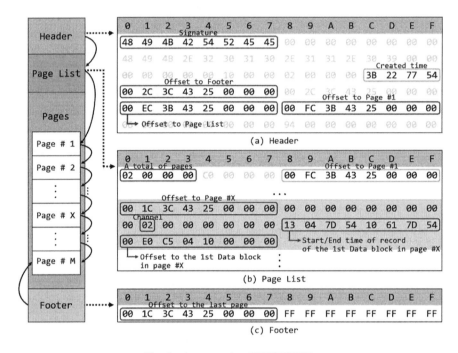

Fig. 5.   An example of HIKBTREE.

The HIKBTREE consists of a number of sections including a header, page list, page number, and footer. The *Header* lists the created time, offset to page list, the first page, and footer. The *Page list* contains a total number of pages, offset to each page, which have information for the connection between video data and metadata, including storage location. Each *page* has numerous data block entries and the size of the page is 4 KB. Every page contains an offset to the next page. Using the offset to next page, one may move to the next page. But if the page is the last page, that field is written by '0xFF' hexadecimal values. The *Footer* is located in the last of the HIKBTREE and contains an offset to the last page.

Each page has numerous data block entries. The *Data block entry* has information about the existence of video data, channel, start/end time records, and offset to the data, as shown in Fig. 6. The field *Existence of video data* has '0x00' hexadecimal values if the data block becomes full of video data or '0xFF' hexadecimal values under the condition that the data block has no video data nor recording. The field *Ch. (channel)* identifies the number of connected cameras which are assigned by the DVR. For example, the value '0x01' means that the video data had recorded from camera #1. The field *Start/End time* records identify the start and end of the UNIX time records in UTC only when the data block is full of video data, otherwise '0xFF FF FF 7F 00 00 00 00'. The field *Offset to the data block* identifies an offset to the data block which have the video data for user to play back.

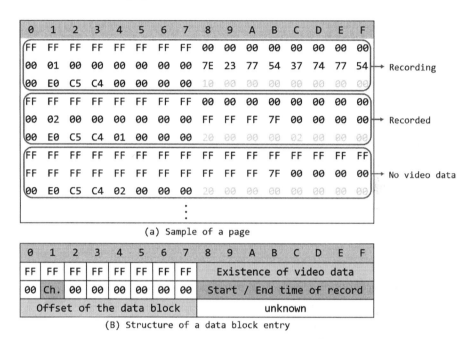

(a) Sample of a page

(B) Structure of a data block entry

Fig. 6. An example of a page and Structure of a data block entry.

In general, different data block entries have different values of the offset to the data block. However, this hexadecimal values of a number of data block entries are sometimes the same. It means that the DVR had been paused or channel had been changed during recording. In this case, the video data can be extracted through the comparison of the IDR table timestamps with the timestamps stored in data block entries.

3   Experiments for DVR System Operation

This study demonstrates ways to access video data in addition to introducing digital forensic analyses after the experiments in initiating or overwriting the system. We conducted a test with the HIKVISION DS-7204HVI-SV (DVR), HIKVISION DS-2CE5582 N (camera), and Seagate Barracuda 7200.9 ST3160811AS SATA 3.5" 160 GB (HDD).

3.1   Video Data Access

The HIKVISION's DVR provides 'Playback' and 'Export' functions. The 'Playback' function allows to play video and the 'Export' function allows to download video file from the DVR to an external device. Using these functions, it is allowed to play video if a hard disk was collected as digital evidence. Once the hard disk becomes connected with DVR, its integrity becomes damaged. Thus, the access method of video data as digital evidence with integrity is necessary.

To access the video data upon user's requests, it is necessary to answer the questions, which of the data blocks store the video data and where the data blocks are. Thus, it is important to inspect the Master Sector prior to reading the offset to the HIKBTREE. After moving to the HIKBTREE, it is also important to verify and scan all pages including the headers. While reading the data block entries on the page, it is essential to find the data block entry that users prefer. If no data block entry is found, it means that there is no video data in the hard disk. Figure 7 shows the procedure for accessing the video data in a HIKVISION file system.

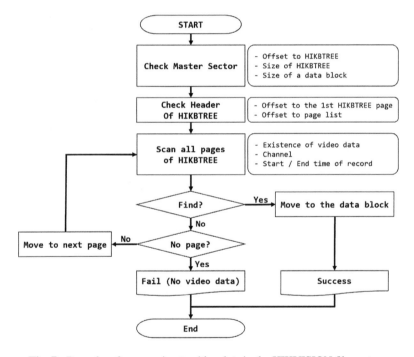

Fig. 7. Procedure for accessing to video data in the HIKVISION file system.

3.2   System Initialization

The HIKVISION DVRs have no delete function. System initialization is the only way to delete video data on a hard disk. When the hard disk is being initialized, the following will be changed: the time of system initialization in the Master Sector, restoration of the system logs to zero, and initialization of the HIKBTREE. After the system initialization, all video data in data blocks will remain. Regardless of system initialization, it is possible to extract video data by scanning all data blocks, for instance, by the carving technique.

In order to determine whether system initialization had been performed (Fig. 8), the value 'Time of system initialization' can be checked in the Master Sector and also be verified by reading the offset to video data and the HIKBTREE. Users can read recording times from the IDR table in the video data and 'Start/End time of record' of data block entries in the HIKBTREE. By comparing the 'Time of system initialization' values with the values of the IDR table and data block entries, users can determine whether system initialization had performed. If any time-reversal happens — the new time is created prior to the old time creation, thereby, users can conclude that this DVR was initialized at that time.

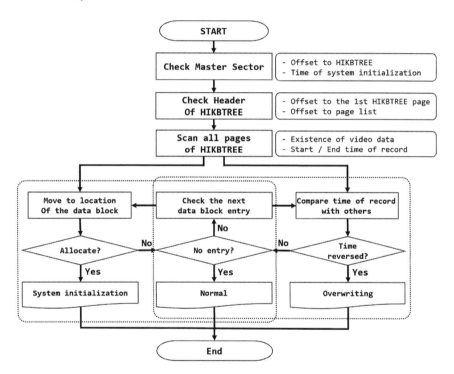

Fig. 8. Procedure of detection for system initialization and overwriting.

3.3 Overwriting

When the data exceeds the capacity of the hard disk, old video data is replaced with new data under the procedure shown in Fig. 9. The old video data could be sometimes stored with the new data in a data block, if device was suddenly stopped or turned off. When the video data become overwritten, the following will change: the values of 'Channel' and 'Start/End time of record' in the data block entry. 'Channel' is updated as the present channel and the 'Start/End time of record' is changed to '0xFF FF FF 7F 00 00 00 00'.

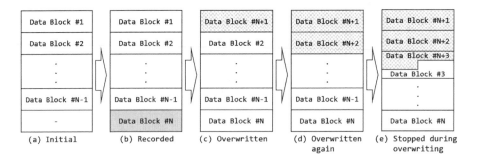

Fig. 9. Process of overwriting in a HIKVISION file system.

In order to determine whether overwriting had been performed (Fig. 8), users can read the recording time from the IDR table in the video database and the 'Start/End time of record' of data block entries from the HIKBTREE. If any recording time from the IDR tables in the video data predates the 'Start/End time of record' of data block entries, it can be understood that the hard disk had been full at least one time and has previously been overwritten.

4   Conclusion

Video recordings of video surveillance systems are the most useful evidence in forensic activities. However, it is difficult to analyze the hard disk using a HIKVISION file system, because there is no related research that are currently available. It is important to evaluate proprietary file systems, otherwise valuable digital evidence can lose its usefulness. Therefore, it is necessary to identify unknown file systems.

This study identifies the structure and mechanism of a HIKVISION file system which is not well-known. Using the result of this study, investigators can analyze hard disks from the HIKVISION products with integrity of the digital evidence. Furthermore, the procedure in the case analysis can be useful to counter anti-forensic activities, such as system initialization or data overwriting. This paper is conducted to provide useful analysis results regarding a HIKVISION file system for investigators in analyzing digital evidence relating video surveillance.

Acknowledgement. This research was supported by the Public Welfare & Safety Research Program through the National Research Foundation of Korea (NRF) funded by the Ministry of Science, IT & Future Planning (2012M3A2A1051106)

References

1. Carrier, B.: File System Forensic Analysis, vol. 3, pp. 156–198. Addison-Wesley, Reading (2005)
2. Hellwig, C.: XFS: the big storage file system for Linux. Mag. USENIX SAG **34**(5), 10–18 (2009)

3. Hikvision Digital Technology Co. http://overseas.hikvision.com/en/
4. Yang, F., Li, R., Wu, C.: Basic principle and application of video recovery software for "Dahua" and "Hikvision" brand. In: SHS Web of Conferences, vol. 14, EDP Sciences (2015)
5. Poole, N.R., Zhou, Q., Abatis, P.: Analysis of CCTV digital video recorder hard disk storage system. Digit. Invest. **5**(3), 85–92 (2009)
6. Tobin, L., Shosha, A., Gladyshev, P.: Reverse engineering a CCTV system, a case study. Digit. Invest. **11**(3), 179–186 (2014)
7. Park, J., Lee, S.: Data fragment forensics for embedded DVR systems. Digit. Invest. **11**(3), 187–200 (2014)
8. ITU-T. H.264, advanced video coding for generic audiovisual services (2004). http://www.itu.int/

Exploring the Effectiveness of Digital Forensics Tools on the Sony PlayStation Vita

Karolina Alvarez and Masooda Bashir[(✉)]

University of Illinois at Urbana-Champaign, Urbana, IL 61801, USA
karolina.a.alvarez@gmail.com, mnb@illinois.edu

Abstract. As gaming consoles become more advanced, their capabilities increase and they can store more information on the users. Because of this, they are becoming viable sources of forensic evidence. This research contributes to the little-explored and growing field of video game console forensics through the examination of current forensic tools on the Sony PlayStation Vita. These tools were used to analyze backups created by the device to better understand the new file types, and what data are stored in them and how. Although most of the files were encrypted, valuable metadata could be acquired from them.

Keywords: Digital forensics · Sony PlayStation Vita · PS Vita · Video game console forensics

1 Introduction

Modern gaming systems are becoming more and more like personal computers. Their functionality and the type of data they store make them potential sources of evidence for criminal investigations. Such data include not only game logs with timestamps, but also personal information, internet history, credit card information, location, pictures, and videos. There have been several instances where gaming consoles have been used for criminal purposes, and became sources of incriminating evidence, especially for child pornography cases. There have been cases where young children were contacted through messaging services on video game consoles and bribed into sending nude pictures [1]. In one case, the only evidence of the crime existed on the gaming console [11]. There have been other cases where gaming logs were used to undermine an alibi or shed new light on a case [2]. However, despite the multitude of information available in gaming systems, investigators have difficulty finding and extracting it in a forensically sound manner. Accessing the contents directly through the console may tamper with the evidence, and typical digital forensics analysis is difficult due to the differences between gaming consoles and regular computers. As a result, investigators typically turn to online forums for advice. They may use community-created tools to view the content, but even those are unable to unveil everything [2]. Because gaming console forensics is still a new field, there is much to learn about how data are stored on these systems. The purpose of this research is to perform preliminary forensics analysis on the Sony PlayStation

© Institute for Computer Sciences, Social Informatics and Telecommunications Engineering 2015
J.I. James and F. Breitinger (Eds.): ICDF2C 2015, LNICST 157, pp. 200–206, 2015.
DOI: 10.1007/978-3-319-25512-5_14

Vita (PS Vita) in order to understand what can be read and accessed using current digital forensic tools.

2   Device Information

From its release in December 2011 to January 2013, over 4 million PS Vitas have been sold worldwide [15]. As with most video game consoles, the technical detail about the operating system and file system of the PS Vita are not publicly released, but various other information is available. As of 2015, there have been 3 models of the PS Vita. The first generation consisted of two models: one with 3G and Wi-Fi support, and one with only Wi-Fi. This research focused on the second generation model, commonly referred to as the PS Vita Slim. All versions use a removable PS Vita Memory Card, but the Slim model has 1 GB of internal storage memory, which is only usable if no card is inserted [17]. In addition to playing games from PS Vita game cards, the PS Vita is also able to stream games from previous PlayStation consoles and connect to a PlayStation 4 through Remote Play. Through Remote Play, the PS Vita can be used as a second screen and controller for the game or can give players the ability to continue to play PlayStation 4 games remotely [10]. PS Vita has proven to be very difficult to mod, as only certain games on a certain firmware can be exploited, and Sony works quickly to fix known security exploits [12]. In this research, firmware version 3.36 was running on a new, unmodified PS Vita Slim.

3   Related Research

As gaming console forensics is relatively new, there are very few papers published on the subject. Most of the research done in this field is on home gaming consoles rather than mobile ones, as the hard drives are simpler to remove and image, and while the effectiveness of traditional forensic analysis is limited, much was learned about these systems. For example, although they produced new file types, the hard drive of the Xbox One used NTFS partitions [7], and the file system of the Xbox 360 was based off an older implementation of the FAT file system. [19], which facilitated analysis of the extracted data. Sony, however, has taken extra measures to prevent reverse engineering on the PlayStation 3, so alternative means had to be found to store and access the data [3]. Some information about the file system of PlayStation Portable, the predecessor of the PS Vita, was found [9], but much of the technology used has been changed, so it is unlikely to be the same for the PS Vita. No other research related to PS Vita forensics could be found. Thus, this research will lay a foundation for future research in PS Vita forensics.

4   Methodology

Because the hard drive of the PS Vita could not be removed, it was connected directly to a computer by the USB cable. However, the device could not be detected without the Content Manager Assistant for PlayStation (CMA). The CMA is an application required to enable data transfer between the device and the PC [10]. Therefore, in order to capture all files on the PS Vita for imaging, the CMA was used to create backups of the system files, saved data, and application data on the computer. Also, to prevent anything from accidentally being written onto the PS Vita, a USB software write blocker by DSi was enabled. This write blocker was tested by attempting to write to another USB device while active.

4.1 Creating Backup Files

To facilitate isolating events, the actions performed on the PS Vita were split into nine phases. After each stage, the system was backed up. By default, the CMA creates a new folder for the backup with a name consisting of the date and time the backup was created. This name was used to keep track of when each backup was made (Table 1).

Table 1. Actions performed in each phase.

Phase I	Initial startup (settings system updates)
Phase II	Connect to WiFi and sign in to PlayStation Network account
Phase III	Insert memory card and transfer data from internal memory
Phase IV	Download Borderlands 2 from PlayStation Store
Phase V	Play Borderlands 2 in single player mode locally
Phase VI	Play Borderlands 2 in multi player mode online
Phase VII	Download Youtube, Facebook, and Skype applications
Phase VIII	Perform regular tasks on each application
Phase IX	Take pictures and videos with and without location enabled

4.2 Acquiring Images of Backups

In order to analyze the image with multiple forensics tools, the file type of the images needed to be compatible with the tools. One such file type is the Encase Image File. However, to create this type of image file using AccessData's Forensic Toolkit Imager, the entire drive where the PS Vita backups were located needed to be imaged.

4.3 Analyzing the Images

Five tools were used to analyze the images: The Forensic Toolkit (FTK) Imager v3.4.0.1, Autopsy v3.1.2, EnCase v7.09.06, Digital Forensic Framework (DFF) v1.3, and Bulk Extractor v1.5.5. Since it was likely that there would be new and unknown file types in the backup, it was uncertain what data each tool would be able to extract. Therefore, multiple tools were used to compare the effectiveness of current digital forensics tools on the PS Vita files.

The examinations in this research were run on 64-bit Windows 7 machine, so the tools selected were those compatible with the machine and widely used by forensic researchers and professionals. FTK Imager is an important component of the Forensic Toolkit, which is a highly regarded forensic analysis tool [8], and Autopsy is a popular open-source tool due to all the modules available [16]. EnCase is a widely accepted tool in the industry and is used in many investigations [14]. DFF is a relatively new open-source tool that has gained popularity due to its capabilities and customizability with modules and scripts [4]. Bulk Extractor has a strong reputation as an open-source forensic tool capable of data carving [7]. Autopsy, DFF, and Bulk Extractor are all packages include in the SANS Investigative Forensics Toolkit (SIFT) [5]. SIFT is a VMware image with multiple open-source forensic tools pre-installed and is widely used for forensic examinations [14].

4.4 Qualitative Measures

In each tool, after adding the image as an evidence file, we navigated to the folder containing the backups. Once there, the folder with the final backup from Phase IX was opened. For each of the files in the backup, several questions were posed, which are listed in Table 2. The results were later compared with the files from other phases.

Table 2. Set of questions for the Phase IX image.

1. What files are in the backup?
2. What are the sizes of the files?
3. What type are these files?
4. What are the timestamps of the files?
5. What are the contents of each of these files?
6. Does the tool recognize anything in terms of file carving?

5   Results

All four tools were able to find three files in the backup folder: 201501262046-01.psvimg, 201501262046-01.psvinf, and 201501262046-01.psvmd. All other images contain these files, with the name of the backup it belongs to as their names. In FTK, another file named $I30 was found as well, which is the Windows NTFS Index Attribute [5]. In Encase, a file called 201501262046-01.psvimg·Attribute List was found instead. This file is created by the NTFS and holds the location of attribute records that do not fit in the MFT record [13].

The tools were also able to find the size of each of these files. The PSVIMG file was 3,483,839,744B, the PSVINF file was 15B, and the PSVMD file was 208B. Additionally, both Encase and FTK provided the physical size of the files. The sizes of the $I30 file and $Attribute List file were 4096B and 1760B, respectively.

In FTK, there is an entry in the metadata table for file type. While $I30 was listed as an NTFS Index Allocation, the PSV* files were listed as Regular Files. In Encase, the "File Type" entry for all files, including $Attribute List, was blank. There was also an entry for "Category", but it was listed as "Unknown" for $Attribute List and "None" for the others. Autopsy and DFF did not have an entry for this information.

All three tools indicated the last accessed, created, and last modified timestamps in each image. All these times matched for each file, after taking into account the time zone. The PSVIMG file was created first and was last modified a few seconds afterwards. Then, the PSVINF and PSVMD files were created. The timestamps from DFF were more detailed. They revealed that the PSVMD files were created before the PSVINF files by about one ten-thousandth of a second. The $I30 file was created at the same time as the PSVIMG file and was last modified at the same time as the other two. There were no timestamps for the $Attribute List file.

In both Autopsy and FTK, the contents of the files could be read in hex and text format. However, the contents of the PSVIMG and PSVMD files were illegible and are possibly encrypted. Future tests will be done to calculate the entropy values to determine if the files are encrypted. The PSVINF file, however, was stored in plaintext, which DFF recognized as ASCII text, and simply contained the name of the backup it belonged to. The $I30 file also contained some encrypted data, but it also held the names of the files in the folder as well as the 8.3 short filenames: 201501~1.PSV, 201501~2.PSV, and 201501~3.PSV.

It was difficult to isolate the backup files from the PS Vita when Bulk Extractor was used on the image. Instead, the original backup folder was used for this test. Bulk Extractor was run with all possible scanners, excluding hashdb and sceadan. The outputted report was empty, except for a file called wordlist.txt. Typically, this file would contain a list of the "words" that were extracted from the folder, but in this case, the only word found was the backup name from the PSVINF file. Other than that, no useful information was found.

6   Conclusion and Future Work

From the results above, much can be learned about the new PSV* file types in each backup. Very little is known about these files, as the system software used by the PS Vita is closed source, and most information posted in forums has yet to be confirmed.

For each phase, the PSVINF file simply contained the name of the backup, most likely for bookkeeping. Since this file type seems more straightforward, most of the discussion in the community is about the other two types. These files are encrypted [17], which the results affirm, possibly through the CMA so that the decrypted data can only be read by the PS Vita that created the backup [18]. The PSVMD files for each phase are different, but they are all the same size. There is speculation in the community that this file contains metadata, "MD," and is stored as an XML file [18]. The PSVIMG file should then be where all the actual data is stored. In each phase, the size of the PSVIMG file grew by relatively small amounts. It should be noted that prior to Phase IV, when Borderlands 2 was downloaded, the backup folders did not include an $Attribute List file, probably because there was enough room for the records to be stored in the MFT. After the game was downloaded, the size of the PSVIMG file grew over 1000 times its size, from 3,208 KB to 3,423,876 KB.

Although the metadata collected from the tools do not match the extent of the data stored on the PS Vita, and may not seem to provide sufficient forensic evidence alone, it can be useful for timelining. At the time the backup was created, the same user would need to be in possession of the PS Vita and the computer where the backup was stored. Therefore, actions performed on the PS Vita around that time are most likely done by the same user. If the identity of the console's user can be found, so can the identity of the computer's user.

The goal of this research was to follow a standard procedure for multiple existing tools in order to find what information could be extracted from the PS Vita in a forensically sound manner, and it is clear that these tools provide limited data. Ideally, a specialized tool will need to be made to properly analyze all the stored data. In order to create more effective tools, more needs to be learned about the system. For example, in future research, we can physically take apart the system and attempt to extract unencrypted data directly from the device. Several members in the community have successfully taken apart a PS Vita [6] and have identified what appears to be a JTAG port on the CPU [18]. Another possibility is to extract the data directly from the PS Vita memory cards and examine how the data are stored in it. A more challenging direction could be to reverse engineer the CMA to attempt to decrypt the files found.

References

1. 10-year-old victimized through Xbox. The Folsom Telegraph (27 August 2010)
2. Anderson, N.: CSI: Xbox - how cops perform Xbox live stakeouts and console searches. Ars Technica (10 January 2012). http://arstechnica.com
3. Conrad, S., Dorn, G., Craiger, P.: Forensics analysis of a PlayStation 3 console. In: Chow, K., Shenoi, S. (eds.) IFIP WG 2010. IFIP AICT, vol. 337, pp. 65–76. Springer, Heidelberg (2010)
4. Digital Forensics Framework. http://www.digital-forensic.org
5. Digital Forensics Training | Incident Response Training | SANS. http://digital-forensics.sans.org
6. Gadget Teardowns | iFixit. https://www.ifixit.com/Teardown/
7. Moore, J., Baggili, I., Marrington, A., Rodrigues, A.: Preliminary forensic analysis of the Xbox One. In: Fourteenth Annual DFRWS Conference. Digital Investigation, vol. 11, supplement 2, pp. S57–S65 (August 2014)
8. Liang, J.: Evaluating a selection of tools for extraction of forensic data: disk imaging. Thesis, Auckland University of Technology (2010)
9. Pancoast, S.: The play station portable: background and forensics analysis of the file system and standard files on the play station portable (2008)
10. PlayStation. http://www.playstation.com
11. Potter, N.: PlayStation sex crime: criminal used video game to get girl's naked pictures. ABC News (13 March 2009)
12. PS Vita Hacks | PS Vita eCFW. https://vitahax.wordpress.com
13. Resources and Tools for IT Professionals | TechNet. https://technet.microsoft.com
14. Shah, M., Paradise, D.: Tool comparison. Research, Champlain College (2013)

15. Stuart, K.: PlayStation 2 manufacture ends after 12 years. The Guardian (4 January 2013)
16. The Sleuth Kit (TSK) and Autopsy: Open Source Digital Forensic Tools. http://www.sleuthkit.org
17. Vita Dev Wiki. http://www.vitadevwiki.com
18. Wololo.net - PS4, PS Vita, PSP Programming, security and homebrews. http://wololo.net
19. Xynos, K., Harries, S., Sutherland, I., Davies, G., Blyth, A.: Xbox 360: a digital forensics investigation of the hard disk drive. Embedded systems forensics: smart phones, GPS devices, and gaming consoles. Digit. Invest. 6(3–4), 104–111 (2010)

Extended Abstracts

Recycling Personal Data:
Data Reuse and Use Limitation in Digital
Forensics (Extended Abstract)

Bart Custers

Faculty of Law, eLaw, Centre for Law in the Information Society,
Leiden University, Steenschuur 25, 2311 ES Leiden The Netherlands
b.h.m.custers@law.leidenuniv.nl

Keywords: Big Data · Risk profiling · Digital forensics · Personal data · Privacy · Data protection · Data reuse · Data recycling · Use limitation principle

The use of Big Data offers tremendous potential in many fields, including digital forensics. A typical example of this is the use of Big Data for risk profiling. Big Data analysis with data mining tools opens the possibilities of finding previously unknown patterns and relations in the data. Such patterns may be useful to identify individuals, to reveal networks in which people are involved and to build dossiers on suspects or potential suspects. This may be useful in solving crime, but it may also be useful in preventing crime. By using Big Data, characteristics may be discovered indicating specific risks of individuals committing a crime or getting involved in crime, identifying situations that may result to crime and addressing groups that may be 'at risk'. Whereas in most forensics there is a lack of data or samples, in Big Data contexts an overload of data exists. This further enables the use of intelligence before a crime takes place as opposed to the more traditional use of forensics after a crime has taken place.

Of course, bigger is not always better. Not all types of data are useful for all types of purposes. But the suggestion that in forensics only data of offenders is required is a misunderstanding. Typically, in order to detect patterns in deviancies (criminal behavior), data of normal people and normal situations is required. In other words, in order to find the 'exception', the 'standard' has to be known. As a result, risk profiling in digital forensics often also requires data of people who do not have criminal records and of people who have not committed a crime.

Obviously, there are also some pitfalls in the use of risk profiling. Because the results heavily depend on the available data, there may be results that qualify as self-fulfilling prophecies. For instance, when police forces only collect data in particular ethnic minority neighborhoods, the risk profiles resulting from data analyses might show that ethnic minorities are more prone to getting involved in crime, whereas a broader, richer dataset might reveal different results. Obviously, such mistakes may also result in stigmatization and discrimination. At the same time, the use of Big Data in risk profiling may increase the objectiveness of risk profiles. For instance, in cases

© Institute for Computer Sciences, Social Informatics and Telecommunications Engineering 2015
J.I. James and F. Breitinger (Eds.): ICDF2C 2015, LNICST 157, pp. 209–211, 2015.
DOI: 10.1007/978-3-319-25512-5

where a particular police officer may have a prejudice, large datasets may prove this perception is wrong. In such cases, it may be helpful to select surveillance areas and people to be searched by law enforcement on the basis of risk profiles rather than by the sole discretion of an individual police officer.

Although there are nowadays many tools that automatically analyze Big Data, such as data mining tools, there is always the risk of data overload or, to be more specific, the risk that human intuition provides insufficient insight in the datasets to choose the right tools for analyses. Data visualization tools may be helpful to counter this.

Another issue is the reliability of data and the resulting risk profiles. Datasets may contain errors or may be incomplete. Risk profiles may contain false positives (e.g., not all Muslims with big black beards taking flight lessons are terrorists) and false negatives (e.g., Muslim terrorists are not the only type of terrorists). However, also in this case, Big Data may yield better results, enabling filtering out data errors, filling gaps in datasets and making more precise predictions.

Apart from the 'garbage-in-garbage-out' argument for datasets, there are also plenty of pitfalls in interpreting datasets and data analysis results. For instance, typical errors may be so-called confirmation bias, i.e., the tendency to search for, interpret or recall information in a way that confirms beliefs or hypotheses. Another mistake may be that statistical relations are interpreted as causal relations or illusory correlations, when people may falsely perceive an association between two events.

Despite these potential pitfalls, there are many benefits of Big Data in forensics. Adding these benefits the question comes to mind why data cannot be reused more often. This may be due to potential unwillingness to share data and to economic, technological, ethical and legal restrictions. In this paper we focus on data protection law. The current European legal framework for personal data protection is based on the idea that there are limits to the collection of personal data (the so-called *collection limitation principle*), that data controllers collect data only for purposes specified in advance (the so-called *purpose specification principle*) and that the data collected are only used for those purposes specified (the so-called *use limitation principle*). Particularly the use limitation principle is relevant in data recycling, since it intends to prevent function creep. The idea behind this principle is obviously to set expectations, especially for data subjects, who have to decide whether or not to provide their personal data in specific contexts and when consenting to the ways in which their personal data may be used.

Data reuse may be widened by renewing models for informed consent. Within the current legal framework, personal data may be anonymized to allow broader use or data subjects may be asked for their consent regarding data reuse. Current practice is to formulate the purposes for data use in very broad ways, encompassing many different types of data use, making consent for data reuse unnecessary. However, limited transparency about the ways in which data are used may be the result. Another approach may be to change the current legislation so that data reuse in some contexts is allowed without bothering data subjects with frequent requests for consent of data reuse. Obviously the question here is when data reuse is close enough to the original consent to assume implicit consent for data reuse and when data reuse should be consented to explicitly. These are just some of the directions in which new solutions can be sought.

This project on modeling the European data economy (EUDECO) is funded by the Research and Innovation Framework Program Horizon 2020 of the European Commission (Grant Agreement No. 645244). The project will assist European science and industry in understanding and exploiting the potentials of data reuse in the context of Big Data and open data, including cloud computing.

Reliability Research about Evidence Acquisition Method of Apple Mac Device (Extended Abstract)

Jisung Choi, Dohyun Kim, and Sangjin Lee

Center for Information Security Technologies (CIST), Korea University, Anam-Dong, Seongbuk-Gu, Seoul Republic of Korea
{chjs207, exdus84, sangjin}@korea.ac.kr

Abstract. Apple Mac devices, which are increasing in global usage, are more likely to be encountered during a digital investigation and may contain digital evidence. Unlike other devices, Apple devices have unique interfaces and operating systems. For such reasons, digital investigators may have difficulty when they attempt acquire digital evidence from such devices. Further, few reliability research on acquisition method from Apple devices have been conducted. Further verification of the reliability of acquisition methods are needed to supplement existing Apple Mac Device acquisition procedures. This paper describes an acquisition method for volatile and non-volatile data on an Apple Mac device that includes the verification of the reliability of the acquisition method.

Keywords: Apple Mac Device · OS X · Acquisition · Reliability · Digital Forensics

1 Introduction

Apple Mac Device is product which globally used. Mac Device uses unique interface and operating system such as OS X, FireWire, and Thunderbolt. These things can be hard to investigate at Mac Device.

This paper classifies evidence acquisition methods according to volatility of evidence (volatile and non-volatile) to make generally reliable evidence acquisition procedure. And this paper describes an existing research about each evidence types. Volatile data acquisition section describes methods about dumping physical memory at PC of investigation and acquisition data by using operating system command. Non-volatile data acquisition section describes method about storage imaging. And we describe limitations of each method and verify reliability through experiments.

2 Related Work

Evidence acquisition methods of Apple Mac Device have been conducted in most part. But there is no a reliability research about each acquisition methods. To acquire Volatile data, acquisition methods that dump physical memory at outside has been used

© Institute for Computer Sciences, Social Informatics and Telecommunications Engineering 2015
J.I. James and F. Breitinger (Eds.): ICDF2C 2015, LNICST 157, pp. 212–214, 2015.
DOI: 10.1007/978-3-319-25512-5

through DMA vulnerability of hardware interface [1]. Pyfw library which use DMA vulnerability of FireWire is opened [2]. And physical memory acquisition research which adopted DMA vulnerability conducted at OS X Lion [3]. Acquisition method which execute on Host PC has been researched by using KVM (Kernel Virtual Memory) [4]. And research which extracts major data from acquired physical memory conducted [5]. Acquisition methods about non-volatile data of Mac Device are conducted Macintosh imaging [6].

3 Acquisition Method and Reliability Verification

Target is Volatile data and Non-volatile data. To acquire volatile data, an investigator must dump physical memory and acquire information through system command. For acquisition physical memory, investigator use FireWire. And they use acquisition software on Host PC. If investigator can't access directly physical memory, they use sleep image or system command. To acquire Non-volatile data, they do storage imaging. These methods are storage separation, using bootable OS, and Target Disk Mode.

Acquisition method with Inception makes kernel panic before 4GiB of physical memory. Thus, we get $3\text{GiB} \sim 3.5\text{GiB}$ physical memory which is below 4GiB of specification. And OSXPmem do normal action on Yosemite (OS X 10.10). And we find Inception minimally affect physical memory during acquisition process of physical memory.

We compare results of MD5 Hash about storage separation, bootable OS, and target disk mode. And we find 3methods can reserve integrity of evidence. But if investigator don't use Write Blocker at target disk mode, evidence can be changed at allocation, catalog, volume header, and alternate volume header. Lastly, we find Bootable OS is the fastest method.

4 Conclusion

This paper describes an existing Mac Device evidence acquisition method which classify by volatile characteristic of evidence. And we experiment about reliability of each method. This paper can be used by investigator as standard guide-line when they does digital forensics about general Mac Device.

References

1. Carrier, B.D., Grand, J.: A hardware-based memory acquisition procedure for digital investigations. Digital Invest. **1**(1), 50–60 (2004)
2. Becher, M., Dornsief, M., Klein, C.N.: FireWire, All your memory are bleong to us. CanSecWest, Vancouver (2005)

3. Mac OS Lion Forensic Memory Acquisition Using IEEE 1394. http://www.frameloss.org/wp-content/uploads/2011/09/Lion-Memory-Acquisition.pdf
4. Singh, A.: Mac OS X Internals. Pearson Education, Boston (2006)
5. Lee, K., Lee, S.: Research on Mac OS X physical memory analysis. J. Korea Inst. Inf. Secur. Crypt. **21**(4), 89–100 (2011)
6. McDonald, K.: To image a Macintosh. Digital Invest. **2**, 175–179 (2005)

Forensic Analysis Using Amcache.hve
(Extended Abstract)

Moonho Kim and Sangjin Lee

Center for Information Security Technologies (CIST), Korea University,
Anam-Dong, Seongbuk-Gu, Seoul Republic of Korea
firstkmh8l@gmail.com, sangjin@korea.ac.kr

Abstract. Amcache.hve is a registry hive file related to the Program Compatibility Assistant, which stores the execution information of application software. Amcache.hve records the execution path of executable files and the time they are first executed. The utility can also be used to estimate when they were first installed and when they were deleted. Using these features, Amcache. hve can be used to draw up overall timelines of application use when used with the Prefetch and Iconcache.db files. Amcache.hve is an important utility for tracking the activities of anti-forensic programs, portable programs, and external storage devices. This paper illustrates the features of Amcache.hve and how it is used in digital forensics, such as when estimating application deletion times.

Keywords: Digital forensics · Amcache.hve · User behavior

1 Introduction

In digital forensic investigation, tracing application execution history is vital. Examining the execution history of applications enables detection of the use of anti-forensic techniques, and a determination of criminal intent.

In order to trace execution history, one can analyze Prefetch files or Iconcache.db files. Analyzing Prefetch files is limited to the number of Prefetch files available, 128 [1]. Analyzing Iconcache.db files is also limited in that it cannot supply application execution times [2]. On the other hand, analyzing Amcache.hve overcomes the limitations of the Prefetch and Iconcache.db files. It enables analysts to draw up general application execution timelines. It can also trace anti-forensic application use, even when portable applications have been used.

Currently, analysis of Amcache.hve is nonexistent except in Yogesh Katri's personal blog. The blog explains the recording in Amcache.hve of application first execution times, execution paths, SHA-l hash values, product names, and file versions [3]. This paper suggests how it could be used in digital forensics.

© Institute for Computer Sciences, Social Informatics and Telecommunications Engineering 2015
J.I. James and F. Breitinger (Eds.): ICDF2C 2015, LNICST 157, pp. 215–216, 2015.
DOI: 10.1007/978-3-319-25512-5

2 Methods for Utilization in Digital Forensics

Amcache.hve is a registry hive file, and "Last Written Time" is saved on each executable file key. This timestamp is created when the executable files are executed for the first time. It is only created upon initial execution and cannot be changed after. Using this feature, the first execution time of the file can be checked.

In the case of package applications, particularly installation files that are installed in the control panel for example, many executable files are tied into a package, allowing the first execution time of each executable to be checked. What the first execution time of each executable file means is described below, using the BCWipe program as an example.

1. bcwipeSetup.exe: install time ("Created Timestamp": this corresponds to the time the exe file was created by being downloaded from internet or copied from an external drive)
2. BCWipe.exe: the first execution time
3. BCUnInstall.exe: deletion time

This will allow us to identify time information regarding the creation, installation and deletion of the BCWipe program.

In addition, it can trace anti-forensic programs and portable program execution histories, through file paths.

3 Conclusion

Amcache.hve, which is a new artifact in Windows 8, holds varied application information, particularly time information, which is especially important in digital forensic investigations.

Utilizing Amcache.hve in conjunction with the Prefetch and IconCache.db file allows the drawing up of an overall timeline of application execution, confirming initial installation time, how many times and the last time of execution, deletion time and even the number of installations. Moreover, analyzing Amcache.hve can allow the identification of traces of even portable programs, which are commonly employed to hinder forensic investigation. Therefore, Amcache.hve can be very useful in digital forensic investigations.

References

1. MSDN. Misinformation and the The Prefetch Flag. http://blogs.msdn.com/b/ryanmy/archive/2005/05/25/421882.aspx
2. Lee, C.-Y., Lee, S.: Structure and application of IconCache.db files for digital forensics. Digital Invest. 11(2), 102–110 (2014)
3. Khatri, Y.: Amcache.hve in Windows 8-Goldmine for malware hunters. http://www.swiftforensics.com/2013/12/amcachehve-in-windows-8-goldmine-for.html

Author Index

14903239R00127

Printed in Great Britain
by Amazon.co.uk, Ltd.,
Marston Gate.